D0387938

For The
Prescott College
Library

with all good wishes

Denis McFadden –

withdrawn

Alexander Hamilton
in the
American Tradition

Books by Louis M. Hacker

UNITED STATES SINCE 1865 (*with B. B. Kendrick*)

THE FARMER IS DOOMED

A SHORT HISTORY OF THE NEW DEAL

THE UNITED STATES: A GRAPHIC HISTORY

AMERICAN PROBLEMS OF TODAY

THE TRIUMPH OF AMERICAN CAPITALISM

SHAPING OF THE AMERICAN TRADITION

NEW INDUSTRIAL RELATIONS (*with others*)

ENGLAND AND AMERICA: THE TIES THAT BIND

GOVERNMENT ASSISTANCE TO UNIVERSITIES IN GREAT BRITAIN
(*with H. W. Dodds and L. Rogers*)

THE UNITED STATES IN THE TWENTIETH CENTURY
(*with H. S. Zahler*)

CAPITALISM AND THE HISTORIANS (*with others*)

ALEXANDER HAMILTON IN THE AMERICAN TRADITION

LOUIS M. HACKER

Alexander Hamilton

in the

American Tradition

New York
Toronto
London

McGRAW-HILL BOOK COMPANY, INC.

Published by the McGraw-Hill Book Company, Inc.
Printed in the United States of America

SECOND PRINTING

To My Wife
Beatrice Larson Hacker

Preface

AMERICANS HAVE NEVER FOUND IT NECESSARY TO APOLOGIZE FOR their return, again and again, to the Founding Fathers for wisdom and inspiration. These were great men, not only because they were capable of encompassing the whole world in which they lived—as students, philosophers, statesmen, men of affairs—but also because, caught up in a period of crisis just as threatening as the one of our own times, they were able to move with courage and determination.

The newly established American states had got off to a bad start. To create a Union that would be lasting and yet not oppressive; to devise a program of fiscal integrity that would furnish public revenues and encourage private capital investments by Americans and foreigners; to protect the young American sovereignty and to save her from the ravages of the war then spreading around the whole world—such were the awesome problems that faced the country's leaders from 1787 to 1800.

The Founding Fathers met these challenges, although not always in perfect agreement as to the courses to be pursued. Their accomplishment was mighty, for they not only created a Union but they also built a nation. Today, among other things, we have these guides to action as we view and treasure their work. The maintenance of the American nation—united, functioning with justice, assuring equality of opportunity—is both a political and a moral responsibility. The honor and faith of government, because these are linked with both public and private credit—the sound management of money and banking; the creation of a climate in which free enterprise and innovation can flourish—are the foundations upon which we continue to build

vii

securely. Our foreign relations are wisely managed if first and foremost we give thought to our own safety.

In laying down these lines of policy, none played a larger role than Alexander Hamilton. He was second to George Washington and was Washington's trusted lieutenant; it was Washington's confidence in him, particularly after the American government was formed, that made possible the realization of his whole program. Earlier Americans understood this and were ready to hail Hamilton's achievements.

Voices of doubt are being raised today. One should not object to them, for in debate reexamination can occur and new agreements can be beaten out, assuming the reasonableness of men. This book is a contribution to that discussion; and it is written in the hope that, as a result of a revaluation of Hamilton's work, not only shall we have a better understanding of the problems facing America at the dawn of its establishment but we shall have clear guidance in our own career and as we confront our own perplexities.

In recent years, Hamilton's intention has been challenged from three different quarters. First, it is being argued—Merrill Jensen's *The New Nation* [1] is a characteristic statement—that the Confederation of 1781 to 1789, rather than plunging the states into irresponsibility and chaos, was moving successfully toward a fusion. The Revolution, in affirming the rights of men, was continuing toward the realization of equalitarianism; the states were arriving at agreement on common action; the peacetime economic processes were being reestablished and put on a firm footing. The Constitution, because it checked the course of the Revolution and made the states subservient to the central government, was usurpation. There was no "critical period"; therefore, the Constitution, with its insistence upon sound money and the sanctity of contracts, was a seizure of power in the interests of a minority.

[1] All footnotes will be found following page 257.

This minority, holds a second view—and here the late Joseph Charles in his "Hamilton and Washington: The Origins of the American Party System" [2] is representative—was made up of the "privileged" or the "moneyed" classes. These were both distrustful of "democracy" and seeking to use government only for their personal aggrandizement. They wanted "the preservation of an old-world society"; they were interested in "exploiting a new continent"; they favored Great Britain, with its hierarchical structure, as against France, the friend and the hope of all mankind. Says Charles:

Hamilton put his trust in the privileged classes and considered their interests as inseparable from those of society as a whole. He wanted a close collaboration between this country and England. He aimed at the closest possible union, even a high degree of consolidation, between the different parts of this country, and he wanted a powerful central government. These aims were so closely related in the conditions of the time that they are perhaps aspects of the same plan, and he probably thought of them as different means toward a single goal. The economic program which he advanced furthered these aims in every respect. It made for the supremacy of the propertied classes; it involved as much consolidation and as great a centralization of power as would have been accepted at that time; and it brought in its train intimate commercial and diplomatic relations with Great Britain.

A third view—and it is that presented by Russell Kirk in his *The Conservative Mind* [3]—maintains that Hamilton was no conservative in the proper sense but only an old-fashioned Tory of the seventeenth century. It was really a mercantilist America he sought to establish, and he equated welfare, through government action, with the encouragement and enrichment of "particular classes and occupations." But he pushed too hard. An industrialized America, its class society, its urbanized population possessing "a newer radicalism," are the fruits of his efforts. Hamilton was "eminently a city-man, and veneration withers upon the pavements. . . . Hamilton never penetrated far beneath the surface of politics to the mysteries of veneration and presumption."

In part, I am seeking to take issue with these positions in this book. It is my contention, here, that not only was the Confederation inadequate but that the Revolution was being perverted: the Constitution saved both the American nation and the Revolution itself. Further, Hamilton united private interest with public policy: without honor, the new nation could not create confidence, and the support of its men of affairs was needed for both stability and progress. Hamilton read the meaning of the capital processes both realistically and imaginatively: Adam Smith was his guide and with Smith he understood that the wealth of a nation and its welfare went hand in hand.

A polity will not survive—and conservatives, because of their love of country, know the significance of stability better than all others—unless justice, equality of opportunity, and therefore the chance to rise are always assured. Industrialization—rather, the diversification of the economy—exactly because it is dynamic, makes possible the realization of well-being and in its processes guarantees class mobility. This is really the message of Alexander Hamilton to the United States today.

This book is appearing in 1957, the year of the observance of the bicentennial of Alexander Hamilton's birth. It accepts the view of other scholars that Hamilton was born in 1755. The only reference in Hamilton's writings to his birth year we find in a letter he wrote in 1797, addressed to his distant Scottish kinsman Alexander Hamilton. He indicated some doubts himself, for he wrote: "Myself at about sixteen came to this country. . . . I was able, by the age of nineteen, to qualify myself for the degree of Bachelor of Arts in the College of New York. . . . The American Revolution supervened. My principles led me to take part in it; at nineteen I entered into the American army as captain of artillery." [4]

Whether born in 1755 or 1757 is of no great moment; and it is fitting, whatever the occasion, that this great man's contributions to the establishment and security of his country be celebrated. This book may add something toward that purpose. It is not a biography in the formal sense nor is it a systematic history; it is an essay in political and economic ideas as they affected public policy. For this reason it draws heavily on Hamilton's own writings and carefully scrutinizes his argument, as he developed it on all those momentous questions that confronted his generation. The general inaccessibility of Hamilton's writings will make the quotations particularly useful, as Americans ponder over what Hamilton's meaning is for us today.

LOUIS M. HACKER

School of General Studies
Columbia University

Contents

Introduction

THERE IS GENERAL AGREEMENT THAT THE ACCEPTANCE OF A COMMON tradition is one of the truly significant binding forces that creates a nation. The distinctive quality of nationality is worth examining constantly: not only do all of us require the security of belonging —of having a home where understanding and affection can be found—but we want certainty about our commitments. We live in time, we have links with the past, and we plan for the future, as much to assure ourselves that our own strivings, however modest, have been meaningful as to provide lines of direction for those who follow us. There is continuity in a national life; and the recognition of this makes it possible for us to postpone immediate benefits for ultimate gains and to compromise extreme positions. We survive by agreement and by making sacrifices, even the extreme one, in our common defense.

A tradition is complex, it has negative and positive aspects, some based on rejection and some on reception. Men live as much in the world as in their country: Americans are aware of Aristotle, Galileo, Descartes, Spinoza, for example, as part of their heritage; on the other hand, because they are Americans, the whole precapitalist system of feudal Europe is outside their ken. Here, if we are to seek uniqueness, if we are to try to set off the American from the rest of western culture, and, indeed, from that of the East as well, is a significant point of departure.

One of the fundamental aspects of the American tradition is that all Americans, from the seventeenth century until today, have been brought up in a capitalist world of private striving and individual ownership. The European emigrants who departed for America in the seventeenth, eighteenth, nineteenth, and twentieth centuries were largely the unwanted simple and underprivileged folk of the countryside and the smaller communities. Many departed voluntarily; some were forced; a few were assisted. They came—when they could pay their passage in the seventeenth and eighteenth centuries—as freemen; the larger number, certainly in the one hundred years between 1650–1750, came as bond servants. They came, as young men and women who had been the victims either of war and famine, or of religious persecution, or of ecclesiastical or economic oppression, or of unequal land systems and guild restrictions, or of racial discrimination.

The settlers of America came lightly burdened with this world's goods—and with loyalties. To understand the American tradition one must note what these left behind, or rejected, and how, therefore, the ways of life and attitudes they created were sharply opposed to those with which they had been familiar.

They left behind the medieval land system of tenure and organization and the class society linked with it. It is true that in England that system had been in process of dissolution since the fourteenth century; but there were many hangovers that continued to survive, all of which made for concentrated land ownership and backward agricultural practices. On the European continent, right into the nineteenth century, feudalism still flourished in many areas. In Europe, the possession of a freehold for the little men was next to impossible; the common lands, with their harmful effect on animal husbandry, continued to exist; landlords persisted in exacting their dues and obligations and increasingly contracted the common lands; the village still dominated planting programs; but the newcomers to America left all these practices behind.

In consequence, land tenure, in America, was revolutionized: for the first time men of little or no means could hope to become freeholders, or the owners of property. Whether as purchasers, squatters, or homesteaders, they had easy access to the land. This was the hope of America. This was its most significant attraction, which drew millions of Europeans out of the British Isles, Germany, Scandinavia, and Central Europe, for 250 years. Because of freeholds, the village as a method of organization, and the public utilities as the right of landlords, could be abandoned. The American freeholder could live where he pleased; he could plant what he pleased; he had water rights, subsoil rights, and the right to bequeath and devise his property as he chose. The right to possessions was unencumbered: because there were many freeholders there were many freemen in America.

The dearth of labor that existed right to the beginning of the twentieth century in America was an extraordinary consequence of this. Men could become farmers, or owners of property, rather than industrial workers, with the result that, from the seventeenth century on, real wages were always higher in the United States. And because costs of labor were high, whether on the farms or in the factories, mechanization was an early concern of Americans; that Yankee ingenuity Americans pride themselves on was the child of necessity.

The newcomers also left behind them Europe's corporate organization—in industry, trade, the churches, and the state. And with their rejection of corporativism they rejected authoritarianism. The medieval world has been founded on corporate authority—whether of manor, guild, or church. Even as the medieval world dissolved, remnants of it persisted in modern Europe. The corporate guilds survived; new corporations made their appearance as regulated companies and joint-stock companies; monopolies flourished.

The guild system, with its controls over wages, apprentices, production, new capital investments, and innovation, was not transplanted into the New World of North America. Whether as worker or enterpriser, the American was free to open his own establishment, move where he pleased, trade where and when and under whatever conditions he chose. The European system of monopolies, however, had important effects upon Americans, for they continued to be fearful of it. Not only did Jefferson express

his misgivings about monopoly, but also Hamilton. Corporate
charters—except in banking and transportation—were granted
only with the utmost caution in early America. Indeed, it was not
until the 1840s that the doors were thrown open wide to the creation of corporations. Concern over concentrated economic power
is part of the American tradition, to be found in attitudes and in
basic law.

In every country of Europe from which the seventeenth- and
eighteenth-century colonists came, established churches existed.
(Many established churches survived into the nineteenth century.)
Established churches meant not only the curbing of dissent but
the domination of education and the possession of great legal and
financial powers. Americans were fearful about the corporate authority of established churches and they moved against them.
During the Revolution, churches were disestablished in some of
the states; the first Amendment of the Constitution prevented the
federal government from setting up an established ecclesiastical
authority in America; by the end of the first quarter of the nineteenth century, the surviving state-established churches of New
England had disappeared.

Thus, freedom of religious worship, the separation of church
and state, and—a corollary arising from these ideas—public support
of education and easy access to it have always been basic American
commitments. As the pioneers (and freemen) moved westward,
everywhere there sprang up in their midst the little white churches
and the litttle red schoolhouses—both local, both symbols of their
independence of authority.

These were institutions of restriction, privilege, and control
Europeans coming to America left behind. They also left behind
an attitude which regarded human labor as inferior and the role
of the worker as debased. The dignity of human labor has, of
course, been at the heart of the Christian system of ethics, notably
Protestantism. Because it linked the idea of his calling with salvation, Protestantism did much to ennoble man in his humble pur-

suits. But practices and professions did not always go hand in hand. The medieval serf was despised by his lord; he repaid ill will with the treachery and violence that have so darkened the pages of medieval life. The seventeenth and eighteenth centuries also saw the same gulf widening; the theory of mercantilism—against which Americans rebelled in the Revolution—also was founded on the inferior status of labor.

If wealth, according to mercantilism, flowed from a nation's foreign trade and the favorable balances obtained therein, the key factor was low costs of production. The wealth of a nation, therefore, was in its labor supply engaged in the production of goods and services for export; the size, docility, and poverty of its workers made possible the riches of the whole body politic. It is ironic and revealing that England called its workers collectively "The Poor"; right into the last quarter of the nineteenth century this designation of the English working class persisted. Arthur Young, in the third quarter of the eighteenth century, could say of his own countrymen, "Everyone but an idiot knows that the lower classes must be kept poor or they will never be industrious." [1]

From such a world, the humble Europeans fled. It is easy to account for the new values they created as they rejected those of the old world. Freedom meant a freehold, or the possession of property, and acquisition had a universal stamp of approval. Freedom meant mobility, geographically but socially, too. Men could rise—here is the real heart of the concept of "equality of opportunity"—because work was noble and natural and not demeaning, because property ownership was a right and not a privilege, and because talents could emerge, for education for all was available. This, and only this, was the meaning of equalitarianism to Americans.

This equalitarianism could be supported by equality in political institutions and equality before the law. Here is the other side of the shield: the reception, or transmission, of English law was one of America's great heritages, woven into the warp and woof of its tradition. What are the leading components of this political tradition? These, certainly: the rule of law; constitutional government; republican institutions, based on the representative principle and the separation of powers; the safeguarding of the rights of the individual through exact procedural guarantees.

Because these protections exist, the responsibilities of citizenship have been accepted. The citizen functions as a party member and as a voter; he also functions freely, with many loyalties which act and interact on politics, in a rich associational life. He is a member of a trade association or a trade union, of a veterans' organization or a community club, of a parents' group or a cooperative society. The state may grow bigger; but as the citizen's interests expand and become more articulate, he develops new devices for the scrutiny of public authority and to keep its affairs manageable.

THIS IS OUR COMMON BACKGROUND OF BELIEF AND ACCEPTANCE. Within its terms, Americans seek tranquility, stability, and welfare or progress. They hope to achieve these by maintaining their national security under honorable conditions. Having said this and accepted its validity, we are ready to admit that two main tendencies have developed in America for the realization of these aims, one the Hamiltonian, the other, the Jeffersonian. These are not necessarily contradictory; it is imperative that Americans always have in mind that both Hamilton and Jefferson were dedicated to the same broad principles. They wanted to see a free, secure, progressing America. And the contributions of both have been mighty.

If we believe in human freedom, the dignity of the individual and his right to dissent, the wide dispersion of political power, we recognize Jefferson's enduring contributions; and if we believe in the necessity for stable political institutions, honorable government in its relations at home and abroad, and freedom of economic enterprise as the real key to national progress, we recognize Hamilton's. We are all Jeffersonians, we are all Hamiltonians; yet, so profound has been the impact of these two great men, the American today is either largely a Hamiltonian or he is largely a Jeffersonian. It is equally true that an American can be a Hamiltonian, logically and consistently, and yet reject some of Hamilton's eighteenth-century positions. The same is true in the case of a present-day Jeffersonian. It will be useful, then, to examine the basic differences between the two protean antagonists, as they contemplated their own world.

Jefferson and Hamilton, because they were political thinkers, started out with a theory of human nature. Hamilton's was in the older Christian tradition: man inherited and transmitted Original Sin because of Adam's fall, and, because man was capable of good but also of evil, government was necessary to prevent him —and groups of men—from preying on his fellows. Men were creatures of passion and guided by their immediate interests; they were "ambitious, vindictive, and rapacious"; these qualities were keys to their actions, rather than "policy, utility, or justice." At the end of the same sixth essay of *The Federalist*, in which these observations were made, Hamilton, looking at the world about him, remarked, "Is it not time to awake from the deceitful dream of a golden age, and to adopt as a practical maxim for the direction of our political conduct that we, as well as the other inhabitants of the globe, are yet remote from the happy empire of perfect wisdom and perfect virtue?"

Government was necessary for external defense, to support society's normal activities, and to protect the community from the aggrandizement of individuals and the irresponsibility of groups. Hamilton feared internal disorders and sought an "energetic" government to assure tranquility; but he was worried more about power, and the danger of its seizure by willful, self-seeking persons; to this extent, a government had to be "coercive." It can be seen that it is a far cry from coercion under a totalitarian scheme to coercion to prevent selfish men from despoiling society. "Great power, commerce, and riches," said Hamilton in 1782, "may ... be denominated evils; for they lead to insolence, an inordinate ambititon, a vicious luxury, licentiousness of morals, and all those vices which corrupt government, enslave the people, and precipitate the ruin of a nation." It was the role of government, therefore, "to guard against encroachments upon the rights of the community." [2]

Jefferson's position was the reverse: a "very energetic" government was "always oppressive." [3] This was so because man—and here Jefferson drew his inspiration from his own Age of the Enlightenment—was not only rational but capable of continuing self-improvement. Science and education contributed their share, as they broke down anicent prejudices and prerogatives, to release the spirit of men; of equal importance to Americans was their escape from European ties; in a boundless new continent, where equality really existed, free institutions now for the first time could take root and flourish. Therefore, notably in America, it was proper to expect that reason would curb egoism, prudence would temper selfishness, and self-improvement and social well-being would become inextricably linked. Given freedom, under the beneficent auspices of science—science as the eighteenth century understood it, that the wide world was orderly and ruled by invariant law—and men must grow to new intellectual, if not moral, heights.

It is obvious that such a canon of not only improvement but perfectibility, ends in anarchism—no government at all. Jefferson's economics also had the same quality of utopianism that we find in that long line of dreamers from Plato through More to Marx and William Morris. Production, largely in a self-sufficing agriculture, can dispense with markets, credit, and the accumulative process; notably, it prevents human exploitation by the wage system. This is far different from the "equality of opportunity," where men may rise and fall, dependent upon their talents. This is the equalitarianism of the leveler, who would eradicate different stations for men and differences in wealth and income.

There is another contrast in the positions of Jefferson and Hamilton which follows from their theories of society. Hamilton saw the unequal capacities and rewards of men, and the necessity for protecting the community against internal aggression. From time to time, society required re-examination; change had to occur. It was to be orderly change, conforming to the traditions, habits, and duties of men, and it had to be change under the dispensation of law. During the Revolution and in the troubled reconstruction following it, again and again Hamilton requested that legal procedures be rigorously followed. He was no friend of the loyalists, but they had personal and property rights. If redistribution had to occur it must not take place without legal sanctions, or a full weighing of putative losses and gains. In 1783, he wrote: [4]

Individuals have been already too long sacrificed to public convenience. It will be shocking, and, indeed, an eternal reproach to this country, if we begin the peaceable enjoyment of our independence by a violation of all the principles of honesty and true policy.

Jefferson's equalitarianism led him down strange paths. Oppression might suddenly spring up; imbalances could appear. Then men had the right to take the law into their own hands and establish their ideas of justice. The smashing of all normal relations as a result of revolution, the chaos that ensues and the violence that is unleashed, the danger of dictatorship, whether of the majority or of an individual—these are risks, but less portentous than the perpetuation of old wrongs.

Repeatedly, the two men take sharp issue when gradualism and extremism are the choices. Hamilton follows the careers of the states, during and after the Revolution, with concern; Jefferson is untroubled. Hamilton takes alarm at the Shays Rebellion; Jefferson thinks the embattled farmers, closing down the courts, were in the right. Hamilton from the beginning, sees the French Revolution as imperiling human rights, and with every changing phase in it—Jacobinism, Girondism, Bonapartism—he sounds a warn-

ing; Jefferson refuses to express concern. What if some innocent
blood is shed? The gains for humanity will be immense. Frenchmen, even after they have begun their aggression on the whole of
Europe, are still fighting the battle of universal freedom. Hamilton
must put down the Whiskey Rebellion, for now constituted government is threatened; Jefferson wants to debate the equities or
inequities of an excise tax, and looks with complacency on the
violence of the western farmers.

It is on the question of welfare—the devices men employ to
improve their economic lot—that the greatest disparities appear.
Jefferson is indifferent to the economic processes; all questions
involving them are political in their nature. Men can be free
if they are the possessors of small properties given over largely
to self-sufficing agriculture. A policy based on such a wide diffu-
sion of ownership cannot be an oppressive one; nor has government any significant functions to perform. Commerce, banking,
and manufactures bring in their train all sorts of evils, and utopia
is invaded. Accumulation undermines his conception of the equality of men; commerce and industry cause cities to rise and underprivileged laborers (a "canaille") to appear; banking is only usury.
Commerce involves the nation with other nations; it also encourages capital transfers, and the foreign investor is among us.
Jefferson is willing to see commerce atrophy and is even ready
to take reprisals against foreign investors in order to force their
governments to change their policies toward America.

Progress, in short, needs no encouragement under the Jeffersonian dispensation; the heart's desire has already been realized.
Hamilton, on the other hand, is clear, realistic, imaginative, and
bold. The United States is a poor nation on insecure foundations.
It is surrounded by unfriendly powers on the American continent
and caught in the crossfire of the two great nations of Europe,
the English and the French, engaged in a struggle to the death.
If the United States is to survive and if it is to grow—absorbing
more peoples, diversifying its economy, increasing its "revenue

and capital"—it must establish a climate in which the accumulative process, "under the direction of a private interest," can flourish. Hamilton starts with fiscal integrity and he ends with a "system of perfect liberty." Hamilton, in short, profoundly influenced by both John Locke and Adam Smith, sees the wealth of America in basic libertarian terms: in the productivity and "parsimony" of its people as free enterprisers, so that, as rounds of working and spending become more complex, income is advanced and the defense of the nation is assured. Hamilton's political economy is always that of a patriot; the honor and the security of his country stand highest on his agenda.

A nation, to grow, must establish its financial faith, honor its obligations, provide a revenue for governmental purposes, service its debt, and protect its money supply. Only if it does so will "the moneyed men," "the most enlightened friends of good government," [5] cooperate and invest in the country's economy. The same applies to foreigners; almost alone among his contemporaries, Hamilton saw the necessity for creating a state of affairs which would encourage foreign capital to move into the United States. An economy, to grow, must diversify its interests: dependence upon agriculture is not enough. Commerce and manufactures, particularly the latter, will augment the country's wealth and establish that domestic market in which alone agriculture can thrive.

Public credit and private credit are irrefragably linked: credit is the foundation of the country's "increase of national and individual welfare": a treasury, zealous in defense of its obligations, works hand in hand with a national bank, which regulates the rise and fall of private credit. It can do so because the money of the government is based on gold and silver and because bank notes can be kept on a specie basis.

Should government intervene? If a "system of perfect liberty" existed throughout the world—and that meant universal peace and free exchanges in terms of the "peculiar advantages" nations possessed in the production of goods—government could remain quiescent. But because nations continue to resort to mercantilist devices and American's defense is a prime consideration, government must be called upon to help in the diversification and strengthening of the economy. Government should use short-run devices—bounties are better than tariffs, because tariffs breed monopolies—to encourage domestic manufactures toward that time when our "peculiar advantages" will become significant and intervention can be relaxed, even terminated.

It is extraordinary how Hamilton has been misread throughout history, by both his fellow countrymen and his admirers abroad. Because he saw the need for industrialization as the road to welfare, or progress, and because he made the case for the support of infant industries so eloquently, his advocacy of protection has been pondered over and repeated again and again. But we have lost sight of the fact that he regarded governmental assistance (of which protective tariffs constituted but one and the least desirable of the devices to be employed) as an expedient necessary only because new, young, and underdeveloped nations were unequal in a race where the more powerful nations had every advantage for the very reason that their governments used intervention on their behalf.

His own preferences are clear. He follows Adam Smith so plainly and completely that one can only express wonder that the Hamilton text has been misunderstood for so long. Hamilton says:[6]

If the system of perfect liberty to industry and commerce were the prevailing system of nations, the arguments which dissuade a country, in the predicament of the United States, from the zealous pursuit of manufactures, would doubtless have great force. It will not be affirmed that they might not be permitted, with few exceptions, to serve as a rule of national conduct. In such a state of things, each country would have the full benefit of its peculiar advantages to compensate for its deficiencies or disadvantages.

Hamilton thought of his country constantly. In 1782, he said, "There is something noble and magnificent in the perspective of a great Federal Republic, closely linked in the pursuit of a common interest, tranquil and prosperous at home, respectable abroad." [7] In 1798, even amidst the alarums of war, he could say, "I anticipate with you that this country will, ere long, assume an attitude correspondent with its great destinies—majestic, efficient, and operative of great things. A noble career lies before it." [8] It is natural that his views on foreign relations would be in the same vein: America, in its dealings with other nations, was to regard its self-interest as its only guide; benevolence, moral principle, gratitude were irrelevant. The United States, then, should keep free of entangling alliances; it was to remain neutral, despite France's claims upon it; it was, however, to make the best possible bargain with Britain, for English trade and English good will, in the final analysis, were our best friends.

Such intelligent counsels stood the country in excellent stead. America was not embroiled in war on the side of France; her commerce and therefore her public revenues were safeguarded; settlements were effected with Spain and Britain—and we continued to expand and grow prosperous at the same time that national honor was preserved. For espousing these principles, Hamilton was taxed with perfidy: he was abandoning those republican ideals for which France was fighting and to which we ourselves were dedicated; he was an "Anglo-man." Yet, except once—and this was during "Mr. Madison's War," in 1812—these have been America's guides to foreign policy, until recent times.

HAMILTON'S GREAT CONTRIBUTION IN THE BUILDING OF THE AMERIcan nation thus takes shape. He sought a strong central government only to assure tranquility and welfare. In 1783, he wrote that every state had to be guided by the "superior motives" of "national faith, honor, and reputation." [9] In their sequestration of property, assaults on contracts, inability or refusal to pay public debts and to provide a public revenue, and in the launching of runaway paper inflations, the leveling forces at work in the states, during and after the Revolution, had done great damage. When he expressed his fear about "democracy" he meant this legislative irresponsibility; Madison had had the same concern in mind when he referred to the "mutability of the laws of the states." [10]

Hamilton, however, was no foe of popular government; as early as 1777, he had declared his confidence in it, for then he had said, "That instability is inherent in the nature of popular governments, I think very disputable." [11] He had repeated the same sentiments in the "Phocion" letters in 1784.[12] In 1788, at the New York ratifying convention, he had made an open and frank declaration along similar lines: "The true principle of a republic is, that the people should choose whom they please to govern them"; and again: "In whatever direction the popular weight leans, the current of power will flow. Whatever the popular attachments be, there will rest the political superiority." [13]

By the same token, he was not hostile to the states, nor was he prepared to see them swallowed up in a "vigorous" central scheme. They had their legitimate functions to perform; it was possible to attach the loyalties of the citizens to them. Here there would exist that greater play and interplay between government and its subjects which results in the response of authority that republicanism demanded. As early as 1781, he saw the solid basis of federalism, when he alluded to the states in these words: "The particular governments will have more empire over the minds of their subjects than the general one, because their agency will be more direct, more uniform, and more apparent." [14]

It is absurd to call such a man a monarchist or an aristocrat in the European sense; yet his contemporaries did so, and the slander continues to die hard. Hamilton believed in inequality of talents, as did all the men of his generation, Jefferson among them. But, having pondered deeply over the British Constitution, he saw the significance of continuity in the head of state and of the public services performed by the House of Lords. Government should be in the hands of the capable and those who had a stake in society. Let tenure of office, then, be based on a "responsible and temporary or defeasible" term. Equally desirable was service by the "rich and well-born," for these would assure good government "as they cannot receive any advantage by a change." [15] The idea of noblesse oblige was a feudal one and has always been highly praiseworthy; but it was a counsel of perfection that Hamilton, normally so realistic about the motives of men, should have been on his guard against. Because he spoke in these sanguine terms of dedication to the public welfare, it is absurd to charge him with aristocratic principles or authoritarian ideas, as his opponents did, and as some commentators do today.

He was committed to republicanism; again and again he asserted he would accept no other form, even granted its shortcomings. "We ought to go as far in order to attain stability and permanency, as republican principles will admit," [16] he said at the Constitutional Convention. In *The Federalist* he declared, "The republican principle demands that the deliberate sense of the community should govern the conduct of those to whom they entrust the management of their affairs." [17] And, in 1792, when the attacks on him had become particularly virulent, he said, "As to my own political creed, I give it to you with the utmost sincerity, I am affectionately attached to the republican principle. I desire above all things to see the equality of political rights, exclusive of all hereditary distinction. . . ." [18]

These were the political ideas upon which a firm and secure union was to be built. It was to be American—as fully American as Jefferson sought. A sense of nationality was always at the heart of Hamilton's striving. In 1796, he wrote, "We are laboring hard to establish in this country principles more and more *national* and free from all foreign ingredients, so that we may be neither 'Greeks nor Trojans' but truly Americans." [19]

Only within such a framework could welfare be pursued. If the American nation was to be "majestic, efficient, and operative of great things," [20] it could be so because government, by protecting its own honor through its fiscal responsibility, created a climate where the private citizen could labor, accumulate, and invest. Public and private credit went hand in hand; the money supply was to be safeguarded; a revenue was to be assured. But the country's credit was the foundation stone, "the palladium of public safety," America's "invigorating principle," the basis for the "increase of national and individual welfare." [21]

So much for government's function: otherwise, it was to keep hands off; the individual's self interest was the only guide to economic policy; in consequence, the "industry of a people ... will, upon equal terms, find out the most beneficial employment for itself." [22] Similarly, the best order, viewed internationally, to permit of full mobility of trade, labor, and capital, was a "system of perfect liberty." Then nations could pursue their "peculiar advantages" in their intercourse with one another, as at home they developed that complex program of commerce, industry, and agriculture which their natural resources, skills, and predilections directed them to. All this would increase their productivity and augment their "revenue and capital"; by these processes, progress was realizable in a free climate.

However, as long as other nations burdened American commerce with disabilities, and as long as the country's safety was in jeopardy, government intervention was justifiable. American manufactures should have public assistance; but bounties, rather than tariffs, were the most desirable forms of public aid. Bounties had the advantages of being easily determined and of encouraging competition; they were essentially short-run devices, used as expedient in bargaining with other nations to achieve reciprocity.

Hamilton said flatly, "The continuance of bounties on manufactures long established must almost always be of questionable
policy." [23]

For all this, foreign capital was imperative: to finance trade,
to buy the public "stock" and the shares of private banks, to
build highways, waterworks, navigation systems, and factories.
Hamilton, from his childhood, knew the part foreign credit
played in making trade possible. It is understandable, in consequence, that he should early advocate honoring the mercantile
debts of the colonies to Great Britain. The United States was a
poor country; the transfer of foreign capital was just as vital to
its growth as the "parsimony" of its own citizens.

Hamilton was, then, in the best sense, both nationalist and internationalist, quick to defend his country's honor in political and
fiscal terms, but ever ready to expand the movement of goods,
workers, and capital into and outside of the American borders.
This was the creed of a libertarian; and because the United States
followed Alexander Hamilton's lead and built a strong union,
honored its debts, and encouraged and protected the domestic
and foreign investor, it was able to survive the first uncertain
years of its founding. This was the measure of his accomplishment;
by these processes the American nation was built.

THE WHOLE HUMAN SCENE WAS NOT HAMILTON'S STAGE AND TO THIS
extent he was no typical child of the eighteenth century. He was
no Diderot, Voltaire, Johnson, or Burke, no Franklin or Jefferson:
he did not have that wide curiosity or large appetite for knowledge that made so many of his contemporaries range freely and
with so much pleasure in the many different areas of human
aspiration. The opening Newtonian world, as it sought to find
order and chart the course of accomplishment in nature's and
man's growth, apparently never caught his imagination. He
listened to music and bought pictures; he was familiar with the

accomplishments of antiquity; but he never speculated about art and life. He was religious, but again in the formal sense, contenting himself with the knowledge that there was to be a redemption—men were to be judged by their deportment among and their obligations to their fellows.

One does not read Hamilton's letters, pamphlets, and reports for any purpose other than that for which they were intended. He was always immersed in affairs, and he wrote only of these matters. Hamilton was no Chesterfield, whose work one peruses in an idle moment for amusement or even general guidance. He operated in a narrow sphere and yet, in an imperfect world, it was the most important one affecting the relations of men in society. This was statecraft. It is idle to say that Hamilton was no political philosopher and that none of his contributions to political economy was original. Burke and Jefferson, in this sense, were more important; but can either match Hamilton in the management of the business of government, that rare capacity, which he possessed, of recognizing a crisis and knowing how to meet it? What significance are such strictures in the face of the impressive facts that Hamilton knew how to establish the security and honor of a new nation and how to lay out the lines of direction for its future development, nay, survival?

To lose sight of this achievement—to introduce wholly extraneous matters having to do with supposed motivations or even personal aspirations—is to be almost frivolous. Hamilton was ambitious. Hamilton sought the Presidency. Hamilton appealed for support to the "most enlightened friends of good government." Granted; but of what statesman, from Pericles through Disraeli into our own times, cannot such observations be made? They really have no relevance, once we are prepared to acknowledge that the true statesman always has before him the greater good of the society with which he identifies himself. To this extent, the statesman is selfless and classless; indeed no public program devised through statecraft can be successful unless it has general (not necessarily universal) support. Hamilton was a statesman whose policies remained the staples of American government long after his personal retirement—indeed, his defeat —and which continue to furnish guidance for our contemporary world.

One must not seem to yield too much before Hamilton's critics. He was a man with a mission but not therefore one whose presence made one uneasy. Because he worked so hard and yet so quickly, because he was able to master detail so competently, one must not assume he was superior, overbearing, churlish. Quite the contrary, Hamilton had hosts of friends who delighted in his company. He liked human society and sought it out; he was witty; he was devoted to those who were loyal to him; he was trusted. He continued in touch with his youthful companions until his death. Women were at ease with him and he knew how to please them. He had harmless human vanities that are distinctly in his favor: he liked to dress well and he took pleasure in his home.

This is not the picture of a man possessed: a person who drives himself and breaks down opposition ruthlessly. His origins were obscure (none knew that better than he); and he had married well. The first made him want to succeed—is there a better reason for a man's striving? The second was helpful, but his was no marriage of convenience. Hamilton loved his wife and was deeply devoted to his children. Because of his origins, because of the need for proving himself (to his wealthy father-in-law as well as to the world at large), Hamilton was single-minded. Such men frequently triumph. They prepare themselves well; they take risks (as Hamilton did, when he challenged Washington and quarreled with him); they fight hard; they know how to overcome opposition. He had enemies, as what man of accomplishment does not.

Here, in short, is a complex and fascinating personality: ambitious, restless, resourceful, tenacious; and also devoted, honest, and faithful. In a time of crisis no country dare seek another kind of public servant. This is Hamilton's particular quality and his notable significance in American affairs. Well might it be said of him, as Pericles did of his fellow Athenians: "For there is justice in the claim that steadfastness in his country's battles should be as a cloak to cover a man's other imperfections; since the good action has blotted out the bad, and his merit as a citizen more than outweighed his demerits as an individual."

1

West Indian Background

WHAT ARE THE FORCES THAT SHAPE A MAN'S LIFE? WHAT ARE THE influences—the early conditioning and frustrations, the dreams of youth, the hopes and fears of personal ambition—that give plan, scope, and variety to his public conduct and his private relations? Sometimes he himself seeks to tell—as did Pepys, Johnson, and Rousseau, for example; such a man seems to be endlessly fascinated with himself and, in consequence, one knows why there is acceptance or rejection of his efforts.

What if a man is as silent as the tomb, however? What if he never talks of his childhood and youth and never writes of his dreams or their failure to those dear to him who may reasonably be expected to share his confidences? Are we of necessity to assume that such silence itself is significant?

One is confronted by such a puzzle in the personality and character of Alexander Hamilton. Of that great generation of the Founding Fathers, he, along with Thomas Jefferson, left the mightiest impress on his times and a towering heritage to succeeding American generations. While it was still disunited, Alexander Hamilton saw what elements were necessary to bind the American states together. When it was still weak, he already had a vision of a growing and powerful nation. While it was still ringed around by hostile powers, its newly created sovereignty threatened, he laid out a course of action which preserved the American people against the perils of international involvement.

If Thomas Jefferson—with his deep and abiding confidence in the intelligence, integrity, and humanity of man—unerringly guided America to a democratic commitment, Alexander Hamilton as surely and as permanently laid the basis for its success. Alexander Hamilton, in political and economic terms, built the American nation; Thomas Jefferson, in democratic and humanist terms, gave it its unique dedication. Despite this, paradoxically enough, these two great men mistrusted and fought each other, and were responsible for the development of two opposing tendencies in American life.

This is so because Americans have looked not at the grand design to which both gave their loyalty, but to the devices each employed to achieve his particular end. We forget too readily that each labored constantly to establish and assure a free America; we remember unnecessarily—and by doing so exacerbate our own differences—the transitory quarrels that kept them apart. Both men had powerful intellects and wills, and therefore both triumphed. If the United States is to endure, it is because of this simple and yet impressive fact.

Of Jefferson—as of Washington, Franklin, Madison, Adams, indeed scores of their contemporaries in that extraordinary time —we know much that curiosity prompts us to learn. We know of his birth, youth, early maturity; we know what he read and who influenced him; we know of his family and friends and their almost daily relations; we know of the trivial as well as the momentous events of his life.

We know of none or little of these things in the life of Alexander Hamilton. We cannot say, Here is a reticent man, too shy to wear his affections on his sleeve, or too correct and impersonal to share a confidence. He was devoted to his family and true to his friends; he was gay and warm in company—he earned people's devotion and affections. Yet rarely does he tell his wife, children, friends about himself and his purposes.

The analyst, sympathetic or not, is driven back upon conjecture. Is Alexander Hamilton silent about his origins and youth because he was sensitive to the fact that he was born out of wedlock? As a young man, having gained the favor of George Washington, does he risk all in a sudden burst of temper because of this same sensitivity? Having married well into the rich, highborn, and influential Schuyler family, does he throw in his lot with the aristocratic tradition because of a gnawing insecurity? Why does he seek military eminence on the field at Yorktown, to lead armed men against the embattled farmers of western Pennsylvania, to be the Inspector-General of the American Army? Is it because in war, reputations can be made despite birth and family?

These things are so; yet it is too easy to say that Hamilton was an arrivist, an aristocrat, a militarist because of his sensitivity and his insecurity. It is perhaps nearer the truth to say that Hamilton was a great man just because there was an awareness of early failure and, therefore, a necessity to overcome its stultifying restraints. For surely—possibly in the eighteenth century this was more the case—a young man without legitimate birth or family starts out with terrifying handicaps. It requires a powerful character to emerge from such a background. Alexander Hamilton did so, and by looking at his youth, one can gain a clue to the great purposes of his life. His youth was insecure and he sought security; but not, curiously enough, for himself but for the new nation with whose destiny his was linked.

Hamilton was personally ambitious, yet again and again he subordinated his own interests to those of his country. A patriot is selfless, single-minded, energetic; he sees a crisis, devises the means for handling it, risks all in its successful resolution. He is determined in overcoming opposition, skillful in obtaining allies, endlessly resourceful in the means to be employed. Wounds are inflicted; he hopes they will heal and that he will in time be forgiven. A patriot sometimes is a friendless man.

One of the keys to Hamilton's life was his patriotism. Another was his narrow association, in planning for a stable America, with a specific class. The United States would survive if it gained the "reason and the interest" of the men of affairs: they would save and invest, and their private enterprise would advance the welfare of the whole community. To these, then, he addressed himself constantly, never concealing his fears of the havoc a "democracy" could bring upon his country. He believed in republican government, which to him meant the indirect choice, with all sorts of checks, of its rulers. The direct and full suffrage of all the people is what he understood by "democracy," and of this Hamilton was as distrustful as were most of his contemporaries.

This is not the way a political career is built or a party created. Politics frequently means accommodation: one bargains, one temporizes, one adjusts to prejudices and sectional and local loyalties; a sense of urgency is abandoned in favor of the education of a following. And no party, in the democratic meaning, can succeed unless it can make its appeal on national lines and above class concerns. To this extent, a party is always an alliance, held together by a common interest conceived in the broadest sense but functioning because sooner or later every element in it will be heard and its claims allowed. For this reason, upon the order of the party leaders, directions of policy are developed and followed— the day of those who individually dissent will come, too.

In these terms, Hamilton was neither a politician nor the head of a party. Because times were out of joint, because he had great personal rectitude, because of his brilliance as a planner and organizer, because he was so close to George Washington, as Secretary of the Treasury, he obtained agreement. But, except from his own small company of friends who were dearly devoted to him, he got no enduring support or gratitude. When the crisis was over—and it lasted through the decade of the 1790s—Alexander Hamilton could be safely shelved. His work was done; the Republic was saved and its future assured; and a private life was his inevitable reward. His impatience with "democracy," his failure to build a party on broad lines, his constant and even narrow preoccupation with measures of direct immediacy—although his purpose was nothing less than the preservation of his country—now bore their unhappy fruit.

One records all those impressive qualities that Alexander Hamilton possessed, and yet one must disregard them. He had friends and kept their devotion, but not that of his countrymen. He was a fluent public speaker, but his discourses appealed to the mind and not the heart. He was brilliant, affable, and persuasive—but at the dinner table rather than before a public assembly. He was restless and energetic; but he required promptness and accuracy from those who worked for him. Finally, one must note that he was in reality an anachronism, or a sport, in that eighteenth-century world which was leisurely in its habits, simple in its outlook, and more given to speculating about the universe than to concerning itself with the rigorous discipline practical affairs required.

A clue then, to Alexander Hamilton's character and conduct was his need for a safe and stable world. His own youth, in its personal and broad economic relations, had been the reverse of that.

ALEXANDER HAMILTON WAS BORN IN 1755, IT WOULD SEEM, AND NOT in 1757, as he claimed. He was born in one and brought up in another of the islands lying at the eastern end of the Caribbean Sea, known as the Lesser Antilles. Into these islands, toward the end of the sixteenth century, came French, Dutch, and English adventurers, buccaneers, and smugglers—all from poor countries—to prey on the Spanish treasure ships and to engage in illicit trade with the Spanish settlements. The silver and gold of Mexico and

Peru aroused the cupidity of all Europe; and the precious metals ultimately made at least one of the European countries, England, great.

These early marauders were not powerful enough to despoil the mighty Spanish Empire. Initially, their trade with it yielded only a meager harvest. But the settlement of the islands, notably by the English, created an empire; and from the Lesser Antilles (as from the North American mainland) came those plantation wares which, by the eighteenth century, gave England its impressive favorable trade balances and its wealth.

England poured its "surplus" men and women into its American plantations. These grew the sugar, indigo, cotton, and tobacco —the products of a plantation economy linked with Negro slavery—that England sold in the European markets as manufactured wares.

Many forces combined to make these island settlements successful. Britain, despite its escape from a feudal economy centuries before, still lived half in the old ways, half in the new. Its land system, guild restrictions, and trade monopolies were incapable of providing opportunities for a growing population. Its church was oppressive; its poor law and penal code were heartless and savage. The unwanted humble men and women—as freeman, indentured servants, articled boys and girls—migrated out of the British Isles by the hundreds of thousands, some to die miserably, most to live obscurely, a few to succeed magnificently in the hazards and fortunes of the Americas. It was in this world that Alexander Hamilton was born and raised.

Three of the small islands in the Lesser Antilles are associated with his name: St. Kitts, where his mother lived for a time; Nevis, where he was born; and St. Croix, where he spent his boyhood and youth.

A narrow strait separates Nevis from St. Kitts. The open sea lies between them and St. Croix. The first two islands, always held by Britain, had been settled by the English and the French.

St. Croix had had a more chequered history. Dutch and English colonists had come early in the seventeenth century; they had been joined by Frenchmen, Germans, and Irish. The Spaniards took the island only to be driven out by the French who sold it to the Danes in 1733. St. Croix now became a part of the Danish West Indies—the Virgin Islands of today—and as such was a proprietary colony of the Danish West India and Guinea Company when it was added to the Danish crown in 1754.

Hamilton's maternal grandfather was John Faucitt, a French Huguenot who, because of the revocation of the Edict of Nantes, was compelled to flee his native land. He came to Nevis, where, after an apprenticeship, he set himself up as a physician; he became a sugar planter as well. In the beginning of his career he prospered: he married, acquired an estate, and built a great house on it. He had one daughter by his first wife and another by a second. In 1718, we find him marrying Mary Uppington, white, an Englishwoman, widowed like himself. It was Mary Uppington Faucitt who bore him Rachael, who was to become Alexander Hamilton's mother.

Faucitt's daughters married well. Ann, the elder, took as her husband James Lytton, a planter of St. Croix; Rachael married John Michael Lavien, a merchant and planter of either Danish or North German extraction, also of St. Croix.

The Faucitt women were intelligent, spirited—and ill-starred. Mary divorced Faucitt; Rachael, considerably her husband's junior, bore Lavien one son and then left him in 1750. In that year the two women returned to the British islands and it was at St. Kitts or Nevis that Rachael met James Hamilton.

James Hamilton, fourth son of Alexander Hamilton, Laird of Cambuskeith, in the parish of Stevenston, Ayrshire, was a typical young Scotsman without patrimony. He had come to the Lesser Antilles to seek his fortune. Possessing great charm and no skills, he had drifted from island to island as small trader, bookkeeper, or estate's overseer. There was a steady emigration out of Scot-

land of such penniless young men who wandered up and down the
Leeward and Windward Islands and across to Jamaica and even
to Honduras. They came with the sugar and the Negroes. Initially,
sugar was white gold. The great fortunes created by it produced
absenteeism; white managers were wanted on the estates. If successful, they rose; if not, they drifted away. James Hamilton belonged to the latter company.

Rachael and James fell in love and without benefit of clergy
set up their home in Nevis. Here James Hamilton was born in
1753 and Alexander Hamilton in 1755. We may assume that the
natal date was January 11, for it was this date that Alexander
Hamilton recognized as his birthday. When Alexander was seven,
the small family crossed to St. Croix where the father became
manager of one of the Lytton properties. The estate did not
prosper nor was James very competent. He was discharged, and
the Hamiltons took up residence in Christiansted, St. Croix's capital city. We know that, in 1765, Rachael became the precarious
support of the little family.

Aided by a firm of New York merchants—that of David Beekman and Nicholas Cruger—newly established in St. Croix, she
opened a small shop dealing in plantation necessities. A year later,
at the age of eleven, Alexander was working for Beekman and
Cruger. This must have been the final humiliation for the father.
He was at the end of his rope, or ready to move on, for he
deserted Rachael and the two boys that same year. Meanwhile,
Lavien had obtained a divorce from Rachael; her mother had died;
the Lyttons had gone back to Nevis; Rachael's spirit was crushed.
She died in 1768, leaving James's two boys without resources, for
under Danish law her modest property—the few slaves her mother
had willed her—went to Lavien's son now resident in South Carolina.

James was fifteen, Alexander thirteen: so the probate court of
St. Croix listed their ages. For a year they were the wards of the
Lyttons, and when the Lyttons, father and son, died, they were
alone. James was apprenticed to a carpenter and he soon dis-

appeared. Alexander was befriended by the merchant Thomas Stevens into whose home he was taken for a time and whose son Edward became his close companion. And Alexander continued to work for Beekman and Cruger, and then Cruger alone, most of the time in Christiansted, for a brief period in Fredericksted, St. Croix's other city at the western end of the island.

It was a dazzling yet strangely unstable society on whose outer edges the youthful Alexander moved. Sugar dominated it; an uncertain foreign trade kept it uneasy; debt ate away at its insecure supports. With the conclusion of the war against France and Spain in 1763, sugar planting took even a firmer hold upon all the islands of the Antilles, and with sugar, estates became even larger and living outwardly more splendid. The planters—really their managers and attorneys, for absenteeism was a characteristic and a fatal flaw of the West Indian world—lived in great houses thronged with Negro house servants; they drove fine teams of horses; they moved in a constant round of feasting, heavy drinking, and gaming.

It seemed a captivating world—proper, polite, rich. But the ways and attitudes that make a society stable—religion, learning, theater, music, cultivated conversation—were lacking. There was an unreal quality, a feverishness about the living, in part a result of the war's alarms. (There was also the uncertainty of hurricane weather, the uneasiness over the great growth of the slave population.) However, the main cause undoubtedly lay in the sword of debt that hung over the whole economy.

Sugar was both an agricultural and a manufacturing product. The sugar cane, after being cut, was brought to the grinding mills and the extracted juice flowed into the boiling house. There it was boiled and skimmed until crystallized; and after cooling, the coarse brown crystals, the muscavado of commerce, were separated from the viscous part, the molasses. The muscavado for the most part went to Britain for refining; the molasses to the northern mainland colonies for distilling into rum. It was this rum that sustained so much of the commerce of the eighteenth century.

With rum, furs and hides were purchased from the Indians; with rum, Negro slaves were acquired on the Gold Coast; rum accompanied the fishermen as they worked the Newfoundland Banks. Muscavado, molasses, and rum moved along all the sides of the triangular trades that characterized the economy of the age.

And because sugar was staple farming and manufacturing, its capital requirements were heavy. Capital was needed to plant and cut the crop, to erect the mills and boiling and cooling houses, to buy the work animals, and to acquire the Negro slaves. Sugar carried equally heavy obligations to the absentee owners, the mortgagees, the English merchant creditors who bought their luxury goods for the islands in England, and to the home merchant creditors who sold them their provisions, lumber, and iron goods.

Credit and debt went hand in hand; indeed, credit led to mounting debt, for the central weakness of sugar cultivation was the unfavorable balance of payments under which the British islands labored. British West India sugar—with its fluctuating prices, its overproduction, and the extending competition of the French and Dutch islands—had to bear the burden of higher slave costs, freights, outlays for supplies, commissions, and interest. No better proof was needed of the essential flaws in the economy than the constant movement of currency out of the islands and the large premiums demanded by the dealers in London who bought the island bills of exchange. The wealth of the islands was drained off; more and more English merchant bankers became the mortgagees and ultimately the owners of the estates and slaves.

All these things an alert youngster like Alexander Hamilton (without parents and little formal education, with only his wits to sustain him) could see and understand, for he worked for merchants and merchants were at the center of this well-spun but fragile web. Nicholas Cruger, the senior partner, later the sole owner of the firm, was a typical merchant of the period, bold and enterprising. His ventures ranged over the whole Atlantic world.

The Crugers were New Yorkers with mercantile and banking

ties in Jamaica, Honduras, Curaçao, and Bristol. They owned warehouses, docks and a distillery in New York. They sailed ships, financed slaving voyages, bought and sold bills of exchange, advanced credit. They dealt in West India sugar, molasses, and mahogany, which they carried to the mainland; mules, horses, packed meats and fish, flour, barrels and staves, which they brought from the mainland to the islands. From England they obtained mixed cargoes of dry goods, metals, and luxury ware; to England they transported sugar, tobacco, rice, hides and furs.

The little ships, moving in and out of the southern islands, were usually on trading voyages: they picked up and discharged cargoes, carried on their transactions in the varied coinage of all the foreign settlements, bought European ware in Dutch or Danish ports—and made profits as traders, privateers, and smugglers. To avoid British mercantilist restrictions and British taxes, it was not uncommon for colonial merchants to have an entrepôt in a foreign settlement. It was with this idea in mind that Nicholas Cruger came to St. Croix, where he soon became one of its leading merchants. It was in the Cruger warehouse, store, and counting house—from the time he was eleven years old until he was eighteen—that Alexander Hamilton, under Cruger's benevolent eye, learned the skills and risks of a merchant.

By 1771, Alexander must have been the senior clerk. He kept books, drew up commercial documents, and wrote and copied letters to captains and correspondents carrying on the firm's affairs. He probably engaged in small trading ventures on his own. From November, 1771, to March, 1772, when Cruger was ill in New York, under the supervision of Beekman, Alexander may have run the business. He was learning other things as well.

ST. CROIX WAS AN EXCELLENT VANTAGE POINT FROM WHICH TO BE-hold a great drama unfolding; for the British Empire, at the height of its glory, now that France and Spain had finally been humbled and compelled to yield up vast territories, was being challenged, this time from within. The Old Empire—begun under Cromwell and not ended until the mid-nineteenth century—had really a single interest, the metropolis. Trade was its lifeblood; the wealth of England—to support its landed gentry and merchant classes, to maintain its fleets and protect it in war—was its one concern.

Colonies were established to produce unfinished goods: the hardwoods of Honduras and the sugar of West India; the tobacco and rice of Virginia, Maryland, and the Carolinas; the furs, hides, naval stores, and lumber of New England, New York, and Pennsylvania—which the English could use and fabricate at home or sell abroad. Colonies, in their turn, were to buy their finished products from the mother country and use its banking services. To maintain this system, which, in the eighteenth century, filled her great country houses with the spoils of every land, and amassed that wealth out of which the industrial revolution was financed, England exploited the slave trade and debased her own working populations. Two great Englishmen were later to deliver mighty blows to help end the Old Empire: Adam Smith and William Wilberforce. The first linked public policy and human welfare with a free commerce, and the second, with Christianity and the end of the slave trade.

To safeguard the metropolis, all manner of restraints were devised. Exports to and imports from the English plantations overseas could be carried only in English ships manned by English crews. The leading raw materials of the colonies were put on "enumerated lists" and could be sold only in England. Europe could not trade directly with the English possessions; European cargoes had to be discharged in England first. An export duty of 4½ per cent was placed on West India sugar, while mainland merchants had to buy their sugar and molasses from the British islands alone. Colonial assemblies were forbidden to revalue foreign coinage, strike off their own, or issue legal-tender paper

currency. Efforts at the support of colonial manufactures were
sternly checked. Interlopers were to be watched carefully by
governors, colonial and vice-admiralty courts, customshouse officials. In London the Board of Trade and the Privy Council sat
to view with a suspicious eye any attempts of colonials to free
themselves from this tangled web of coercion and prohibition.

The web was finely spun; yet it was possible for the bold and
the ingenious to slip through. Northern mainland merchants could
meet their unfavorable balances with England by pursuing an
illegal commerce with the foreign sugar islands—and by supplying
the enemy during war. Southern mainland merchants and planters
could discharge their debts by moving into the wild lands of the
West and engaging in land speculation and the Indian trade. Despite laws to the contrary, all the colonies sought escape from
financial pressures by tinkering with the coinage and by issuing
an inflated paper currency.

When the Seven Years' War was over in 1763, Whitehall set
out to repair these breaks in its system, in fact, to re-examine and
strengthen every aspect of its imperial policy. The times were
ready for such a change. Not only had the great new territories
of Canada, the eastern Mississippi Valley, and Florida been wrested
from France and Spain and France's influence in India destroyed;
not only were the sugar islands declining; the mainland colonies
had arrived at man's estate—politically mature, ready for great
economic adventures. And England, too, was changing, as it
shifted from an agricultural and commercial axis to an industrial
one. (Adam Smith, in Glasgow, just ending his career as professor
of moral philosophy at the university, saw this; but his contemporaries were too close to their day-to-day perplexities to catch
his vision of an expanding and improving free world.)

A period of great decision, however, produced little men. And
because no imperial conception of consultation, widening opportunity, the uninhibited flow of capital emerged; because, in-

deed, the constitutional guarantees which the Glorious Revolution had gained for England in the end seemed threatened, the Old Empire was shaken.

By statutes, by orders, by instructions to governors and by the establishment of new Admiralty courts, London made every effort to break up the trade of the northern colonies with the foreign sugar islands. To strike at Pennsylvania and New Jersey manufacturing and commerce, it put iron on the "enumerated list" and prohibited the erection of a new iron and steel mill. A general currency act forbade all the colonies to issue legal-tender bills of credit and ordered all outstanding bills retired. The West was shut off, ostensibly for the reordering of Indian relations, but as much to end the forays of colonial fur traders and land promoters. The whole area beyond the crest of the Appalachians was put in charge of imperial agents and settlements already planted were ordered abandoned; the control of the fur trade was centered in Quebec.

The conduct of the wars had left Britain with a heavy burden of debt; its victories had only added to the costs of the Empire's maintenance in the larger armies and navies it had to support. London decided to tax the colonies overseas directly—it had never done so before—at the same time using the revenue acts to tighten mercantilist controls over colonial trade and industry and confine within even narrower limits colonial enterprise. The Sugar Act of 1764 and the Stamp Act of 1765 were the chief, although not the only, devices employed for regulation and taxation.

The Sugar Act once more taxed the entry of foreign-produced molasses and sugar and prohibited the importation of foreign rum. The Stamp Act placed a tax on colonial newspapers, pamphlets, almanacs, legal documents, and ship's papers, licenses, playing cards, and dice. Duties and taxes were to be paid in specie, thus further draining the colonies of hard money. To divert colonial capital into raw materials, these measures increased the bounties paid for the colonial production of hemp and flax and placed high duties on the colonial importation of foreign indigo. Lumber, hides and skins, pig and bar iron, and potash and pearl ashes were put on the "enumerated list." Heavy duties were imposed on foreign wines, fruit, and oils; the importation of many kinds of foreign luxury articles was stopped altogether.

The end of war had been followed by a check to colonial prosperity; the new restraints on trade and the deflationary measures affecting bills of credit and currency deepened the financial crisis. John Dickinson, one of the first of the colonial pamphleteers to sound the alarm, wrote in 1765: [1]

Trade is decaying and all credit is expiring. Money is becoming so extremely scarce that reputable freeholders find it impossible to pay debts which are trifling in comparison to their estates.... The debtors are ruined. The creditors get back but part of their debt and that ruins them. Thus the consumers break the shopkeepers; they break the merchants; and the shock must be felt so far as London.

All this was the heavy-handed work of uninspired politicians and placemen in London. No two-party system functioned with its play and interplay of opposition and responsibility; the "rotten boroughs," speaking for rural constituencies and not the new great commercial and industrial interests of London, the midlands, and the eastern ports, still dominated Parliament; England was governed by Whig factions and the King, George III, was too close to their center. He regarded himself as a constitutional monarch, indeed he was a Whig: thus he and his ministers belonged to the same party. He could intervene in affairs of state; he frequently obtained compliance through corruption. A dull, opinionated, inflexible person himself—he was to be insane for a good part of his long life—George leaned upon second- and third-rate men. One of these was George Grenville, first Lord of the Treasury, responsible for the trade and revenue acts that were beginning to shake the British Empire.

THESE SHOCKS WERE QUICKLY FELT ON THE AMERICAN MAINLAND, and in the sugar islands as well. The young Alexander Hamilton, growing up in St. Croix, but British by birth and therefore curious about and sensitive to all that was taking place in the nearby islands of St. Kitts and Nevis, could see that the times were out of joint. Debt and absentee landlordism were stripping the islands of wealth and talents; assemblies were wrangling with governors endlessly and fruitlessly over supply bills and currency. Political debate had degenerated into quarrels among men whose tempers were short—in the trying climate, the constantly threatening hurricanes, with the soft-spoken, polite, but watching blacks all about them. Could men's nerves be anything but edgy in this southern paradise?

This was the past out of which Alexander Hamilton emerged. He was not the only young British colonial to feel and measure the inequities of the imperial system: Jefferson in Virginia too was living in the midst of a plantation economy where debt was destroying the hard-won wealth cut out of the wilderness; Adams in Massachusetts was seeing restraints threaten the very life of the New England ports. Curiously enough, however, Jefferson and Adams were to remain always suspicious of the economic processes by which wealth was being created. Not so Hamilton, for he learned his youthful lessons well. He was to remember what he had thus acquired all his life; indeed, here is the key to his constant preoccupation with public affairs. An economy had to be diversified in order to grow and flourish; the rigorous ordering of money and credit was vital; without solvency in government as in private affairs, there could be no confidence and therefore no progress.

In any case, the islands were a prison from which escape was imperative. And when the opportunity presented itself, in 1772, the young Hamilton seized it. Whether the immediate cause for his departure was the attention he attracted by a newspaper article that he wrote on the effects of a hurricane sweeping over St.

Croix, or whether it was due to the small capital he had built up, or to the continuing interest of his employer Nicholas Cruger, we have no means of knowing. Armed with letters of introduction from Dr. Hugh Knox, a young Presbyterian minister trained in Princeton College, and a letter of credit drawn on Cruger's mercantile correspondents in New York, Alexander Hamilton left the West Indies in the early summer of 1772 never to return. The ship on which he sailed was bound for Boston. Upon landing, he proceeded at once by coach to New York.

He came to a mainland already challenging the British crown. He came to a city just as sensitive as St. Croix to the needs of a balanced and stable economy.

2

New York in the Revolution

ALEXANDER HAMILTON WAS SEVENTEEN WHEN HE ARRIVED IN NEW York. He had come to study; for a few years he did so. Having had little formal preparation, upon the advice of his New York friends, he entered a secondary school. It is here, probably because he was in the company of boys considerably his junior, that Hamilton first falsified his age. He was slender, fair, and quite short; his reddish-brown hair, high color, and lively spirits helped in the deception.

He attended, then, a grammar school at Elizabethtown in New Jersey; here he got up his Latin, Greek, and mathematics with such success that in a year he was ready for college. He applied at Princeton to pursue an accelerated program, was refused, and then gained admission to King's College in New York (later Columbia College). In all likelihood, Hamilton was a serious and devoted student, for he became a highly educated man. He worked at his Latin, Greek, logic, rhetoric, and natural philosophy (physics). He had a tutor in mathematics. He found time for reading in French, history, literature, and philosophy.

When he led away his company of volunteers, in 1776, he took with him, among others, the following books: Demosthenes,

Cicero, Plutarch, Bacon, Hobbes, Rousseau's *Emile,* a number of histories, and Ralt's *Dictionary of Trade and Commerce.* Only the last, in all likelihood, was unfamiliar to Jefferson and Madison: Hamilton's peculiar interest was already fully formed. His notes on his readings and his observations relating to trade, population, and money have been preserved. There is even an outline of a proposed book on the political and commercial history of British America.

New York was precisely the place for such speculations. Covering not more than a square mile in area and with a population of but 20,000, New York already was one of the great ports of the world. Into it, in one year, came 700 ships; its merchants had an interest in every land and every product of the Atlantic community.

On all sides were to be found the shops and warehouses of the merchants—with their shipyards, docks, and rope walks. The merchants, in fact, dominated the city socially and politically. They constituted the largest segment of the upper class; they were allied by marriage and financial interest with the great landowners of Manhattan Island and the Hudson Valley; they had links—through family and business ties—with Britain and West India. The public officials of the crown as well as other public officials moved in the same company—for New York was the capital of the province, and the crown's business required a numerous office-holding class. Here, too, were the lawyers who, when they were prosperous, were as much men of affairs as advocates. When the Revolution ended, Hamilton became a lawyer; he pleaded causes and rode the circuit; but he was also a promoter of manufacturing, banking, and land companies.

All these persons, because they owned property, were freeholders and therefore possessed the franchise. In this group, too, were the city's "freemen": those skilled mechanics and artisans

who, by dint of a long apprenticeship, had become master workmen, had shops of their own, and hired lesser workers. The "freedom of the city" was hereditary; it could also be granted by the
city's council; the right was jealously guarded and its members
restricted. In all there were not more than 1,500 freeholders and
freemen in New York in the early 1770s.

Such was the narrow apex of New York's society. The rest of
its population—the smaller tradesmen, the countinghouse clerks,
the street hawkers and venders, the laborers, carters, porters,
dock workers, seamen, apprentices—were without the franchise
and without economic privilege. It was a volatile community,
as the inhabitants of a seaport usually are. When commerce was
thriving, as it was during the Seven Years' War, all elements of
the population prospered, for wages were high in the New World:
then journeymen could become master mechanics, or with small
capitals acquire farms on Long Island, or become itinerant ped-
dlers and tinkers.

When affairs fell on hard times—as they did during the greater
part of the period 1763–1775—the "mob" (the gentry's appellation
for the largest portion of the city's population) stirred. The "mob"
complained about restrictions in the crafts and the inadequacy of
town relief; the "mob," easily inflamed by popular leaders, demonstrated against the crown officials, destroyed property, rioted.
When the Stamp Act troubles began, the "mob" formed secret
societies—the Sons of Liberty was the most important—and these
played significant roles in the Revolution's preliminaries. They
joined hands across the boundaries of the provinces; they brought
pressure on merchants to boycott English goods; they helped
form and participated in committees of correspondence; they set
up, after 1774, extralegal provincial congresses.

The gentry watched such maneuvers uneasily. It was one thing
by petition, argument, private representation, to insist that London
was abridging and violating the constitutional rights of Englishmen in the plantations overseas; it was another to flout and under-

mine authority. A young and alert New Yorker, Gouverneur Morris, thus described a protest meeting of 1774: [1]

The spirit of the English Constitution has yet a little influence left, and but a little. The remains of it, however, will give the wealthy people a superiority this time, but the mob begins to think and reason, poor reptiles! It is with them a vernal morning; they are struggling to cast off their winter's slough, they bask in the sunshine and ere noon they will bite, depend upon it.

It was into such a supercharged atmosphere that Alexander Hamilton came. It was true, the Stamp Act had been quickly repealed, but not before the colonials had acquired valuable lessons in political and economic action. A Stamp Act Congress had met in New York: it protested against taxation without representation and demanded a trial by jury in all cases affecting the Admiralty. At the same time New York merchants—their lead was quickly followed elsewhere—agreed to the nonimportation of English goods to compel parliamentary compliance. A new ministry in London passed another set of measures, in 1767, called the Townshend duties; these imposed import taxes on tea, paper, paint, lead, and glass. In 1770, again after the successful threat of embargo, all those but the one on tea were lifted. And even the tea tax was lightened in 1773 when the new Tea Act provided for a full drawback of English import duties on British tea shipped to the American colonies.

This Tea Act—and the Quebec Act of 1774—revealed London's hand. Raising a revenue for defense was only one aspect, and the lesser one, of the crown's purpose; the monopoly of the colonial trade and the exploitation of the new empire in the Ohio Valley and Canada, in the interests of the metropolis, were the greater, the transcendent ones.

To save the great East India Company from bankruptcy, it was to be permitted to ship in its own vessels and through its own agents to dispose of a surplus stock of 17,000,000 pounds of tea in America. Thus, American merchants, who carried, imported, and sold British tea at retail were to be undermined. It was not only the tea handlers. Would not the same plight—with the precedent established—in time affect merchants concerned with other commodities, as well? For the East India Company also dealt in eastern wares of all kinds—silks and cottons, spices and drugs, chinaware and fine woods.

Americans were quick to see the intention behind the querulous talk of parliamentary right. To them, this meant, as a pamphleteer of Philadelphia pointed out, the monopoly of the whole colonial trade. "Thus our merchants are ruined, ship building ceases. They will then sell goods at any exorbitant price. Our artificers will be unemployed, and every tradesman will groan under dire oppression." [2]

If seaboard merchants were thus put in jeopardy, the threat to the western land dealers and fur traders was no whit less real. The pacification and protection of the Indian tribes—the stated intention of the Proclamation of 1763—were lost sight of; in the Quebec Act of 1774, London proceeded to exclude colonial interests and enterprises from the vast domain north of the Ohio. By this law, in order to divert the movement of western furs away from Philadelphia and New York, London provided for the regulation of traders by the governor of the province of Quebec (its boundaries pushed southward to the Ohio River) seated in Montreal. By the same token, colonial land companies— for a long time interested in the Ohio country—were checked in their plans of development and settlement. Well-to-do New Yorkers, Pennsylvanians, Virginians were involved in these promotions; so antagonisms were multiplied. Another sensitive nerve was exposed by the law: the Catholic populations of the Quebec province were recognized; they could vote and their priests were to be publicly supported.

Thus, 1773, 1774, and 1775 became years of decision. Tea was destroyed in Boston harbor, turned back unloaded from New York and Philadelphia, and landed but not sold in Charleston. In

1774 the First Continental Congress met in Philadelphia, with delegates from all the provinces attending; it passed the Continental Association, an embargo agreement affecting both imports from and exports to Great Britain, Ireland, and the West Indies.

London returned fire with fire. In 1774 and 1775, Parliament passed first the Coercive and then the Restraining Acts: once again, control over trade was the weapon. The port of Boston was closed; the government of Massachusetts was reduced to the status of a crown colony; the quartering of troops was demanded; almost all the colonies were cut off from the northern fisheries, and their trade limited entirely to Great Britain, Ireland, and the British West Indies. Yet as late as 1775, colonial lawyers and pamphleteers still talked of reconciliation: if only Parliament could understand that the English Constitution recognized the rights of all Englishmen; that taxation without representation struck at England's fundamental liberties!

Popular demonstrations accompanied the formal acts of protest and the meeting of extralegal assemblies. Hamilton participated in these street affairs as did undoubtedly many of his youthful contemporaries. He harangued crowds; he joined a band of young patriots, wore a uniform, and engaged in forays on crown property. He and his companions proceeded to collect arms. The same process was going on all over America; a revolutionary situation was developing.

ALTHOUGH FROM THE BEGINNING THEIR LEADERS SEEK TO CONFINE their grievances to constitutional questions—what is really involved is the restoration of ancient liberties—revolutions always threaten to get out of hand. Violence inevitably appears and human rights are jeopardized; equally significant is the tendency to push the whole revolutionary apparatus upon the tracks of equalitarianism.

For this reason, it is idle to argue that the American Revolution did not seek to make over the world, that it did not concern itself with an elaborate and universal scheme for the establishment of the authority of the "people." One aspect of it did; and to the extent that it was committed to equalitarianism, it was as "revolutionary" as were the Levelers in the English Revolution of 1649, the Jacobins in the French Revolution of 1789, and the Bolsheviks in the Russian Revolution of 1917. Revolutions have their right and left wings; and these were to be found in America. Indeed, it was not until the Constitutional Convention met that the danger of left seizure of power finally was allayed.

Alexander Hamilton from the beginning—after his youthful escapades—was alarmed at the excesses of which revolutions are capable. As early as 1775, when he was twenty, having watched a band of bravoes from Connecticut descend upon New York to wreck the press of a loyalist printer, he was able to write to John Jay: [3]

In times of such commotion as the present, while the passions of men are worked up to an uncommon pitch there is great danger of fatal extremes.... The due medium is hardly to be found among the more intelligent, it is almost impossible among the unthinking populace. When the minds of these are loosened from their attachment to ancient establishments and courses, they seem to grow giddy and are apt more or less to run into anarchy. These principles, too true in themselves and confirmed to me both by reading and my own experience, deserve extremely the attention of those, who have the direction of public affairs. In such tempestuous times, it requires the greatest skill in the political pilots to keep men steady and within proper bounds....

This is an impressive wisdom on the part of one so young. Hamilton, thus, accepted the validity of the Revolution, but he was constantly alert to the anarchy it could bring in its train and the equalitarianism that always threatened. Hamilton, in short, was a libertarian in his devotion to personal and property rights under law; but he was no equalitarian, in the sense that he was willing to place the good of the "people" above individual welfare.

Hamilton accepted the constitutional theory of the American

Revolution and, in his earliest writings, contributed not a little to the building up of the argument. This ran as follows:

The oppression of the English crown, disregarding those fundamental laws which were the basis of orderly government—the laws of nature, Holy Writ, the evidences of history, the English Constitution, the charters of the colonies—justified resistance. Government was a contract; it operated on the basis of universally known and accepted moral and legal principles; its purpose was to assure the liberty and happiness of men. They, on their part, were equally bound to one another: to maintain a community based on law; to keep open the avenues of opportunity for the recognition and reward of talents; to respect those rights and possessions—of the person, conscience, property—which virtuous, sober, hard-working, and law-abiding citizens had earned.

Men were unequal in their capacities and labors: the superior had their rewards and their responsibilities. They governed according to the rules of a moral universe. Their obligations were heavy; they were to assure the existence of a balanced society, in which not only justice and order reigned but where progress—man's ability to improve his physical lot—was possible. For if society was open, fluid, and not stratified, concerned with individuals and not the community, accepting the rationality and capacities of men rather than their weaknesses and hostilities, it was ever changing.

The failure of the British crown, in addition to its flouting of fundamental law, lay in its inability to understand how restrictive it had become to the growth of the colonies. But the genius of good government lay in sensitivity to new opportunity, in a capacity to adjust to the needs of the changing times; an ability to conserve old and tried virtues and at the same time to move forward, accepting the risks of change. In these terms the American Revolution was in the Whig tradition and simply sought the reaffirmation of the principles of 1688, when constitutional monarchy had been once and for all established.

Hamilton took up his pen and wrote three pamphlets in 1774 along these lines. The first two, called *A Full Vindication* and *The Farmer Refuted,* were in defense of the Continental Congress' nonimportation, nonconsumption, and nonexportation agreements. The third, called *Remarks on the Quebec Act,* attacked the Quebec Act for its suppression of civil and political liberties and its establishment of the Catholic Church.

These are not youthful exercises; they are the work of an imaginative and subtle mind. Hamilton shows his familiarity with the British constitutional tradition and the natural-rights debate. He quotes Pope, Hume, Blackstone, and Coke; he cites Grotius, Puffendorf, Locke, Montesquieu, and Burlemaqui; he refers to Hobbes and Calvin and—already pointing up his particular preoccupation with political economy—the mercantilist writers. The whole content of the constitutional discussion appears in these pamphlets—the compact theory of government, the real nature of liberty, government by consent, natural right. There is a rhetorical flight like this, in *The Farmer Refuted:* "The sacred rights of mankind are not to be rummaged for among old parchments or musty records. They are written, as with a sunbeam, in the whole volume of human nature, by the Hand of the Divinity itself, and can never be erased or obscured by mortal power." [4]

But there is also this mature writing: [5]

...there seems to be already a jealousy of our dawning splendor. It is looked upon as portentous of approaching independence. This, we have reason to believe, is one of the principal incitments to the present rigorous and unconstitutional proceedings against us. And though it may have chiefly originated in the calumnies of designing men, yet it does not entirely depend upon adventitious or partial causes, but is also founded in the circumstances of our country and situation. The boundless extent of territory we possess, the wholesome temperament of our climate, the luxuriance and fertility of our soil, the variety of our products, the rapidity of the growth of our population, the industry of our countrymen, and the commodiousness of our ports, naturally lead to a suspicion of independence, and would always have an influence pernicious to us.

Indeed, at nineteen, Hamilton is seeing—better than Jefferson, better than Adams—how the Revolution is to be won. He looks at balances of payments, production, exchanges, and fiscal management; already he perceives the possibility of America's growth to power and greatness as a manufacturing nation. He senses that, in its struggle for independence, America will have allies. So, we find passages like the following: [6]

We can live without trade of any kind. Food and clothing we have within ourselves. Our climate produces cotton, wool, flax, and hemp. ... Those hands which may be deprived of business by the cessation of commerce, may be occupied in various kinds of manufactures and other internal improvements. If, by the necessity of the thing, manufactures should once be established, and take root among us, they will pave the way still more to the future grandeur and glory of America; and by lessening its need of external commerce, will render it still securer against the encroachments of tyranny.

You ask me: what resources have the colonies to pay, clothe, arm and feed their troops? ... Our country abounds in provisions. We have already materials enough among us, to keep us in clothes longer than Great Britain would have any appetite to continue her hostilities. Several of the colonies are pretty well stored with ammunition. France, Spain, and Holland would find means to supply us with whatever we wanted.

THIS IS A REVOLUTION AT ITS INCEPTION. IT STARTS OUT WITH A stern sense of dedication and with a sober evaluation of the chances of victory; yet it also can release a Pandora's box of horrors before very long. The makers of the Revolution talk of order: but government is weak or incapable of binding in a common cause all those disparate elements it has summoned to its defense. They are committed to responsibility; but the agencies they have established cannot check violence. They hope for orderly change; and, too, men are soon embarked on dangerous and untried courses. Revolutions have been lost from within at the very moment that the victory against ancient wrongs was being brilliantly achieved.

With growing uneasiness Alexander Hamilton watched this happen in America. In one sense, the Revolution was resolving itself into a civil war between patriots and loyalists; in another, it was becoming a struggle for power between the conservative or constitutional, and the radical or equalitarian, wings of the revolutionary host.

The British crown had its defenders in America even after arms had been taken up. Loyalists took to the field as soldiers in the British forces and as irregulars; they plotted and schemed against state governments; they subverted the war effort by defeatism and by open resistance. They were put down harshly and usually without use of orderly legal processes.

Committees of safety, which had sprung up everywhere to replace royal governments provincially and locally, carried on a savage war of reprisal and extermination against the enemies at home. Mob violence was countenanced: loyalists were seized, physically mistreated, shut up in concentration camps, their homes burned, their property confiscated. Not a few were killed; fully 100,000 were compelled to flee. When state governments were finally formed and courts established, these only proceeded to do on a wholesale scale under the color of law what the committees had been doing piecemeal.

In the beginning, in all the states—indeed, in some, throughout the whole period of the Revolution—this mob rule by committees (without legal warrant, with no judicial sanction or review) continued. The committees of safety usually preceded the creation of new governments; and even after such were established, they remained to function as the executive of the legislature. In New Hampshire, for example, which had adopted a new state constitution in 1776, the state committee of safety sat during the recesses of the legislature from 1775 to 1777, and was in continuous session from 1778 to 1784. In those states held by British armies, the committees of safety combined all the agencies of government. The state committees were terminated early in Massachusetts and Virginia; they continued to operate until 1777 in Pennsylvania and until 1778 in New York and New Jersey; until 1783, the committee was still the government in Connecticut.

A revolution is fought desperately; the liberties it is dedicated to recapturing are put in dire jeopardy—and sometimes forfeited. The committees of safety sought to keep the forces in the field supplied with arms and ammunition and with clothing, blankets, horses, and wagons. They sequestered property, all other resources failing. They issued bills of credit on dubious or nonexistent security. Their circles of participation and intervention kept on widening. They sought to fix prices when their debased currencies collapsed; they sat as courts in military and civil cases; they punished profiteers; they granted letters of marque and reprisal to privateers; they even tried to stimulate home manufactures by the payment of bounties.

Property was their particular interest. Crown lands were seized, as were those of the loyalists, and these were granted or sold to patriots. In all, loyalist property losses came to $40,000,000.

During this time, the contest for power between conservatives and radicals in each state was raging. In Pennsylvania, North Carolina, Delaware, New Hampshire, Georgia, the radicals were in the majority and they took control and wrote constitutions in their own interest. A Bill of Rights frequently was incorporated. Qualifications for voting were eased. Equal representation for all districts in the legislature, both the back country as well as the settled tidewater regions, was provided. The powers of the lower legislative house were increased, notably through the right granted it of originating money bills. The executive prerogative was ringed about with all manner of restrictions and the judicial function was severely limited. Thus, the governor's veto was abolished, and he was to be elected either popularly or by the all-powerful legislatures and only for brief terms; the judiciary was to be elected by the voters or chosen by the legislatures and it might be freely removed.

The Pennsylvania Constitution of 1776 was one such leveling frame of government, for it erected a single-chambered house in which even the choice of state civil and judicial officers was deposited. It was so fearful of any encroachments on the rights of the "people" that it provided for a multiple executive and a council of censors which was to meet every seven years to inquire if liberty and justice had been preserved inviolate.

These pretentions were lofty; that they could not invoke confidence—in government, in normal economic processes—was demonstrated by two unhappy circumstances. The states, to finance themselves, issued bills of credit and treasury notes; their total came to the gigantic sum of $250,000,000. Because all this paper was legal tender, an unprecedented inflation took place. And, in an effort to control prices and wages, price-fixing was ordered by statute in a number of states and even by interstate compact in New England. These devices failed; worse, in fact, they led to speculation, black marketing, and hoarding of goods and capital.

Councils of wisdom were not heeded; demagogues, talking of popular rights, were in the saddle. As early as February, 1777, in a debate on price-fixing in the Continental Congress, Benjamin Rush of Pennsylvania, seeking to defend Philadelphia's merchants, tried, without avail, to check the radical tide: [7]

They [the merchants] are disposed to realize their money in lands or goods. And this is not owing to any timidity or disaffection among them. They fear the further depreciation of your money by future emissions. Stop your emissions of money and you will stop speculation. ... I beg your leave to prescribe two remedies for it (1) Raising the interest of the money we borrow to six per cent. This, like a cold bath, will give an immediate spring to our affairs; and (2) taxation. This, like tapping, will diminish the quantity of our money, and give a proper value to what remains.

IN THESE EARLY EXPERIENCES, WE FIND HAMILTON'S VIEWS ON THE Revolution taking firm shape. If its purpose was the preservation of the constitutional guarantees, then government established un-

der it had to be "energetic"; it had to operate with legality; it
had to avoid that its intention be "compounded with other principles." There were, in short, limits of government: government,
for example, had nothing to do with the legislation of a moral
scheme.

Thus, Hamilton was troubled from the start as he watched
the early state-constitution experiments. He saw that New York's
attempts were no better than Pennsylvania's. So, he wrote in May,
1777, to Gouverneur Morris when Morris invited Hamilton's
comments on the draft of the New York document then being
debated: [8]

That instability is inherent in the nature of popular governments I
think very disputable; unstable democracy, is an epithet frequently in
the mouths of politicians; but I believe that from a strict reexamination
of the matter ... it will be found that the fluctuations of governments
in which the popular principle has borne a considerable sway, have
proceeded from its being compounded with other principles. . . .
[The functions of government had to be sharply separated, some indeed, questioned.] Compound governments, though they may be
harmonious in the beginning, will introduce distinct interests, and these
interests will clash, throw the state into convulsions, and produce a
change or dissolution.

At twenty-two Hamilton was already anticipating those perils
to stable government, arising from factions based on special
interests, that Madison was so fearful of when he wrote the
famous Tenth Essay of *The Federalist* a dozen years later. Meanwhile, Hamilton was already in the army.

Among the preparations for war adopted by the New York
Provincial Congress was the establishment of a company of artillery. This took place on January 6, 1776, and Hamilton at once
applied for its command. On March 14, 1776, his petition was
granted and he was commissioned "Captain of the Provincial
Company of the Artillery of this Colony." He was twenty-one
when he set out to raise his volunteers, furnish them with uni-
forms, and whip them into a drilled fighting force. He was to
spend the next year not under fire but in retreat, as Washington's
army fled from New York across the state of New Jersey.

Hamilton in the Revolution

WARS ARE WON IN THE FIELD, AT THE COUNCIL TABLE, AND IN THE countinghouse. They are won because there is courage on one side and indecision and divided purpose on the other. Supply and terrain can be important: for if the attackers, despite superior numbers, find these problems difficult to manage, irregulars can engage in holding actions indefinitely to break down morale.

Every calculation, at the outset, pointed to the defeat of the American patriots. Britain sent an immense expeditionary force led by good, and a few excellent, generals; her fleets constantly patrolled the American waters; treachery helped—in the American army and behind the lines, as loyalists openly gave aid. The war was waged and British victories were gained in the north, the west, along the whole length of the Atlantic seaboard, and at sea.

Yet the British lost and the Americans won. The Americans knew how to shoot and take cover and harass a foe. They were close to their sources of supply; if defeated, they could melt away to re-form later. A defending force of this kind, if it avoids decisive battles, can win by a stalemate. The enemy, made up in considerable part of mercenaries, and foreign ones to boot, fought two months away from their sources of supply in country that was a wilderness once the narrow belt of settlement was passed. At least 2,000 American privateers took to sea—these little ships in all carried 70,000 seamen—and they harried British ports in the Caribbean and Atlantic and destroyed British ships and supplies.

The Americans hoped and prayed for—and before too long obtained—foreign aid. Franklin at Versailles was a tower of strength; the victory at Saratoga was the turning point, and in 1778 France entered into a defensive and offensive alliance with America. Private and public financing, from France, Holland, Spain, which followed, permitted American agents to pay for that vast store of goods that armies in the field burn up and waste in such prodigious quantities. Foreign volunteers came; and then French troops and French ships. At Yorktown, the British met both American and French armies.

Also, the British conduct of the war was marked by extraordinary errors of judgment. Lord George Germain, the Secretary of State for the Colonies, tried to run the war, in every detail, from London. He gave command of the British army in America to Sir William Howe, an avowed Old Whig, politically sympathetic to the colonies. When Howe was replaced by Sir Henry Clinton, Germain permitted a subordinate commander like Cornwallis to strike out independently. And despite their full command of the seas during most of the war, the British rarely effected complete coordination between land and sea forces.

The British won numerous tactical victories in all the theaters of fighting; but they never succeeded in achieving what should have been their aim: the destruction of Washington's army. Washington never quite could be caught; that final advantage of overwhelming force was never utilized. Through defeat and retreat, the Americans continued in the field, learning by doing, until success at Saratoga obtained them the French alliance and widened the conflict into a worldwide war. With British armies engaged in Europe and India and once more fighting to preserve the Empire, Yorktown was too much: London was ready to negotiate a peace.

Finally, there was George Washington to lead the American army. Washington had fine and always human qualities. Because he hated chicanery and cowardice, he was personally brave; formal and correct in his living, he could endure the miseries of camp without a murmur; he could listen, he could temporize—sometimes he faltered, once or twice he lost heart—but always there were times when he could strike boldly. He was wealthy and innately conservative; he hazarded his life and fortune to lead the American rebellion to victory, yet never was he distrustful of the unwieldy and frequently inept processes of civilian government which guided the war.

FOR FOUR YEARS, FROM 1777 TO 1781, AND AGAIN FOR SIX YEARS, from 1789 to 1795, Alexander Hamilton's destiny was closely and inextricably linked with Washington. The first time, the relationship was that of general and aide-de-camp. The older man was remote, polite, yet keenly aware of the younger man's very real capacities. The younger was respectful, but not worshiping: he chewed too much on the cud of his own ambition. The second time, they were equals. They not only admired each other, there was a deep affection between them; and they labored heroically in the common cause of saving the young republic.

Alexander Hamilton had had a year in the field when he was invited to become an aide-de-camp in Washington's official family in 1777. The year had not been without distinction: Washington himself had observed that the youthful captain of artillery knew how to take care of his men and guns, employ his small force to cover retiring foot soldiers, and endure the heartbreak of a defeated and retreating army.

Now, at twenty-two, with the rank of lieutenant-colonel, Hamilton began to move in a more dazzling society. Washington, to make up his official family, had been choosing bright, quick, clever young men—many very well born, some highly ambitious, all fearless and deeply devoted—to act as his aides. In the eight years that the war lasted, some thirty-two of them came and went in his headquarters. They rode with and for the commander-in-chief; they took his dictation, drew up drafts of communications and reports, wrote fair copies; they were his liaison officers and his personal diplomatic agents; they graced his table and helped in the entertainment of his guests.

Alexander Hamilton was one of this company, but not the chief one, and never the one closest to Washington. Washington valued his talents and gave him difficult missions to perform; undoubtedly he consulted Hamilton on the preparation of reports where the young man's keen and subtle mind could unwind a complex argument; but there is no evidence that the youth played a major role in the making of important decisions. They were not friends and therefore not intimate. In consequence, Washington did not know of Hamilton's preoccupation with political and fiscal speculations. Hamilton, on his part, chafed; before long, he began to seek escape from a post that was glamorous but essentially one of dependence.

Perhaps because of his youth, but more probably because of his obscure background and uncertain future, Alexander Hamilton had to be an equal. When he was, he shone. He was gay and affectionate with his peers; they, in turn, made him their confidant. They did not mind his ambitions; indeed they shared with him his hopes for the ultimate recognition of his talents. Among his fellow aides, he was the "Little Lion": a brave soldier, a good and faithful companion. Robert H. Harrison, James McHenry, John Laurens—shining young men—loved him. And so did that other and even more refulgent youth, the Marquis de Lafayette: Hamilton was his closest friend in the American army.

With his elders, too, once having been accepted as an equal, he was respectful but never subservient. When asked for advice, he gave it clearly and firmly: he was every inch the man of affairs being consulted because of his forthrightness, wisdom, and discretion. They valued him so highly that they pushed him for the most important posts.

Thus, in April, 1777, to a committee of the New York Convention (made up of Gouverneur Morris, Robert R. Livingston, and William Allison) he could write, expressing his concerns about the preservation of legality in the face of treachery: [1]

The disposition of the convention, with respect to the disaffected among you, is highly commendable, and justified by every principle of equity and policy....
But in dispensing punishment, the utmost care and caution ought to be used. The power of doing it, or even of bringing the guilty to trial, should be placed in hands that know well how to use it. I believe it would be a prudent rule to meddle with none but those whose crimes are supported by very sufficient evidence, and are of a pretty deep dye. The apprehending innocent persons, or those whose offenses are of so slender a nature as to make it prudent to dismiss them, furnishes an occasion of triumph, and a foundation for a species of animadversion which is very injurious to the public cause.... I believe it would also be in general a good rule either to pardon offenders entirely, or to inflict capital and severe punishments.

As aide-de-camp, Hamilton found there were many routine tasks to be done—as well as some assignments of responsibility. During the battles at the Brandywine and Germantown, Hamilton was active in the field and helped in the reorganization of the army after defeat. He dispatched the warning to Congress to flee Philadelphia; he was sent off to impress blankets, clothing, and shoes "with as much delicacy and discretion as the nature of the business demands"—and given a party of light infantry to assist when discretion could not serve. During the unhappy Valley Forge winter, he and John Laurens polished the translation of the manual of arms which General Steuben—one of the first of the foreign gentlemen of arms (or adventurers) to join Washington—was preparing to help whip Washington's Continentals into a trained fighting force.

Hamilton, in his processes of self-instruction, had learned to speak and write French well; with the French alliance concluded, his abilities were put to use. He was sent to help Admiral D'Estaing get pilots to take his fleet past Sandy Hook; before long, the two men were friends and the Frenchman could write of Hamilton to Washington that "his talents, and his personal qualities have secured him ever my esteem, my confidence, and my friendship." [2]

The next year, Hamilton had an opportunity to meet the English as officers and gentlemen; for he was named a member of a commission to conclude a cartel for an exchange of prisoners. Nothing came of the negotiation, except that Hamilton saw the backing and filling of Congress as it haggled over financial terms; but he learned an important lesson in political integrity. In this connection, he wrote in March, 1778, to Governor George Clinton of New York: [3]

It is thought to be bad policy to go into an exchange; but ... it is much worse policy to commit such frequent breaches of faith and ruin our national character.
Whatever refined politicians may think, it is of great consequence to preserve a national character; and, if it should once seem to be a system in any state to violate its faith whenever it is the least inconvenient to keep it, it will unquestionably have an ill effect upon foreign negotiations, and tend to bring Government at home in contempt, and, of course, to destroy its influence.

Hamilton was the one picked to go on the mission to General Horatio Gates, flushed with victory after Saratoga but reluctant to part with any of his troops—men whom Washington needed so desperately in Pennsylvania. Gates was obdurate; Hamilton was insistent; but many complications arose in which Governor Clinton had to be involved. The militia, who would not leave the state until they were paid, were finally satisfied; General Putnam was dissuaded from marching at once on New York; and at last the troops began to move. Hamilton's letters display none of his customary politeness: he shows his exasperation even in his reports to his commander-in-chief. Of Putnam he writes, "Indeed, sir, I owe it to the service to say, that every part of this gentleman's conduct is marked with blunder and negligence, and gives general disgust." [4] And to Putnam he declared, "My expressions may perhaps have more warmth than is altogether proper, but they proceed from the overflowing of the heart, in a matter where I conceive this continent essentially interested." [5]

ALEXANDER HAMILTON WAS "VERY BUSY, BUT WITHOUT DISTINC-tion," he was "chagrined and unhappy"; he became restive and sought to leave the official family. However, for a time the army, an independent command, recognition, were pushed out of his mind: he had met a charming young creature; he fell in love; soon he was engaged to be married.

In December, 1779, in a letter to John Laurens, he had written out his prescription for a wife: [6]

Take her description—she must be young, handsome (I lay most stress upon a good shape), sensible (a little learning will do), well-bred (but she must have an aversion to the word *ton*), chaste, and tender (I am an enthusiast in my notions of fidelity and fondness), of some good nature, a great deal of generosity (she must neither love money nor scolding, for I dislike equally a termagant and an economist). In politics I am indifferent what side she may be of. I think I have argu-ments that will easily convert her to mine. As to religion, a moderate stock will satisfy me. She must believe in God and hate a saint. But as to fortune, the larger stock of that the better....

Hamilton met his Eliza—she was the second daughter of Philip and Catherine Schuyler—in November, 1777, when on his mis-sion to General Gates. Philip Schuyler was the head of one of the great New York landed families: he had vast holdings in the Mohawk Valley and around Albany; he owned ships; he moved in the company of the mighty. He had thrown in his lot with the Revolution from the start; had had the command of an army in the northern campaign (where he had done well but had been blamed for the loss of Ticonderoga); had been a member of the New York Convention and, more recently, of the Second Continental Congress. The Schuylers, as befitting such powerful clans, were accustomed to making grand alliances; but the penniless young officer was known—the father had met him, had tested the strength and soundness of the metal—and Hamilton was encouraged to press his suit.

Elizabeth was capitivated. She, in turn, had those qualities a young man like Alexander Hamilton valued. She was, as one of his fellow aides wrote of her, "A brunette with the most good-natured, dark, lovely eyes that I ever saw, which threw a beam of good temper and benevolence over the entire countenance." [7] She was not vivacious; Hamilton was enough for two. She was not brilliant; she let her husband sparkle. But she had a deep and warm nature and a good wholesome mind. They complemented each other: such marriages are always a success. Hamilton's grandson says truly of this well-joined pair, "Had she been any other than what she was, despite all his genius and his force of character, Hamilton would never have attained the place he did. His letters show deference to her judgment and opinion, so we may conclude that he confided all his thoughts and plans, and made her a party to much that he did, yet his tender concern for her must have spared her many worries, and the knowledge of much that was harassing in his career." [8]

Elizabeth Schuyler and Alexander Hamilton were married on December 14, 1780, in Albany. Before the year was over, Hamilton was back at headquarters; his bride accompanied him and was made welcome by Martha Washington and the young wives of the official family.

BEFORE THE MARRIAGE, HAMILTON WAS TO BE AN IMPORTANT ACTOR in one of the great and tragic events of the Revolution—the treason of Benedict Arnold. Arnold had been an authentic hero of the struggle and one of the Revolution's greatest generals. He had been charged with financial irregularities—later proved true; Congress had passed him over again and again for important commands; he was constantly under financial pressure. He got in touch with Sir Henry Clinton: for a British post—and for money—he would surrender West Point, the most important fortress dominating the Hudson River.

Arnold obtained command of West Point in August, 1780, and Clinton at once sent his young adjutant-general, Major John André, to complete the arrangements for the surrender. André was luckless, for he moved by land and in disguise; he was captured by American militiamen with the plans of the fortress concealed in his stockings. The alarm was sounded and Arnold fled, leaving his wife behind. Washington now appeared on the scene and directed Hamilton and McHenry, the two aides in his company, to try to catch Arnold. In this they were unsuccessful; but the swiftness with which Hamilton moved nipped the conspiracy and saved West Point.

André was hanged as a spy on October 2. He had asked to be shot, but this Washington had refused, deeply embittering Hamilton, who had become attached to the British officer. On the day of the execution, he wrote to his affianced: [9]

...I must inform you that I urged a compliance with André's request to be shot; and I do not think it would have had an ill effect; but some people are only sensible to motives of policy, and sometimes, from a narrow disposition, mistake it.

This difference between the commander and his aide was more than a passing irritation: Hamilton was becoming increasingly restive as a result of his own minor role in the army and in larger affairs. He saw indecision and fumbling on the field and in civilian management: the war and independence could yet be lost.

In October, 1780, he wrote to one of his political correspondents, putting his finger unerringly on the weaknesses of the Congress: [10]

It is impossible the contest can be much longer supported on the present footing. We must have a government with more power. We must have a tax in kind. We must have a foreign loan. We must have a bank—on the true principle of a bank. We must have an administration distinct from Congress, and in the hands of single men under their orders. We must, above all things, have an army for the war, and an establishment that will interest the officers in the service.

Hamilton's powerful friends urged him for posts in the government—he was even proposed for the suggested office of Superintendent of Finance—but he was too young. Washington, too, was turning a deaf ear to requests for transfer to the line: he needed Hamilton in the family; he did not like pressure; perhaps he was annoyed that Lafayette was so obviously Hamilton's champion. The two young men had become very close: early in 1781, Lafayette wrote his wife that Hamilton was "a man I love very much."

Hamilton—through Lafayette—asked for command for a battalion then without a field officer; he was refused because Washington did not think Hamilton's rank entitled him to the post. Then Hamilton asked for command of another detachment; once again he was rejected. The office of adjutant-general fell vacant and Lafayette wrote to Washington that Hamilton would suit the post "better than any other in the world." [11] But Washington had already named another and would not rescind the appointment.

On February 16, 1781, the break took place. It occurred at headquarters. Washington had requested Hamilton to see him; on his way, he was detained by Lafayette who held him in conversation. Hamilton thus describes what ensued in a letter to his father-in-law two days later: [12]

Instead of finding the General, as is usual, in his room, I met him at the head of the stairs, where, accosting me in an angry tone, "Colonel

Hamilton," said he, "you have kept me waiting at the head of the stairs these ten minutes. I must tell you, sir, you treat me with disrespect." I replied, without petulancy, but with decision: "I am not conscious of it, sir; but since you have thought it necessary to tell me so, we part." "Very well, sir," said he, "if it be your choice," or something to this effect, and we separated. I sincerely believe my absence, which gave so much umbrage, did not last two minutes.

Hamilton, undoubtedly, was deeply hurt, and in his effort to justify himself in the eyes of Schuyler, said harsh things about Washington. He was "neither remarkable for delicacy nor good temper"; "his self-love would never forgive me for what it would regard as a humiliation." "You are too good a judge of human nature not to be sensible how this conduct in me must have operated on a man to whom all the world is offering incense."

But the quarrel must remain a secret; nothing must be done to endanger the successful conduct of the war.

The General is a very honest man. His competitors have slender abilities, and less integrity. His popularity has often been essential to the safety of America, and is still of great importance to it. These considerations have influenced my past conduct respecting him, and will influence my future. I think it necessary he should be supported.

Despite the disagreement, Hamilton continued to press Washington for an active assignment. It finally came just before Yorktown; he was given a battalion in the Second Brigade Light Infantry in the division commanded by Lafayette. On the evening of October 14, 1781, he was under fire. But Cornwallis was already beaten—his retreat by land had been cut off and Clinton had not yet left New York to lift the siege—and on October 17 he beat the parley and two days later he formally laid down his arms.

To all intents and purposes, the war was over, although the British Parliament did not recognize its end until March, 1782. Provisional articles of peace were signed on November 30, 1782; the formal peace treaty was signed in September, 1783.

The States in the Revolution

IN THE MIDST OF WAR, ALEXANDER HAMILTON CONTINUED HIS political education. Before he was twenty-five years old, he was learning that difficult lesson which many leaders today at the heads of new states apparently have not yet acquired: that a nation must have integrity. As he saw the fumbling at Philadelphia, where the Continental Congress sat, fearful of making decisions on fundamental matters of money and finances, he sharpened his understanding of the great requirements of public policy.

A nation survives and advances only if it has integrity. It cannot live beyond its means; it cannot indefinitely postpone the day when its accounts must be balanced; nor can it escape from its obligations by popular exhortation and glittering programs of social reform. In war or in peace, schemes that detract attention from the leading purpose of the state—the creation of an atmosphere of confidence so that the bold, the innovators, enterprisers, adventurers, will take risks—do not serve the general welfare but actually undermine it. A society is healthy when it grows; and it is truly vital when individuals—the risk takers—join their personal interests to those of the common weal. So strength and wealth are assured.

To call this an aristocratic or a conservative tradition of government, and therefore limited to the interests of a single class, is to confuse the issue hopelessly. In war, the root question is survival; in peace, it is stability. In both situations, confidence is bred and government is supported when men hazard their lives and fortunes exactly because the state itself is honorable. What are the characteristics of an honorable commonwealth? It operates under law; it preserves the individual rights of the person, conscience, and property; it cares for the young and the unemployables; notably, it is stern and just about its own obligations. Let it shirk about assuming these and men will abandon it by the most cynical means, by speculation, hoarding, extravagant personal living. And government itself? It would resort to "temporary expedient, fickleness and folly." [1] So Hamilton wrote to Robert Morris in 1782.

HAMILTON HAD CAUSE FOR CONCERN. THE FATAL WEAKNESSES EVIdent in the states were gnawing away at the center; bankruptcy, too, was overwhelming the shadowy government in Philadelphia. The fact is, there was no authority in Philadelphia, for the war was being fought by an alliance of thirteen sovereign states with the Continental Congress only the "superintending power." In the Congress, the delegates from each state voted as a unit; there was no executive, these functions being carried on by committees. Financing was simplicity itself: the war was to be supported by requisitions upon the states.

The states had other ideas and failed to honor their pledge, with the result that the Congress quickly descended into the abyss. It issued paper money, loan-office certificates, and certificates of indebtedness. Driven to desperation, it advised the states to sequester loyalist properties. It moved from expedient to expedient and, by 1780, its credit was wholly gone. If it had not been for the foreign loans, the Revolution might well have been lost.

During the years 1775–1783, Congress raised something like $82,000,000, specie value, to finance the war. State requisitions brought in $5.8 millions; loan-office certificates, $11.6 millions; certificates of indebtedness, $16.7 millions; bills of credit (which only the states could declare legal tender), $37.8 millions. Foreign loans and subsidies produced $9.8 millions. The bills of credit, virtually rejected by the states, for they took no measures to redeem them, and held in contempt by the business world, ended in the customary debacle. By 1779, Congress had issued $241,500,000 in such bills, and they had dropped in value to three cents on the dollar.

Congress played fast and loose with the American people. On the one hand, it angrily denounced those who were hinting that it meant to repudiate; on the other, it was contemplating exactly such measures. In a public address, dated September 13, 1779, Congress said: "A bankrupt, faithless republic would be a novelty in the political world, and appear among respectable nations like a common prostitute among chaste and respectable matrons." [2] And on March 17, 1780, when the ratio of paper to specie stood at almost 100 to 1, Congress did repudiate: it sought the redemption of the old bills at one-fortieth of their nominal value.

These were to be called in through the device of having the states pay taxes with the repudiated paper. In this fashion, $119,-400,000 of the bills were paid in by the states and removed from circulation; the remainder in use—a little less than $100,000,000 —continued to decline in value and by May, 1781, were worthless. Apparently they were destroyed; although by the Funding Act of 1790, these were acceptable for the purchase of the new bonds at a ratio of 100 to 1, only some $6,000,000 were turned in. Meanwhile, "new tenor" notes were to be issued. They were to be redeemed in specie in five years, to bear interest at 5 per cent, and be accepted for taxes; but only $4,400,000 were actually printed.

The assessments upon the states fared no better; heavy requisitions were made upon them—which they failed to honor. In the two years from November 22, 1777, to October 6, 1779, the states were asked for $95 millions (in paper money); they paid about half. From August 26, 1780, to March 16, 1781, a total of $10.6 millions (in specie) was requested; they paid about one-seventh.

Congress was not authorized to borrow until October 3, 1776; then it was permitted to raise $5 millions at an interest rate of 4 per cent. To place these loans, loan offices were established in each state; commissioners were named by state authorities and were remunerated on a commission basis; the loans were to be redeemed in three years. But the interest rate was too low, and it was not until the proceeds of the first French loan (1777) were used to meet the interest on these obligations that some funds from this source began to appear. Quartermasters, commissaries, and purchasing agents generally, in their desperate hunt for supplies, began to issue certificates of indebtedness. Hamilton in 1790 estimated the amount outstanding as $16.7 millions.

Without Europe—first came its money and then its troops and ships—the Revolution would have foundered. Gifts through private subscription (raised by Beaumarchais in France) and government subsidies (from the French and Spanish crowns) produced $2 millions. And between 1777 and 1783, Congress borrowed $6.3 millions from France, $1.3 millions from Holland, and $174,000 from Spain. The French and Spanish loans were almost entirely used to honor bills of exchange drawn upon America's representatives abroad; but the receipts of two of them did come home to help incalculably. One of them, as has been said, was employed to shore up the loan certificates; another produced the specie which helped create the capital of the Bank of North America. By 1782, with victory already certain and the prospects of the country brighter, America secured its first private loan abroad. This was placed with Dutch bankers—more than $1,000,000 was thus raised—at 5 per cent.

AMERICA, IN THESE CRITICAL NEGOTIATIONS, WAS WELL SERVED AT the top by a group of remarkable and devoted men: for Benjamin Franklin represented it in France, John Jay in Spain, and John Adams in Holland. At home, another capable man had appeared: this was Robert Morris, whom the Congress, now certain its committee system was useless, appointed Superintendent of Finance in March, 1781. Morris, a Philadelphian of large affairs, knew what the country required. Government and business needed credit; the first could establish its good faith only by putting its house in order and functioning on a specie basis; the second had to have more than the private loans of merchants for its operations. For government, therefore, revenues had to be regularized, more orderly dealings in foreign exchange created, foreign loans obtained; for business, a bank must be established. Morris was given wide powers, but his proposals were paid small heed. He did succeed in getting Congress to charter the Bank of North America in 1781; this was America's first commercial bank.

The British government had been sternly opposed to the creation of banks in colonial America; this was another way by which the American economy had been kept in leading strings. Morris seized the same opportunity that had been presented to the projectors of the Bank of England, when it was founded in 1694: he tied it to the government's dire necessities. The American Congress required advances against anticipated receipts; a financial institution could perform that function. In addition, a commercial bank, serving private purposes, would be an agency for deposit and discount. Congress therefore authorized the bank with a capitalization of $10,000,000; while private subscriptions were small, part of the French loan, totaling $254,000 in specie, was utilized by Congress for this purpose.

From his vantage point at Washington's headquarters—for the supplying of the army was a matter of growing concern to the commander-in-chief—Alexander Hamilton was able to watch the unfortunate tale of public finance unfold. On two different occasions, Hamilton addressed himself to this central problem of finance, first in a letter to a member of Congress, written in 1780, and then in a letter to Robert Morris, in April, 1781, after he had been appointed Superintendent of Finance.

In his first letter Hamilton came quickly to the reasons for the difficulties that were besetting the American people. The evil of depreciation was a spreading one; but it was an effect and not a cause of America's plight. For the war "required exertions beyond our strength, to which neither our population nor riches were equal." [3] Goods were in short supply; prices therefore mounted; and government—because of its incapacity to raise a revenue through taxation and domestic borrowing—only fed the disorder by its own unfortunate financing devices. The increase of goods, through foreign importation, would help, of course; more important, to get the country's monetary system back in a healthy state, was the establishment of confidence among businessmen. This was Hamilton's simple and flat assertion: "The only plan that can preserve the currency is one that will make it the *immediate* interest of the moneyed men to cooperate with government in its support."

In his letter to Morris, Hamilton expanded on his idea of the joining of private interest and public welfare. Here, in brief, we have the whole design of the Hamiltonian state: [4]

To surmount these obstacles and give individuals ability and inclination to lend in any proportion to the wants of government, a plan must be devised which, by incorporating their means together and uniting them with those of the public, will, on the foundation of that incorporation and union, erect a mass of credit that will supply the defect of moneyed capital, and answer all the purposes of cash; a plan which will offer adventurers [i.e., businessmen] immediate advantages, analogous to those they receive by employing their money in trade, and eventually greater advantages; a plan which will give them the greatest security the nature of the case will admit for what they lend; and which will not only advance their own interest and secure the independence of their country, but, in its progress, have the most beneficial influence upon its future commerce, and be a source of national strength and wealth.

The link between public and private interest was to be found in a national bank, for a bank would increase the credit of both. As for public credit, it "gives power to the state, for the protection of its rights and interests." As for private credit, it "facilitates and extends the operations of commerce among individuals. Industry is increased, commodities are multiplied, agriculture and manufactures flourish: and herein consists the true wealth and prosperity of a state."

There is no need here to examine Hamilton's proposals in detail. Some of the suggestions were fanciful (they did not survive when the First Bank of the United States came to be chartered in 1791); but the basic assumptions Hamilton argued for were sound. A bank was to have public as well as private subscriptions to its capital stock; it was to lend to both public authority and private individuals; it was to have the right of note issue, with redemption in specie; it was to be an agency of deposit; and it should discount commercial paper and bills of exchange.

Hamilton showed, particularly in his communication to Morris, an amazing and thorough familiarity with the public finances of European nations and with banking history generally. One passage will suffice: [5]

Most commercial nations have found it necessary to institute banks; and they have proved to be the happiest engines that ever were invented for advancing trade. Venice, Genoa, Hamburg, Holland, and England are examples of their utility. They owe their riches, commerce, and the figure they have made at different periods, in a great degree to this source. Great Britain is indebted for the immense efforts she had been able to make, in so many illustrious and successful wars, essentially to that vast fabric of credit raised on this foundation. It is by this alone she now menaces our independence.

In these early papers, Hamilton's confidence in his country glows with a steady light. America would grow; emigrants from all parts of the world would be attracted to it; its wealth and capacity for revenue would also increase. A national debt, rather than an encumbrance, would be an aid. It would be, "if it is not excessive, a national blessing." [6] Why? "It will be a powerful cement of our union." Also, taxation would be needed to service it, and this would be a "spur to industry." And he went on, "We labor less now than any civilized nation of Europe: and a habit of labor in the people is as essential to the health and vigor of their minds and bodies, as it is conducive to the welfare of the state. We ought not to suffer our self-love to deceive us in a comparison upon these points." [7]

AT THE SAME TIME THAT HE WAS SHAPING HIS IDEAS ON POLITICAL economy and the key problems of money and credit, Hamilton was giving thought to the central question of government itself. Why was the Congress weak? How were its fundamental defects to be overcome? Between July 12, 1781, and July 4, 1782, he wrote six essays for the *New York Packet*, signing them "The Continentalist." He was, in short, for a powerful central government capable of ruling a continent.

In these papers, Hamilton speculates on the nature of government with a fullness and sweep wholly admirable; he is, at the age of twenty-six, already at the peak of his powers. The writing is sure and felicitous; the arguments skillfully drawn; the recommendations supported from historical experience and an acute personal observation. "We may preach till we are tired of the theme, the necessity of disinterestedness in republics, without making a single proselyte," he writes. [8] And, "we might as well reconcile ourselves to the Spartan community of goods and wives, to their iron coin, their long beards, or their black broth." [9] And this keen note of warning, as he himself lived through a Revolution that was floundering: "An extreme jealousy of power is the attendant on all popular revolutions, and has seldom been without its evils." [10]

Power, then, is important. He rings again and again the changes on this question; there must be so much, neither more nor less, as will assure stability and yet not endanger liberty. There is a fine example of his ability to cut an even furrow in this passage, in the first essay: [11]

History is full of examples where, in contests for liberty, a jealousy of power has either defeated the attempts to recover or preserve it, in the first instance, or has afterward subverted it by clogging government with too great precautions for its felicity, or by leaving too wide a door for sedition and popular licentiousness. In a government frame for durable liberty, not less regard must be paid to giving the magistrate a proper degree of authority to make and execute the laws with rigor, than to guard against encroachments upon the rights of the community. As too much power leads to despotism, too little leads to anarchy, and both, eventually, to the ruin of the people....

There are wholly bad lapses in the conduct of a confederate form of government; there are also real perils in a single central government. It is important to find a middle ground: "The security, therefore, of the public liberty must consist in such a distribution of the sovereign power, as will make it morally impossible for one part to gain an ascendance over the others, or for the whole to unite in a scheme of usurpation." [12]

But he knows that there are deep loyalties attached to the separate states; none has ever phrased as well the reasons why weakness at the center has been more attractive than strength. Thus, he writes: [13]

It is the temper of societies as well as of individuals to be impatient of constraint, and to prefer partial to general interests....

The particular governments [i.e., the states] will have more empire over the minds of their subjects than the general one, because their agency will be more direct, more uniform, and more apparent. The people will be habituated to look up to them as the arbiters and guardians of their personal concerns, by which the passions of the vulgar, if not of all men, are most strongly affected; and in every difference with the confederated body, will side with them against the common sovereign.

In the third essay, Hamilton sounds the alarm; the times are out of joint and quick and drastic remedies are required. "Our whole system is in disorder; our currency depreciated, till in many places it will hardly obtain a circulation at all; public credit at its lowest ebb; our army deficient in members, and unprovided with everything; the Government, in its present condition, unable to command the means to pay, clothe, or feed their troups; the enemy making an alarming progress. . . ." [14]

This same note—of a helpless and do-nothing Congress—Hamilton had struck even earlier, in 1780, in a letter to James Duane, member of Congress from New York. Then, the youth of twenty-five had spoken boldly: "The fundamental defect is a want of power in Congress." This was so partly because the states refused to delegate functions, partly because of an excessive timidity in the Congress itself. The states have too much influence in military affairs, over fiscal matters, and in trade. History, as well as our own experience, has demonstrated again and again the weaknesses of federation. "We have felt the difficulty of drawing out the resources of the country, and inducing the States to combine in equal exertions for a common cause." [15]

What to do? Call immediately a convention of all the states to draw up a new frame of government. "A convention may agree upon a Confederation; the States individually hardly ever will." [16] And Congress ought to confess to them "plainly and unanimously, the impracticability of supporting our affairs on the present footing and without a solid coercive union." [17]

Congress must have complete sovereignty in all matters relating to war, peace, trade, and finance. It must receive, particularly, its own fiscal powers: the right to tax directly and to lay all imposts. Congress must create an administration, or executive departments, headed by individuals and not boards. Congress must have sole charge for the maintenance of the army. And then Hamilton goes on to supply in the greatest detail what the "sovereign" functions of the Congress are to be: they are, almost completely, an anticipation of the powers granted Congress in Article I, Section 8 of the Federal Constitution adopted in 1789.

In the final three essays of *The Continentalist*, Hamilton goes on to discuss how the powers of the Confederation are to be augmented. He talks of encouragement to trade and of proper fiscal management. He is not afraid of government assistance (where "the undertaking may often exceed the influence and capitals of individuals").[18] If there are to be tariffs, "experience has shown that moderate duties are more productive than high ones."[19] In his economics he is part mercantilist, part physiocrat, part libertarian; but the weight, in his thinking, clearly was shifting over to the last.

Always Hamilton sees a community of interest; again he is thinking of the whole state and not of a single or the most influential part of it. "Oppress trade, lands sink in value; make it flourish, their value rises. Incumber husbandry, trade declines; encourage agriculture, commerce revives."[20] To this theme Hamilton was to revert in his famous *Report on Manufactures*. And he ends with this salute, at the same time a warning, to his fellow countrymen. It was written on July 4, 1782. The war was over; he himself was already engaged in civilian pursuits; but his anxiety for the Republic never ceased.[21]

There is something noble and magnificent in the perspective of a great Federal Republic, closely linked in the pursuit of a common interest, tranquil and prosperous at home, respectable abroad; but there is something proportionately diminutive and contemptible in the prospect of a number of petty States, with the appearance only of union, jarring, jealous, and perverse without any determined direction, fluctuating and unhappy at home, weak and insignificant by their dissensions in the eyes of other nations,

The Confederation

ALEXANDER HAMILTON HAD EVERY REASON TO RETURN AGAIN AND again to the inadequacies of the Congress. The Congress had made peace but could not safeguard it; it had been furnished a formula for improving the relations with Great Britain but had proved incapable of using it; it could not defend its own legality because of its incapacity to protect property. Its greatest and its fatal weakness was its inability to create a climate of confidence in America so that stability could be assured and innovation and enterprise encouraged. The Congress, as a war-making body, and the Confederation, as a government of reconstruction, had been failures.

It has become increasingly the fashion among recent historians to seek to rehabilitate the reputation of the American governments of 1775–1789. They take the position that the Revolution was succeeding in its renovation of society; equalitarianism was being measurably established. The independent and sovereign states were discharging their normal obligations; more, they were resolving their differences among themselves. America was beginning to rebuild, overcoming the ravages of war. New industries were making their appearance and fresh avenues of trade —with continental Europe, China, India—were being opened up. Banks had been chartered and they were flourishing, as all sorts of promotions were being financed.

This defense of the Congress and the Confederation has really a political intention; its purpose has been to minimize the emergency that led to the summoning of the Constitutional Convention and therefore to attack the Founding Fathers as enemies of the Revolution. According to this view, the men who met in Philadelphia looked with alarm on the sans-culottism gaining strength in the states; they were hostile to both liberty and equality; they sought, in consequence, to ring around the powers of the states and the actions of individuals with all sorts of restraints. Notably, they placed the rights of property higher on the public agenda than the rights of men. And when they devised a central government which had the powers to check domestic insurrection, guarantee the sanctity of contracts, and protect the money-issuing function—when they deprived the states of the rights to negotiate with foreign nations and to interfere with foreign and domestic commerce—they were counterrevolutionaries. The Constitutional Convention was an illegal seizure of power in the interests of the moneyed classes of America.

The reverse is the case, for the Founding Fathers at Philadelphia made the Revolution secure. They checked its excesses—sans-culottism was a great danger; they restored the rule of legality; they made possible the rehabilitation of the credit of the nation and the states; they laid the basis for an understanding with Great Britain without which the Republic could not have survived. At that time, a strong, energetic central government was America's only salvation; indeed, without it a nation could not be built.

On its face, the treaty of paris of 1783, ending the war with Great Britain, was a great victory for the American cause. The independence of the United States was recognized; British troops were to be withdrawn and the British western posts were to be surrendered; the right to fish on the Newfoundland Banks was conceded; and freedom of navigation on the Mississippi was granted. The new country's boundaries on the north were to be the St. Lawrence and the Great Lakes, on the west, the Mississippi River, and on the south, Spanish Florida. On its part, the United States acknowledged the legality of the private prewar debts due British merchants and assumed the obligation to press the states to the full restoration of the rights and property of loyalists.

The victory was less than complete, however, for full commercial reciprocity between Great Britain and America was not established. In fact, in July, 1783, a British order-in-council shut American ships out of the British West India trade and sharply limited the American produce which could be imported into the islands. These restrictions and the British failure to withdraw from the western posts (Britain argued that the absence of settlements on debts and loyalist property justified its stand) therefore continued to trouble the waters of Anglo-American relations for many years.

To these matters Hamilton constantly reverted. Peace was a cause for rejoicing; it was also a time for patriots to work even harder than before. Thus Hamilton wrote to Washington when the good news from Paris came: [1]

It now only remains to make solid establishments within, to perpetuate our Union, to prevent our being a ball in the hands of European powers, bandied against each other at their pleasure; in fine, to make our independence truly a blessing.

Hamilton did his share by the causes he advocated at the bar and by the business promotions in which he became involved, and by continuing publicly to serve his state and country. In July, 1782, he was admitted to the practice of law while still in residence in Albany, near his father-in-law, Philip Schuyler. In November, 1783, he returned to New York City when the British occupation was finally terminated.

Hamilton came back to a city ravished by war—the occupation had left its mark as heavily as any siege. New York's population had dwindled by almost one-half as a result of the flight of first patriots and then loyalists. Two fires, one in 1776 and the other in 1778, had left one-fourth of the settled area in total ruin. Streets and pavements had been torn up; houses and public buildings were in disrepair; wharves, ships, and wells had been neglected. Commerce was at a standstill; there was a heavy poor roll, and a burdensome public debt. New Yorkers set to work manfully, however, and before long not only was the damage cleared away and repairs made but extensive improvements were begun. Streets were widened; new buildings were erected; the harbor was enlarged; King's College was reopened with the new name of Columbia College. By 1787, the city's population stood at 23,600, compared to 21,800 on the eve of the war. So rapidly did New York grow, thanks to its great maritime advantages and its imaginative business leadership, that in 1790 it was the largest city in the United States.

With its fortunes Alexander Hamilton's were closely joined. He was much sought after as a lawyer, not only because of his skill as a pleader and the care with which he prepared his cases, but because of his great personal charm. Chancellor Kent, having as a young man watched Hamilton in the law courts, later wrote, "His manners were gentle, affable, and kind. He appeared to be frank, liberal, and courteous in all his professional intercourse." [2] It was as a defender of the property rights of loyalists, notably, that Hamilton began to gain a wide reputation.

Conciliatory rather than punitive measures had, from the beginning, been Hamilton's guide in postwar policy; it was improper, he told Governor Clinton, in 1783, to drive out useful citizens by unwise laws. But sans-culottism was in the saddle, and the New York legislature treated the loyalists vindictively. It refused to permit loyalists to re-enter the state and buy back their confiscated lands; it disfranchised those who had only pas-

sively assisted the British during the occupation; and it ordered
those loyalist properties sold which hitherto had escaped con-
fiscation because they had been within the British lines.

All this not only was bad law but disregarded the Peace Treaty
which had promised no additional discrimination against loyalists.
In 1783, the New York legislature, going farther, passed the
so-called Trespass Act which permitted returning New Yorkers
to claim damages against loyalists who had occupied and misused
their property. When a suit arose in 1784, under this act, Hamilton took the unpopular side, defending a wealthy loyalist merchant against the claims of a widow who had been a fugitive
and had been impoverished by the war. Hamilton, nevertheless,
proceeded with the case, sensing at once its broad constitutional
involvements. Was it not necessary to maintain that the Articles
of Confederation were supreme over the laws of the individual
states? And was it not imperative that the United States demonstrate its bona fides under the Treaty of Peace?

Hamilton's pleading ran along such lines, but he lost the case
on a technicality. Nevertheless, he gained his chief point, for the
court agreed with him in principle, ruling that the Trespass Act
violated the Treaty for "no State in this Union can alter or
abridge, in a single point, the Federal Articles or the Treaty."
There was widespread hostility to the decision: the sovereignty
of the State of New York had been questioned for the first time:
and bitter public attacks were made on Hamilton. He replied,
in 1784, in two pamphlets under the name of "Phocion." The
second one is an impressive plea for the maintenance of constitutional government and the safeguarding of the legal processes.

His argument ran as follows: Constitutions were to be respected for they were the devising of the people. If the people
were dissatisfied with their handiwork, they could abrogate the
old compact and establish a new one; but until that was done,
society and individuals both were bound by their own agreement. The legislature could not supercede the constitution; nor

could "the sense of the people" do so. There was no danger that government would fall into the hands of hostile and special interests.[3]

The body of the people in this state are too firmly attached to the democracy, to permit the principles of a small number to give a different tone to that spirit. *The present law of inheritance, making an equal division among the children of the parent's property,* will soon melt down those great estates, which, if they continued, might favor the power of the few. [Italics original.]

And he ended with this plea for the preservation of the integrity of "these infant republics": [4]

Our governments hitherto have no habits. How important to the happiness, not of America alone, but of mankind, that they should acquire good ones! If we set out with justice, moderation, liberality, and a scrupulous regard to the Constitution, the government will acquire a spirit and tone productive of permanent blessings to the community. If, on the contrary, the public councils are guided by humor, passion, and prejudice ... the future spirit of government will be feeble, distracted, and arbitrary. The rights of the subject will be the sport of every vicissitude. There will be no settled rule of conduct, but everything will fluctuate with the alternate prevalency of contending factions.

The law kept Hamilton very busy; at the same time his private interests also widened. He speculated in wild lands; and he discussed with his friends the establishment of companies to improve inland navigation, build roads, erect bridges, create water supply systems, and begin manufacturing enterprises. In the 1780s—in the face of government's inadequate and frequently dangerous fiscal measures—a few starts had already been made. In the 1790s these were to burgeon richly. Hamilton's celebrated *Report on Manufactures* was to show how closely he was following America's economic development.

One of his early promotions was the Bank of New York which made its appearance in 1784. The Bank of North America, the country's first commercial bank, had justified all its projectors' fondest hopes. Founded in 1781, not only had it lent $400,000 to the Continental government but, by 1784, the debt had been discharged and the bank had been able to pay a dividend of 14 per cent. Businessmen from all over the east were pleased to become its shareholders, so that in 1784, $500,000 new capital was sought. One of the largest shareholders was Jeremiah Wadsworth of Hartford; Hamilton's wealthy brother-in-law, John B. Church, was equally interested. They encouraged Hamilton, in the light of these successes, to establish a bank in New York. A charter would be highly desirable.

Hamilton soon met with opposition. Chancellor Robert R. Livingston was already in the field, seeking legislative sanction and an exclusive charter for a land bank with the right of note issue against land and land mortgages. Colonial America, for want of other banking institutions, had experimented with land banks; they had only ended by precipitating paper-money inflations. These unhappy experiences were remembered, and a rival group, therefore, pressed for "a money bank." They set up a subscription to raise a special capital of $500,000 in $500 shares; Hamilton joined these men.

Hamilton drew up the constitution of the bank and became one of its directors. To this extent he was successful: while the Bank of New York received no charter (it did so, finally, in 1791), Livingston's land bank scheme was rejected. On June 9, 1784, the bank opened for deposits and on June 16 for discounts.

The bank became successful at once because of the sound practices it inaugurated. It was prepared to discount notes and bills for thirty days without renewal; payments were to be made in bank notes or specie; deposits would be accepted but overdrafts would not be permitted. Its original capital was only $51,500; but by May, 1785, this had grown to $75,000, and by May, 1791, to $318,250. It paid regular semiannual dividends of 3 per cent; it weathered the hard times of 1785–1789; and it did yeoman service in financing the business needs of New Yorkers, who were rebuilding the city and extending New York's commercial interests into every corner of the globe. By 1791, its deposits were $773,700 and its loans and discounts $899,200.

An aside reflecting on the uncertainties of business enterprise during the Confederation period is of interest here. The bank could not stay on an exclusively specie basis because of the dearth of hard money in America generally; it was compelled to accept the notes of the states. Pennsylvania and New Jersey began to issue legal tenders in 1785; New York followed in 1786 with $200,000 in notes. These flowed into banks and they depreciated in value. It was necessary to segregate them, and before long to stop their circulation altogether. By the end of the century, the Bank of New York possessed more than $100,000 of these frozen and dubious "assets." It is small wonder that first on his agenda for fiscal reform, Alexander Hamilton always put the restoration of the public credit.

DESPITE HIS PERSONAL REQUIREMENTS, IT WAS DIFFICULT FOR Hamilton to avoid public service. Finally yielding to Robert Morris's pleas, for a short time in 1782 he became the collector of the Continental revenues in New York. It was an unsuccessful and a thankless task. The state's quota had been set at $375,598; although the legislature voted to grant Morris about a fourth of this, Hamilton's collections came to only $6,250. However, there had been other accomplishments. He had had an opportunity to address a joint committee of the legislature on the state's hopelessly inadequate revenue system; he had prevailed on the legislature to pass joint resolutions calling on all the states to meet in convention to enlarge the powers of Congress; he had seen himself picked as one of New York's five delegates to the Continental Congress. This had been in July, 1782.

The resolutions for a general convention of the states were drawn up by Hamilton. Danger still threatened from Britain; America had allies but needed to depend more upon its own capacities; the "radical source of most of our embarrassments is the want of sufficient power in Congress"; [5] the Confederation was particularly defective in not granting the federal government the right to provide its own revenue or assure funds from the states.

Therefore, "these defects ought to be without loss of time repaired, the powers of Congress extended, a solid security established for the payment of debts already incurred, and competent means provided for future credit and for supplying the current demands of the war." [6] And for this purpose Congress was called upon to recommend to the states the meeting of a general convention of the states to revise and amend the Confederation.

Hamilton sat in the Continental Congress from November, 1782, to July, 1783. Personally, the experience was a rewarding one. Hamilton had learned from early youth the blessed discipline of hard and organized labor; he not only worked well alone, but he was a good member of the groups with which he was associated. In the Congress he attended faithfully: he drew up resolutions, served on committees, wrote reports, participated in debates; he was a firm but a fair antagonist. Here, as at Washington's headquarters, before the New York legislature, and in the law courts, he had the esteem of his colleagues, so that when he quit Congress, there was general regret.

But Hamilton had labored in vain. Congress had lost repute. Those who might have been the leaders in guiding the first faltering steps of the new nation were either in the service of their states or were with foreign missions. Washington was soon to retire from public life to manage his properties. Attendance was irregular; often no quorums could be assembled; some of the states remained unrepresented for long periods of time. When Hamilton left, in July, 1783, only six of the thirteen states had delegates to speak for them. And this unhappy state of affairs existed in the face of the requirement that, on most of the business the Congress could transact, the concurrence of nine states was necessary. Hamilton became completely confirmed in his conviction that the Confederation would not do.

As always, sooner or later, he came back to the central point: the survival of the nation and the maintenance of the public credit were irrefragably linked. It guided his hand everywhere: in the policies he was urging, the private letters he wrote, the public statements he made.

Early in 1781, when the instructions were being drawn up for one of Washington's aides, young John Laurens, about to leave on a mission to France, these striking observations appeared. The letter was signed by Washington; the thinking, the turns of phrase, are clearly Hamilton's.[7]

... from that inexperience in affairs necessarily incident to a nation in its commencement, some errors may have been committed in the administration of our finances, to which a part of our embarrassments may be attributed; yet they are principally to be ascribed to an essential defect of means, the want of a sufficient stock of wealth ... which want ... will make it impossible, by any merely interior exertions, to extricate ourselves from these embarrassments, restore the public credit, and furnish the requisite funds for the support of the war.

Here is the essence of Hamilton's public policy: that combination of economic understanding and state action which makes for survival. In a new country, whose wealth is modest, unless the public credit is sound, neither men of means at home will support it nor will foreigners come to its succor. In 1781, America needed foreign financial aid to win the war; during the 1790s— when Hamilton was devising the country's fiscal and financial programs and institutions—it needed foreign assistance for its economic development and progress. This was Hamilton's accomplishment and his personal triumph.

When he wrote to Washington, in April, 1783, justifying his interest in the army's demands for back pay and some recognition of its sacrifices, Hamilton reverted to the theme: "But the question was not merely how to do justice to the creditors, but how to restore public credit." [8] And when he wrote to Governor

Clinton, in May, 1783, urging New York's approval for a plan to regularize the revenues of Congress and fund the public debt, he once more declared: [9]

> But there are superior motives that ought to operate in every state—the obligations of national faith, honor, and reputation.
> Individuals have been already too long sacrificed to public convenience. It will be shocking, and, indeed, an eternal reproach to this country, if we begin the peaceable enjoyment of our independence by a violation of all the principles of honesty and true policy.

It was with these two matters of the Congress' revenues and the army that Hamilton largely concerned himself when in the Congress. The system of requisitions on the states simply was not functioning; it was vitally necessary to guarantee a revenue from at least one source. In 1781 import duties were singled out; would not the states agree to permit Congress to lay a 5 per cent impost, or duty, on all imports?

By December, 1782, all the states but Rhode Island had assented. Hamilton had just appeared in Philadelphia; he at once threw himself into the fray. Rhode Island had written out its reasons for refusing to approve the impost; Hamilton was made the head of a committee (on which Madison also served) to draw up a reply. It was a characteristically forthright and lucid statement, answering point for point the objections Rhode Island raised. And these general considerations were stressed: failure to fund the national debt "would stamp the national character with indelible disgrace"; funding would increase the "active stock," or working capital, of the nation "by the whole amount of the domestic debt"; the national credit would revive.[10] Rhode Island, however, could not be budged; and, stunning blow to Hamilton's hopes, Virginia withdrew her ratification.

Another plan was drawn up in 1783; this impost sought to use both specific and ad valorem duties, to run for twenty-five years, and to apply the revenues thus obtained to the principal and interest on the public debt. Collections were to be made by state officials. But the impost of 1783 fared no better than its predecessor: for, though by 1782, Rhode Island had finally agreed to participate, this time New York held back. In 1786, Hamilton was sitting in the New York legislature; and the refusal of New York to reconsider gave Hamilton the immediate occasion for moving that New York participate in the Convention of 1787.

TROUBLE WAS BREWING IN THE ARMY: THERE WERE ARREARS IN pay, no plans for demobilization, and no financial arrangements for returning officers and men to their homes. Hamilton was aware of the mounting discontent; in fact, army leaders, memorializing Congress, sought him out for advice and help. Hamilton wrote to Washington in February, 1783, once more pointing up the unhappy state of the Congressional finances and asking him to champion the cause of the country's soldiers. "In order to do it," he said, "it will be advisable not to discountenance their endeavor to procure redress, but rather, by the intervention of confidential and prudent persons, *to take the direction of them.*" [11] (Italics original.) Here, too, was an opportunity to link the army's proper grievance with the general scheme of fiscal stabilization.

Washington took alarm: rumors had come to him that officers would not lay down their arms until their accounts had been settled. He had to appear before his officers in Newburgh to demand that they desist; but he recognized the justice of their complaints and sent their petitions on to Congress. These stated that "until their accounts are liquidated, the balances accurately ascertained, and adequate funds established for payment" demobilization was out of the question. He wrote to Hamilton: there was talk of a "combination" of public creditors and the army to force Congress' hand.[12]

Hamilton replied March 17. It is apparent that he was flirting with dangerous expedients, that while the end he sought was meritorious in the highest degree, the means were just as dubious. He admitted he was playing politics with the army's needs, that he was joining their demands with those of other creditors. His hope was to force Congress to act to "adopt such a plan as would embrace the relief of all the public creditors, including the army"; that the states, under popular pressure, would yield. But not a combination to seize power. "As to any combination of *force*, it would only be productive of the horrors of a civil war." [13]

On March 25, Hamilton wrote again—in fact, he wrote twice. In his first letter, he asked Washington to point out to the officers that constitutionally Congress could not establish funds with which to provide for the soldiers' requirements; it could only recommend to the states such action. He thought, however, events were moving toward a solution. In his second, he showed he still was unaware of how close he was to the brink of disaster; only the failure of his efforts in Congress can account —but not justify—the reckless position he took.

He was afraid the army's "distrusts have too much foundation." Republican governments have notoriously been hostile and ungrateful to their military. This temper was to be found among his colleagues. What can the army do? It must accept rebuff; it must not rise. Yet: [14]

I make these observations, not that I imagine your Excellency can want motives to continue your influence in the path of moderation, but merely to show why I cannot myself enter into the views of coercion which some gentlemen entertain, for I confess, could force avail, I should almost wish to see it employed. I have indifferent opinion of the honesty of this country, and ill forebodings as to its future system.

To Hamilton, Washington sent back a proper rebuke. What Hamilton had said, Washington read with "astonishment and horror . . . the idea of redress by force, is too chimerical to have had a place in the imagination of any serious mind in this army." The army "is a dangerous instrument to play with." [15] A settlement had to take place at once and the army should be disbanded.

A settlement with the officers—they received five-years' full pay in the form of interest-bearing securities—was finally arranged.

Despite this fundamental disagreement between the two men —and Hamilton's faltering—Washington did not lose confidence in Hamilton, and the older man continued to consult the younger; their correspondence remained on a friendly footing. A year later, as we have seen, Hamilton had returned to his faith in the constitutional processes: his statement, in the second "Phocion" pamphlet, was a clear call for the maintenance of all the institutions of free government.

Discontent in the army was not yet over, as noncommissioned officers and soldiers rioted and made representations to the commander-in-chief and to Congress. By June, 1783, the army had begun to melt away; but not until there was a last flare up at Philadelphia. A band of Pennsylvania troops, refusing to be discharged, marched on Congress in June and threatened force unless they were paid. Congress, taking alarm, fled to Princeton. Hamilton took the lead in championing the cause of the soldiers; they were paid off and a full pardon was agreed upon. Congress never returned to Philadelphia; from Princeton it moved to Annapolis and then, in 1785, to New York.

Hamilton took his leave of Congress by proposing a set of resolutions, on June 30, 1783, which called for the summoning of a general convention to revise and strengthen the Confederation. Here we have, in masterly fashion, a dispassionate and complete exposure of the inadequacies of the Confederation, as well as a previsioning of some of the basic settlements incorporated into the Constitution.

These resolutions took the following position. The power of the federal government was too narrowly confined: there was withheld from it "that efficacious authority and influence, in all matters of general concern, which are indispensable to the harmony and welfare of the whole." [16] There was no proper division of functions in the government: the legislative, executive, and judicial authorities ought to be distinct and separate. In fact, there was no federal judiciary at all, to prevent infringement of national laws and treaties by state action; and as for legislative authority, it was strikingly weak. Congress was given the power of general taxation, with no right to impose and collect taxes. It could borrow money and emit bills of credit, but it could not assure the repayment of the moneys borrowed or the redemption of the bills. And again, the recurrent theme: there must result from this "either a want of sufficient credit, in the first instance, to borrow, or to circulate the bills emitted . . . ; or, in the second instance, frequent infractions of the public engagements, disappointments of lenders, repetitions of the calamities of depreciating paper, a continuance of the injustice and mischiefs of an unfunded debt, and, first or last, the annihilation of public credit." [17]

There was no real control over foreign affairs; no adequate provision for interior and exterior defense; no supervision over foreign coins in circulation.

The Confederation had failed to vest in the federal government a general control over trade, for both revenue and regulation. It was the role of government to discourage injurious branches of commerce and encourage favorable ones, and to promote useful products and manufactures.

The requirement that nine states approve proposed legislation on important matters only stultified the Congress; delays occurred, the majority had to give way before the minority, "and must always make the spirit of government a spirit of compromise and expedient rather than of system and energy." [18]

The feebleness of the Confederation made the United States weak in war and unjust to the army and the public creditors; it involved the states in "all the disgrace and mischiefs of violated faith and national bankruptcy." [19] These could be avoided and security and happiness attained only through "a government capable both in peace and in war, of making every member of the

Union contribute, in just proportion, to the common necessities, and of combining and directing the forces and wills of the several parts to the general end...." [20]

WHAT WAS THE TRUTH ABOUT THE CONFEDERATION? THE ARTICLES OF Confederation had been drawn up in 1776 and 1777 but had not been finally ratified until March 1, 1781, largely because of the resistance of Maryland. The western claims of Virginia concerned her, and when Virginia agreed to yield at least part of her domains to the federal government, Maryland fell into line.

The new government, which functioned from 1781 to 1789, was both a league of friendship and a confederation of sovereign states. As a league, the states were combined for "their common defense, the security of their liberties, and mutual and general welfare." In the league, each state had one vote. The vote of nine states was needed for all important measures: those affecting war and peace, international relations, and the borrowing of money. Unanimous consent was required for amendments. No independent executive or judiciary was set up. Each state retained control over taxation and commerce; gave full faith and credit to the records, acts, and judicial proceedings of the others; extended to the "free inhabitants" of one "all the privileges and immunities" of citizens of the others. Freedom of access and trade and freedom to deal in property were singled out for mention.

As a confederation, however, the states surrendered specific sovereign rights to the Congress. Congress could make war and peace; send and receive ambassadors; make treaties of alliance and draw up commercial conventions; regulate coinage, weights and measures; establish a post office; manage Indian affairs; determine interstate disputes over boundaries and certain land titles; borrow money on the credit of the United States; raise an army and equip a navy, make requisitions upon the states for funds, supplies, and men. Congress might appoint committees and civil officers to manage its business and it could set up a "Committee on the States" to act during recess periods.

The states were not to undertake diplomatic dealings with foreign nations or conclude compacts with each other unless Congress consented. They were not to lay duties interfering with treaty stipulations. They were not to keep land or naval forces in peace except as Congress deemed necessary (but the militia was to be maintained on a sound footing), nor could they engage in war without the consent of Congress.

Some of the accomplishments of the Confederation were significant. Congress concluded peace in 1783. It made some progress in the enormous task of settling accounts between the states and "the Continent" for expenses incurred during the war. It even contrived to set up a civil service of sorts, so that a permanent staff could deal with details in Indian affairs, foreign relations, and finance.

Perhaps the Confederation's most important achievement was the acquisition of a national domain and the development of a policy for governing the territory and speeding its settlement. Under their colonial charters, several states extended "from sea to sea" and so claimed huge areas of unsettled land. In 1780, New York ceded its claims to the United States, a course which the other states followed. The Virginia grant—to territory northwest of the Ohio—was accepted in 1784, without voiding private land claims (as Virginia had wished) or guaranteeing her the rest of her western territory.

"The United States in Congress assembled" now had a national domain, vast in area (although largely unsettled) and a source of revenue; it was at the same time a bond of union and a bone of contention. In June, 1783, Theodore Bland of Virginia proposed (with Hamilton seconding) that ceded territory be divided into districts and that these, when sufficiently populated, be admitted into the Union. Jefferson's Ordinance of 1784 (he was then sitting in the Congress) provided for some free grants to settlers, self-government, and, ultimately, admission to the Union. An ordinance regulating land sales was passed in 1785, and provision was made for the erection of public schools. In July, 1787, Congress finally adopted the ordinance which became the core of United States territorial policy. The Northwest Territory was to be set up; a system of limited government was created with territorial legislatures to be elected when an adequate population had settled; civil and property rights and schools were guaranteed and slavery was barred. It had been the hope that the sales of lands to settlers in the government's public lands would relieve Congress' financial embarrassments; but only disappointment resulted. Cash sales were small—although squatters did move in—so that the revenues derived from this source came to less than $1,000,000 by 1789.

The economic problems of the nation were handled by the Confederation with only indifferent success. American merchants managed the transition from war to peace and colonial to independent status with a fair measure of smoothness, in part aided by the expenditures of British and French commissaries during hostilities, in part by the balance of the Dutch loan. During 1783–1785, imports could be financed, and merchants hastened to fill the shelves that had been emptied by the war. America set to work cleaning up, restoring the ravages of combat and occupation and starting new construction in cities. Small industries, many of them new, also began to flourish—in paper, iron, woolens. In Philadelphia, New York, and Boston—for in the last a bank too had been created in 1784—financial assistance was available to private enterprise. Not so, however, in the countryside: the want of credit was agriculture's leading and constantly besetting concern.

Direct trade with France, the Netherlands, the Baltic region, and the Orient was now open; but the direct trade with Britain continued the main support of the country's economy. The order in council of 1783 created serious barriers in the direct trade with British West India and, while there was a certain amount of smuggling, the regulations hurt New England shipping and products. The balance of payments was heavily against the United States: in the two years 1784 and 1785 imports from England came to £6,000,000 and exports to England totaled only £2,000,000. True, the United States had a favorable balance in the total West India trade and freights earned by ships were measurable; but interest on public and private loans, commissions, and insurance ate these away. It was clearly evident, despite all the new ventures in trade and industry, and the great future promise of America —in its vast, unsettled continent, its rich natural resources, the skills and energy of its population—that America was living beyond its means. In 1785 and 1786 this became known to all, for specie began to flow out of the country, credit became tight, agricultural prices dropped: the brief boom was over.

The disproportionate role played by speculation was another factor that made America's economy an uneasy one. Men of means—denied opportunities in industrial enterprise because of the difficulty of obtaining general articles of incorporation for companies and because of the absence of protection for infant industries—plunged heavily in land speculation and the purchase of returned soldiers' land warrants. They further immobilized their funds by buying old state public issues—at large discounts, it is true. The unsoundness of this kind of activity was demonstrated by the melting away in the 1790s of great paper fortunes: the failures of Robert Morris, James Wilson, and William Duer were typical and outstanding.

There was no economic collapse in America: nor was there a basis for sound and continuing expectations. The recession of 1785–1786 was followed by spotty revival; in 1787 business was better, although recovery was not general. Toward the end of 1787, wholesale prices again were slipping and they continued to decline until the middle of 1789. It was not until the new government was established, that a steady, upward advance began to take place.

ONE MUST NOTE THE ELEMENTS OF INSTABILITY AND THE ESSENTIAL want of confidence in the country's broad economic intention. A new country cannot live on prospects alone; it must demonstrate —by work, abstinence, and saving—its ability to balance its public and private accounts and its capacities for accumulating wealth. When savings flow into speculation and not productive enterprise, when income from international trade generally is less than outlays, when government—by its own reckless course or for want of power—is incapable of encouraging foreign investment, then the economy's career is a fitful one. This was America's dilemma during the years 1784–1789. It was inevitable that there should be a mounting concern on the part of responsible persons, notably those who viewed America's problems in their international setting. Hamilton understood all this: and this is his significance, for from 1780 to 1795, he constantly exposed the country's weaknesses and unerringly defined the lines of policy for building up its strength.

Public finance, as has been said here, lay at the very center of the matter. The government, to all intents and purposes, was bankrupt.

At the beginning of 1784—apart from outstanding bills of credit —its indebtedness in specie was $39,000,000, broken down as follows:

Foreign debt, including arrears of interest	$ 7,921,886
Loan Office certificates	11,585,000
Unliquidated certificates of indebtedness	16,708,000
Arrears of interest on domestic debt	3,109,000
	$39,323,886

To this must be added the indebtedness of the states—most of them incurred for war purposes—and these stood at $21 millions. The annual interest charges on the federal foreign debt came to $375,000; and on the domestic debt, $1,500,000. The government was incapable of paying interest on its obligations: the arrears therefore piled up. The arrears of foreign interest grew from

$67,037 to $1,640,071 between 1784 and 1789; the arrears of domestic interest grew from $3 millions to $11.5 millions in the same period.

During these years 1784–1789, the receipts of the government totaled $4.6 millions. Requisitions on the states brought in $1,945,-000; miscellaneous sums produced $338,000; while foreign loans —from Dutch bankers—brought in $2,296,000. More than half of the Dutch funds came in in the single year 1784, and these were used to pay interest on foreign loans and finance imports from Holland. In the two years 1785 and 1786, Dutch loans totaled only $100,000; it was not until there were prospects of a more powerful federal union that the Dutch bankers indicated a willingness to help America's financing.

A further word about the breakdown of the requisitions system. During 1784–1789, Congress called upon the states for $5.2 millions in specie; it received $1.9 millions. It asked from the states $7.7 millions in indents: scrip with which the federal government was paying the interest on the domestic debt. It received $1.5 millions. During 1786, less than $200,000 was paid in, and that by only two or three states. The federal government needed funds for its civil and military requirements: and it had to resort to the further issue of certificates of indebtedness. These sank so low—for such was the credit of the Confederation—that they were publicly valued at fifteen cents on the dollar.

Davis R. Dewey made this analysis in 1902; the judgment still stands as an informed one: [21]

At heart the country was economically sound, but the national financial system was weak, and in 1786 it broke down completely; further borrowing at home or abroad was almost impossible; requisitions were of slight avail; domestic creditors were thoroughly alarmed, and when the efforts to secure unanimous consent for a national tax failed, it was agreed that, if a federated republic were to continue, the government, particularly in its relations to finance and commerce, must be remodelled.

The states, in their separate actions, were equally a cause for concern. The erection of barriers to impede the free movement of transport and goods across state boundaries did not exist; quite the reverse. Reciprocity generally took place among the states: American-made goods and American ships were exempt from imposts and tonnage duties, and foreign goods imported in American ships enjoyed lower rates. This did not prevent quarrels from breaking out, however. New Jersey and Connecticut sought to win away some of the foreign trade entering New York; New York retaliated by taxing foreign goods reaching her by way of these states. Control over trade was used as a weapon and an irritant.

Into the bargain, there developed a complex of regulations, imposts, and tariffs with which state legislatures tinkered almost annually. All the states laid duties for revenue purposes; beginning with 1785 they began—frequently on top of earlier schedules—to establish tariffs for protection. Rhode Island was the first to do so, and it was quickly followed by Pennsylvania, Massachusetts, Connecticut, Georgia, and Virginia. The tariff rates were uneven from state to state and, because some had no tariffs at all, all hopes for uniformity and protection went aglimmering. So, too, did the opportunity of bringing commercial pressure to bear on those foreign countries, like Britain and Spain, which were discriminating against American ships and goods.

States also were wrangling among themselves about boundaries and land claims. In northern Pennsylvania—an area claimed by Connecticut—blows were exchanged and lives were lost. New York, New Hampshire, and Massachusetts for a long time could not settle amicably the disposition of what is now the state of Vermont. All claimed the region, or parts of it. Formal war did not break out: but there were border forays and much bitterness publicly expressed.

Worse, in this particular, was the attitude toward paper-money emissions and contract obligations. By the end of the war, most states had voided their old bills of credit as legal tender. But the outflow of the country's specie and mounting debt, particularly in rural districts, prompted seven of them to reissue paper-money legal tenders during 1785–1786. These states were Pennsylvania, South Carolina, North Carolina, New York, New Jersey, Georgia, and Rhode Island. All kinds of motives were adduced: states wanted to pay their shares of the Confederation foreign debt; pay the bounties soldiers had been promised; redeem Loan Office certificates, lend on farm mortgages, buy up surplus farm crops.

Whatever the intention, a good deal of this paper got out of hand. The Pennsylvania issue depreciated slightly; the North Carolina paper dropped by 50 per cent in value in three years; in New Jersey, by 1789, its paper was unacceptable for private obligations; and the paper of Georgia and Rhode Island ended by being worthless. Rhode Island went so far as to include a "forcing" provision in its law, imposing an initial fine of £100 and a second fine of £100, with a loss of citizenship, upon those who would not accept the legal tenders. The law courts were filled with heated wranglings between debtors and creditors.

With paper issues went demands for stay, or mortgage-moratorium laws, and laws to write down the face values of mortgages themselves and to abolish imprisonment for debt. Judges, authorizing the seizure of properties and jailing debtors, were bitterly denounced and even threatened with physical violence. North Carolina, to protect them, went so far as to shut down its courts altogether.

It was this uncertainty about the status of contracts, this inability suddenly to count upon the states to safeguard normal business activities and obligations, that caused the most alarm. Currency tinkering and stay laws—paper issues that depreciated and contracts that were violated—jeopardized any chance of economic betterment in America. Edmund Randolph, in his opening address at the Convention of 1787, had this example before him when he referred to the danger arising "from the democratic parts of our constitutions." [22] James Madison, after the Convention was over, felt that this state of affairs—this inability to protect individual property rights—was in the minds of the delegates more than any other concern. He said, writing to Jefferson, "The mutability of the laws of the States is found to be a serious evil." [23] And "the evils issuing from these sources contributed more to the uneasiness which produced the Convention ... than those which occurred to our national character and interest from the inadequacy of the Confederation to its immediate objects."

Agrarian debtors took up arms, too; government itself seemed endangered as a result of the Shays Rebellion in western Massachusetts in the fall of 1786. Massachusetts, to restore its public finances, was proceeding to fund its debt, and to do so was seeking to raise a revenue from poll taxes and to require payments in specie. This, and its effort to protect private obligations—by specie payments and foreclosures—aroused hard-pressed farmers. Appeals to the Massachusetts General Court for paper emissions and stay laws were in vain. Captain Daniel Shays organized a band of farmers to prevent seizures for debt and force the closing of the courts. The Springfield Arsenal was in the heart of the troubled area; there was concern lest it be seized and its weapons used to overthrow the government of Massachusetts.

Congress offered Massachusetts federal aid; the state's governor moved vigorously; the General Court called upon citizens to put down "lawless and violent" men; and the Shaysites were quickly disbanded. The rising shocked opinion all over the country: General Knox, writing to Washington, said of the embattled and embittered farmers, "In a word, they are determined to annihilate all debts, public and private, and have agrarian laws, which are easily effected by means of unfunded paper money which shall be a tender in all cases whatever." [24] The troubles in Massachusetts were alluded to, again and again, by speakers at the Convention of 1787.

Finally, there was no glory for the United States in its management of foreign affairs: America's place in the company of nations was turning out to be an uncertain and an insecure one. There were some gains: France, the Netherlands, Sweden, Prussia, and Morocco concluded commercial treaties with the United States between 1782 and 1787. On the other hand, Britain continued in its refusal either to establish commercial reciprocity or to evacuate the western posts. American ships were not permitted to sail on the Great Lakes; British customs officers were stationed on American territory; Indian relations continued disordered because of the British control over the fur trade. To justify all this, Britain took its stand on the Treaty of 1783: state laws were continuing to harass loyalists and to hinder the collection of prewar debts. The incapacity of the United States to retaliate—particularly against the order in council of 1783—through discriminatory commercial regulations, undoubtedly held the British to their course.

Relations with Spain were no better. Spain would not accept the northern boundary of Florida agreed on between Britain and the United States at the same time that it fomented discontent among the Indians and supported southwestern secessionists. In 1784, Spain, refusing to surrender Natchez on the river's eastern bank, also closed the mouth of the Mississippi to American ships and commerce. In 1785, Congress instructed John Jay, then its foreign minister, to negotiate a commercial treaty with Spain. Such a treaty was drawn up the next year and submitted to Congress; but Jay's willingness to see the Mississippi closed for twenty-five or thirty years, in return for trade concessions by Spain elsewhere, provoked a bitter storm. The Congress—and the country —divided on regional and economic lines, with the mercantile North and East supporting the treaty and the agricultural and expansionist South opposing it. The treaty received seven votes in the Congress, and therefore failed: but the hostilities brought out into the open left deep scars.

THIS WAS THE STATE OF AFFAIRS UNDER THE ARTICLES OF CONFEDERATION in 1786 and the early months of 1787. Impatient, and perhaps desperate, men were talking of the dismemberment of the Confederation; others were proposing separate and independent leagues. These were not idle rumors: James Monroe, Benjamin Rush, Daniel Humphreys, in their private correspondence, reported such discussions. So Benjamin Rush, from Philadelphia, wrote to his English friend Richard Price, in October, 1786, "Some of our enlightened men who begin to despair of a more complete union of the States in Congress have secretly proposed an Eastern, Middle and Southern Confederacy, to be united by an alliance offensive and defensive. These Confederacies, they say, will be united by nature, by interest, and by manners, and consequently they will be safe, agreeable, and durable." [25]

Again and again, in this uncertain time, responsible men were expressing their forebodings. Thus, Washington wrote to Madison in November, 1786: [26]

No morn ever dawned more favorably than ours did; and no day was ever more clouded than the present. Wisdom and good examples are necessary at this time to rescue the political machine from the impending storm.... Without an alteration in our political creed, the superstructure we have been seven years in raising at the expense of so much treasure and blood, must fall. We are fast verging to anarchy and confusion.... Thirteen sovereignties pulling against each other, and all tugging at the Federal head, will soon bring ruin on the whole....

And, in February, 1787, Madison wrote that if "some very strong props are not applied," [27] the present system will quickly tumble to the ground: no funds were coming into the federal government and no respect was being paid it. Under these circumstances, it could not last. Alexander Hamilton had long be-

fore—as early as 1780, as we have seen—come to the same conclusion. With his characteristic energy, he was to move twice to
create a machinery for the re-examination of the purposes of the
Articles of Confederation and the strengthening of the federal
Union. The first was in the prominent role he played at the
Annapolis Convention; the second, in obtaining the participation
of New York in the Constitutional Convention of 1787.

The Constitution

WHAT ARE THE DUTIES OF A GOVERNMENT? IT SHOULD PROVIDE FOR the national defense; it should assure the rule of legality, functioning through an incorruptible judiciary; it should encourage and safeguard freedom of religion, communication, and association; it should employ the police power to defend and improve the life, health, and morals of its people. It must protect its own survival, allowing for change through orderly processes at the same time that it maintains balances within the commonwealth. Shifts of power from time to time occur: majorities through the passage of time may be converted into minorities. Oppression, either at the hands of government or those dominating the state, must always be guarded against.

Madison well understood this last danger. Speaking at the Constitutional Convention, he issued this warning: [1]

An increase of population will of necessity increase the proportion of those who will labor under all the hardships of life and secretly sigh for a more equal distribution of its blessings. These may in time outnumber those who are placed above the feelings of indigence. According to the equal law of suffrage, the power will slide into the hands of the former. No agrarian attempts have yet been made in this country, but symptoms of a leveling spirit, as we have understood, have sufficiently appeared, in a certain quarter, to give notice of the future danger.

Government, notably, must create a climate in which welfare is realizable. This is a function of individual initiative and enterprise; and the state can both help and stultify. In consequence, the protection of private property is an important concern of government. If innovation is the only significant spur to increases in production; if capital formation—in a world always poor—is a constant necessity; if the saving process needs regular stimulation; if, from historical experiences, we know that unless risks are taken—and fortunes made by the successful—the idea of economic progress cannot be sustained, then private property and private business decisions must be assured.

Equalitarianism, a leveling spirit, the substitution of security for welfare, threatens government and stability.

In a free society, there must be free consumer choices and unequal compensation. The first guarantees the efficient employment of scarce resources, the second provides proper social incentives. Unequal wages and salaries—leading to private fortunes—are the great aids to innovation. If social progress is a legitimate public interest, then adventurers must be permitted to invest, take risks, and save for further investments from their successful ventures.

All this does not mean that privilege is to be tolerated. Encouragement for a short time, yes: tariffs to nurture infant industries, patents to permit inventors and discoverers to get some recompense for their labors, tax exemption and quick obsolescence when national emergencies or massive shortages threaten to weaken the state. Idle funds or excessive fortunes used for antisocial purposes always are a danger. Every political thinker of consequence, from Aristotle to John Stuart Mill, knew that no society could endure for long, or ward off social discontent, unless it concerned itself with redistribution. There was always a wealthy group in the top layer and a poor one in the bottom. In between was to remain that broad sector of the middle class which had the fluidity and opportunity to reach above or—if unsuccessful—to fall below.

The power to tax, as John Marshall said, is the power to destroy. But the power to tax can also make possible society's stability, because it can be employed for the redistribution of wealth. Redistribution, then, keeps opportunity alive and equal and permits the regular emergence of new adventurers or innovators. So does the maintenance of the luxury industries, although in a minor way. Mandeville, in part, was right: the luxury industries are useful—not, of course, because they give employment, but because they help the profligate and stupid to speed the processes of redistribution. Thus, taxation is a double-edged sword: it can both encourage and threaten the life of incentive.

Given the possession of that awesome weapon, fiscal power—to tax, to create money—the state has a great responsibility: the protection of society's credit structure is in its own hands. The state cannot be heedless in the management of its own finances; any recklessness on its part must have a blighting effect on enterprise at once. A sound monetary and credit system and a manageable public debt are the first concerns of virtuous lawmakers; otherwise economic chaos inevitably follows.

This warning, particularly, must be taken to heart by new or underdeveloped nations. The formula of inflation (or repudiation) and—more recently—that of price and exchange controls seem such simple and magical ones; but only one's own people—and not for long—can be bemused by them. Certainly the stranger—the foreign investor and trader—smells out the danger at once. As has been said, Alexander Hamilton, almost alone among the public leaders of his day understood this; he knew how vital it was that a new nation's public and private credit be built on an indestructible foundation.

Is a state to be a monolithic one? Is there no place for a division of public functions? And should not private associations also assume some measure of social responsibility? The answer is in the affirmative to both questions. Liberty must flourish, and pluralistic loyalties keep the tree of liberty in a healthy condition. The devolution of power—through a federal scheme, through private association—must be the key to proper political thinking. The monolithic state, because it seeks to assure both progress and protection, ends by sapping initiative; associations are weakened and finally converted into pale satellites without lives of their own.

A federal scheme of government will work if such a division of responsibilities is rigorously maintained. The central government will live and thrive if it accepts as its exclusive role the assurance of welfare, or progress, through the exercise of the fiscal authority, the protection of property, and the constant defense of the liberty of the individual—to communicate, to assemble and associate, and to accumulate. The separate states will survive and gather about them the loyalties of their citizens if they protect the police power, and defend and improve the life, health, and morals of their people. The separate states have in their charge the care and needs of the young; they assure decent working and housing conditions; they facilitate mobility.

SUCH ARE THE BROAD AND GENERAL CONSIDERATIONS NECESSARY TO keep a polity healthy. And the Founding Fathers, when they assembled in Philadelphia to devise a new frame of government, were aware of much, if not all, of these needs. They were neither visionaries nor pleaders of special causes. Because, among them, there were few spokesmen for the "popularity"; because they regarded with so many misgivings the inadequacies of the Confederation and the errors committed by the states, it is a grave injustice to them and to the Constitution to assume that their labors were not in the common interest.

There was no conspiracy at work: the Constitution was not a "counterrevolution," or usurpation; the principles of the Declaration of Independence and the "rights of man" were not undermined or even threatened. Here was a body of devoted Americans only too well aware how time was running out, how heavy were the stakes involved. The survival of the Republic was really the issue. If their political ideas were conservative—and Alexander Hamilton enunciated these honestly and openly—it was because there was a general feeling that only with such leadership, and not with a leadership of those who were the unyielding spokesmen for factions, could a favorable outcome be assured. A strong union, a "coercive" central government, to check the states in their headlong career, was the difference between the existence of a United States of America and disintegration.

A number of circumstances combined to make possible the meeting of the Constitutional Convention and the completion of its work. The rise of a new leveling spirit—the assaults on contracts, the resort to paper emissions, the threat to authority from the Shaysites and the turbulences in Rhode Island—sounded the alarm. Conflicts among the states, because of the erection of trade barriers, particularly in a time of economic contraction, created the immediate reason for discussion among them. The most important of these was the Annapolis Convention of 1786. In this Hamilton played a leading part.

In 1785, Virginia and Maryland representatives began to examine the problems arising out of their common interest in the Potomac and the Chesapeake Rivers in order to report back to their legislatures. Early in 1786, a compact was agreed upon to regulate the mutual commercial concerns of the two states; and Virginia sent out a call to all the states for a general meeting to consider the creation of a "uniform system of taxation in their commercial intercourse and regulations."

This was the origin of the Annapolis Convention of September, 1786. New York accepted Virginia's invitation and named six delegates, Hamilton among them; but only New Jersey, Pennsylvania, Delaware, and New York joined with Virginia in the proceedings. In all there were twelve men in attendance, and, with so few states represented and so small a company, very little could be hoped for. Hamilton seized the opportunity, nevertheless. He drew up the draft of the address to all the states out of which the Constitutional Convention of 1787 emerged.

The statement called attention to the fact that the New Jersey commissioners had been empowered to discuss uniform commercial regulations and "other important matters"; but because there had been no point in considering the questions of trade and commerce when so few states had had spokesmen, the time was ripe for a general examination of these problems "and such other purposes as the situation of public affairs may be found to require." [2]

All the states, therefore, were asked to send commissioners to meet at Philadelphia on the second Monday in May, 1787, "to take into consideration the situation of the United States, to devise such further provisions as shall appear to them necessary to render the constitution of the federal government adequate to the exigencies of the Union," and to place their views before Congress. In October, Virginia voted to attend; at last, it began to appear, the momentous issue of the survival of the Union was going to be faced.

Hamilton hurried back to New York. He had been elected to the Assembly, or lower house, of the New York legislature; all his skill and resources would be needed to obtain New York's participation. For New York, its politics largely dominated by agrarian, debtor interests, under the skillful leadership of Governor George Clinton, was hostile to any measures calculated to strengthen the hand of the federal government. It itself had issued new paper currency; it still had on its statute books discriminating measures against the loyalists; it had ringed around its acceptance of the impost of 1783 with so many exceptions that the Congress had refused to take its action as approval. These momentous matters were all to be discussed in the 1787 legislature.

Hamilton immediately entered the lists against Clinton on the question of the impost and the mode of its collection. The latter was really the heart of the matter, for unless collections were made by the agents of the federal government, the voting of financial assistance was a futile gesture. But the Clintonian forces held firm and Hamilton's resolutions were lost. His efforts to have the Trespass Law repealed also ended in failure. But there was one triumph, and it turned out to be the important one: over the opposition of Clinton, both houses of the legislature voted that New York's representatives in Congress recommend the summoning of a convention for the purpose of revising the Articles of Confederation.

Congress immediately passed such a resolution; and New York was pledged. Hamilton had been a leader in all these maneuvers; and it would have been difficult to pass him over when the New York delegation came to be named. With him, from New York, however, went two Antifederalists, John Lansing and Robert Yates. So the lines were already drawn. Those in favor of a strong national union were coming to be called Federalists; and those opposed, Antifederalists. These groups persisted; the two-party system had emerged in the United States.

It was not until May 25, 1787, that the Philadelphia Convention assembled. All the states but Rhode Island had voted to take part; there were named sixty-two delegates of whom fifty-five attended at one time or another; however, only thirty-nine signed the Constitution. George Washington came, as did the venerable Benjamin Franklin. There were seven governors or former governors of states, twenty-eight members or former members of Congress, eight signers of the Declaration of Independence. There were some distinguished absentees, among them Thomas Jefferson (then minister to France), John Adams (occupying a similar post in England), and Patrick Henry and Samuel Adams.

The business of organization was quickly settled: George Washington was named President; each state was to have a single vote;

a quorum was to be made up of seven states; the proceedings were to be held behind closed doors with no official record taken. What we know of the debates we have learned largely from the notes of James Madison; indeed, it was this quick, dapper little man from Virginia who left the largest single impress on the proceedings. Like Hamilton, he was a nationalist from the beginning, and his indefatigable co-laborer first in Congress, now at the Convention, later in the struggle for ratification. He was "the Father of the Constitution." But there were other leaders; perhaps there were five men among this extraordinary company of talents assembled in Philadelphia whose indelible mark was to be found upon the finished document: these were James Madison, Alexander Hamilton, Gouverneur Morris, James Wilson, and C. C. Pinckney.

It has too commonly been supposed that the deliberations of the Convention were marked by bitter controversy and that an understanding was finally beaten out only because reasonable men were prepared to mediate extreme positions. There was, indeed, one important issue over which long discussion took place—how were the small states to be protected from being overwhelmed by the large ones? This having been resolved, there was never any question about ultimate agreement.

Only one compromise, therefore, had to be worked out, and this was the reconciliation of the so-called Virginia and New Jersey Plans. The Virginia Plan, submitted May 29, presented the position of the large states; the New Jersey Plan, submitted June 15, that of the small states. The Virginia Plan, of course, was more than a proposal to enhance the power of the large states: it was so broad and thorough in its scope that it represented an entirely new frame of government. In fact, out of it, with the necessary concessions to the small states, emerged the Constitution. These agreements are well known: they had to do with the nature of representation in the Senate, the method of the Constitution's amendment, and the choice of the President by electoral rather than popular vote. Otherwise, the discussions concerned themselves largely with two matters, that of overcoming the defects of the Articles of Confederation and that of limiting the powers of the states.

The Convention sat from May 25 to September 17. From May 30 to June 13, it debated the Virginia Plan; from June 19 to July 26, the New Jersey Plan. As a result of these deliberations, twenty-three resolutions were approved and submitted to a committee on detail. When the Convention reassembled, on August 6, it began to examine the specific proposals of this committee and continued to do so until September 10. Then a committee on style, headed by Gouverneur Morris, was authorized to draw up a final draft. This it presented September 12; there was further debate; on September 15, the Constitution was agreed upon; and two days later the Convention disbanded.

Disregarding its instructions, the Convention did not revise the Articles of Confederation; it replaced them. It reported back to Congress and the several legislatures only formally; actually, it asked for the approval of its labors by specially elected state conventions. And the new Constitution was to be installed after nine of the states had given their approval, instead of all, as the Articles of Confederation required.

The major accomplishments of the Convention, in strengthening the hand of the federal government, were these: There were to be three separate and independent departments of government, the legislative, the executive, and the judicial. The new Congress was to have the powers of defense and taxation. In fact, "it was to pay the debts and provide for the common defense and general welfare of the United States." It could regulate foreign and interstate commerce. The states could not disregard treaties made by the United States: these were to be the "supreme law of the land." The judicial power of the United States was to "extend to all cases, in law and equity, arising under this Constitution, the laws of the United States, and treaties made . . . under their authority." The Congress was to consist of two houses, with voting by individuals and not states. Instead of the approval of nine states on all important matters, only bare majorities were to be required in both houses. And amendments to the Constitution might be made by two-thirds votes in both houses, with ratification by three-fourths of the state legislatures.

When it came to the curbing of the powers of the states, there were no uncertainties. That "mutability of the laws of the States," to which Madison referred, was in the minds of all the delegates: legal-tender and stay laws and laws impairing contracts were even more pernicious than the processes by which the old Congress had been stultified. The Constitution, in consequence, had these provisions. All debts and contracts entered into, by Congress, whether before or after the Constitution's adoption, were valid. The states could not, under any circumstances, emit bills of credit. They could not make anything but gold and silver legal tender for the payment of debts. They could not impair the obligations of contract. These requirements and prohibitions made property rights secure, of course: but more, they gave legal protection to the processes of accumulation and, therefore, economic welfare in the young America.

In this wise, the framers of the Constitution sought "to form a more perfect union, establish justice, insure domestic tranquility, provide for the common defense, promote the general welfare, and secure the blessings of liberty" for the United States.

And in this spirit of great hope—as Madison described it—the delegates entered upon their final formal action: [3]

Whilst the last members were signing the Constitution Doctor Franklin, looking towards the President's chair, at the back of which a rising sun happened to be painted, observed to a few members near him, that Painters had found it difficult to distinguish in their art a rising from a setting sun. I have, said he, often and often in the course of the Session, and the vicissitudes of my hopes and fears as to its issue, looked at that behind the President without being able to tell whether it was rising or setting: But now at length I have the happiness to know that it is a rising and not a setting sun.

AT THE CONVENTION—DESPITE THE FACT THAT HE HAD DONE SO MUCH to bring it about—Hamilton's role was a difficult one. His fellow delegates from New York were Antifederalists and hostile to much that was taking place; in fact, they quit early in July and did not return. In consequence, it would have been impossible for Hamilton to have presented a plan, similar to Virginia's and New Jersey's, that had his state's backing. For the same reason, he avoided participating on points of detail; and he engaged in none of the prolonged debates. He made one long speech—perhaps the best at the Convention—and he submitted a group of propositions, more as his articles of faith than in any hope they could carry persuasion. These set forth his theoretical position.

At the end, he signed the Constitution and urged all the others to do so. The final plan could not have been more remote from his own ideas; "but is it possible to deliberate between anarchy and convulsion on one side, and the chance of good to be expected from the plan on the other?" [4] So Hamilton, the good member, expressed his concern; and, despite his misgivings, he became at once the Constitution's most stalwart defender.

Hamilton was present from May 18 to June 29; he was again in Philadelphia during August 13–20; and he attended the final sessions during September 2–17. He sat on two of the Convention's important committees: that on rules, at the beginning, and that on style, at the end.

He engaged in one exchange that demonstrated the earnestness, and, at the same time, the capacity for accommodation, of the delegates. They had reached, after weeks of debate, an impasse on the question of representation brought so sharply before the Convention by the New Jersey Plan: and Franklin arose to suggest that Divine Providence be called upon for guidance. Let the proceedings every day open with prayer through the agency of the clergy of the city. Hamilton objected: such a move might have been proper at the beginning of the Convention, but appointing a chaplain at this late date might lead the public to believe that "embarrassments and dissensions within the Convention" [5] had prompted the measure. Franklin rejoined that rejection of the proposal would cause more unpleasant talk than would its adoption. Williamson (of North Carolina) observed, perhaps dryly, that the Convention had no money to pay a chaplain; and Randolph (of Virginia) moved that the Convention attend church in a body on July 4 and ask that a special sermon be preached for its benefit. The Convention voted then to adjourn; and it continued deliberating thereafter without opening prayers.

To what extent legend and malice have grown about the Constitutional Convention, the subsequent reporting of this incident displays. In 1825, Jonathan Dayton, a New Jersey delegate, remembered the exchange in this wise: [6]

Franklin proposed present adjournment and future prayer at the crisis of dissension between the large and the small states. Hamilton opposed the motion. He was willing to adjourn, but not to have a chaplain. He "said he was confidently of opinion that *they were competent* to transact the business which had been entrusted to their care" without "calling in *foreign aid*."

On June 18, with the New Jersey and Virginia Plans already before the Convention, Hamilton arose to make his longest speech and set forth his personal philosophy of government. It was the credo of a patriot: the survival of his country and the creation of stability were his two concerns. He had seen the "violence and turbulence" [7] of the democratic spirit; he was too realistic about the motives and passions that guided human conduct to seek to discount them; every safeguard to assure good government ought to be created. The best government was that which was in the hands of those with a personal stake in society and who, in their private and public lives, were guided by noblesse oblige. This was an aristocratic principle, but it was also a conservative one, for it offered liberty, justice, and, most of all stability. It was for this reason that Hamilton appealed to British experience and the British Constitution: with its monarchy and its House of Lords, it stood above corruption.

Hamilton admired such a monarchy, but did not propose it for America; he had his misgivings about republicanism, but he did not suggest that it be abolished. He wanted to see established a "national" plan; at the same time he was aware of the powerful loyalties gathering about the states. They were to continue to exist, but their potentialities for mischief were to be sharply checked. It was a courageous, honest, and thoughtful statement; but his political enemies always continued to misrepresent it, never ceasing to maintain that Hamilton was really trying to fasten monarchy on America.

As late as 1803, Hamilton was compelled to defend himself against this canard. Writing to Timothy Pickering of Massachusetts, in reply to an inquiry, he said that the plan he had presented in 1787 was "conformable with the strict theory of a government purely republican, the essential criteria of which are that the principle organs of the executive and legislative departments be elected by the people, and hold their offices by a *responsible* and temporary or *defeasible* tenure." [8] And he ended: "These were the genuine sentiments of my heart, and upon them I acted. I sincerely hope that it may not hereafter be discovered that... the experiment of republican government, even in this country, has not been as complete, as satisfactory, and as decisive as could be wished."

The thrusts that Hamilton directed against the two plans before the Convention unerringly hit their weaknesses. The New Jersey Plan was too much like the Articles of Confederation, particularly in the weight it gave the states as sovereign bodies. It did grant the general government power to regulate trade, but it did not help provide a revenue; and the United States, with a debt to pay, required assured funds. The Virginia Plan was not essentially better. It checked a democratic House of Representatives by a democratic Senate and both by a democratic Executive. Ultimately, the people might tire of an "excess of democracy"; and what was the Virginia Plan, but " 'pork still, with a little change of the sauce.' " [9]

For the most part, Hamilton declared, he had been silent from respect to the "abilities, age, and experience" of his colleagues and because of his "delicate situation," opposed as he was by both his fellow delegates from New York. He could accept neither of the plans suggested for a new government because he was "fully convinced that no amendment of the Confederation, leaving the States in possession of their sovereignty, could possibly answer the purpose." He fully realized, however, that the alternative was equally distasteful: the amazing extent of country the United States had to govern discouraged hope of "the desired blessings from any general sovereignty that could be substituted."

The next question was "what provision shall we make for the happiness of our country?" That happiness was interfered with by the fact that the states had too much power. At present, few active interests were concerned with supporting the federal government, while many such were intertwined with the states.

All the passions, then, we see, of avarice, ambition, interest, which govern most individuals and all public bodies, fall into the current of the States, and do not flow into the stream of the General Government.

Therefore, ultimate emasculation of the central authority could be avoided "only by such a complete sovereignty in the General Government as will turn all the strong principles and passions" to its side.

The New Jersey Plan, with its provision of equal votes for all the states large and small, prevented proper use of power by Congress. "The general power, whatever be its form, if it preserves itself must swallow up the state powers. Otherwise it will be swallowed up by them. . . . Two sovereignties cannot coexist within the same limits." Undoubtedly, it would be cheaper to eliminate the state governments. Such a measure would shock public opinion; and to such opinion he was prepared to yield. Ultimately perhaps, because the states were not essential for commerce, revenue, or agriculture, the necessary subordinate authority could be supplied by local courts and the cities. If the general government did grow strong, the state governments might be extinguished.

In so large an area as the United States must rule, Hamilton went on, he almost despaired of republican government; yet he knew it was not desirable to propose any other. To be sure, he was supported "by the opinion of so many of the wise and good, that the British government is the best in the world; and that I doubt much whether anything short of it will do in America." Since even those "most tenacious of republicanism" were loud in declaiming against the "vices of democracy" he hoped for further "progress of the public mind" toward a better view of government.

The many must be kept from oppressing the few; the few from imposing on the many. Both, therefore, ought to have power, so that each could defend itself against the other. But it was the few who were in greatest danger. The "rich and well born" should have a "distinct, permanent share in the government" so that they could check the unruly changeable people, who "seldom judge or determine right." The rich and wellborn would always maintain good government "as they cannot receive any advantage by a change." Exactly because it recognized this principle of the responsibility of aristocracy, the British Constitution was great. "Their House of Lords is a most noble institution. Having nothing to hope for by a change, and a sufficient interest, by means of their property, in being faithful to the national interest, they form a permanent barrier against every pernicious innovation." In the United States, the proposed seven-year term would not be enough to give a Senate firmness against the "amazing violence and turbulence of the democratic spirit."

As to the Executive, Hamilton continued, it seemed to "be admitted that no good one could be established on republican principles." Yet was "not this giving up the merits of the question; for can there be a good government without a good Executive?"

Indeed, the entire "goodness of a government" consisted "in a vigorous execution." Therefore "we ought to go as far in order to attain stability and permanency, as republican principles will admit."

Hamilton concluded his speech by offering, in a series of propositions, a sketch of a plan of government, that would be vigorous, stable, and balanced. His plan would be unacceptable to most delegates and to the people. But the Union was "dissolving or already dissolved." The current evils of the state governments "must soon cure the people of their fondness for democracies." On that score, progress was being made daily. And, once the people had been "unshackled from their prejudices," as they would be in time, they would be ready to go as far as he proposed.

Hamilton's plan of government exists in two forms; he read his propositions to the Convention as part of his June 18 speech, and he gave Madison a more carefully drawn version as the Convention disbanded in September.[10]

There were to be three departments of government: legislative, executive, and judicial. The legislature was to be made up of two houses, an "Assembly" chosen by the free male citizens for three years, and a "Senate," chosen indirectly by electors, who, in turn were to be chosen by voters with a property qualification. The senators were to hold office during good behavior. Money bills were to originate in the Assembly but the Senate might modify them. The Senate was to have exclusive power to declare war, to confirm appointments made by the President, and to ratify treaties.

The President, who represented the executive branch, was to be chosen by a double set of electors, also named in turn by voters with a property qualification; and he too was to serve during good behavior. He was to have an absolute veto over legislation, make appointments, arrange treaties, and be commander-in-chief. The President might be impeached by a two-thirds vote in each house.

The judicial department was to consist of a Supreme Court

holding office during good behavior. It was to hear cases in which the United States, the states, or foreign governments were represented; and it was to have appellate jurisdiction in cases involving citizens of foreign nations, citizens of different states, and cases in which "the fundamental rights of this Constitution are involved."

The legislature was to have "power to pass all laws which they shall judge necessary to the common defense and general welfare of the Union." The legislature was to enact no bill of attainder or ex post facto law, to grant no titles of nobility, or permit acceptance of titles or presents from foreign states or princes. Nor might it establish religious sects or tests by law. Direct taxes were to be levied in proportion to the number of free persons plus three-fifths of all the others.

The laws and treaties of the United States were the supreme law of the land and to be construed as such by the state courts. Further, state governors were to be appointed "under the authority of the United States." They might veto state laws, subject to regulations made by the federal legislators. The states were guaranteed a republican form of government and assured protection against domestic violence and foreign invasion.

So much for Hamilton's scheme. In many important particulars, it can be seen, Hamilton had a powerful influence on the Convention. The Convention would not accept his idea of office to be held during good behavior (except for the judiciary); but he sharpened up its thinking about how a separation of powers could truly work, and what it adopted about the place and function of a national government it drew from him. The concept of judicial review is clearly stated by Hamilton; and so are many of the principles subsequently incorporated into the Bill of Rights.

THE LINES FOR AND AGAINST A NATIONAL UNION HAD FORMED EVEN before the Convention had met. With the Constitution's presentation, by Congress, to the states for ratification, the battle was joined. In almost every state a bitter struggle between Federalists and Antifederalists broke out: and only patience, adroit political maneuvering, and superior talent—skillfully, and sometimes irregularly, employed by the Federalists—won the day for them. Had the Constitution been submitted to a popular mandate, it probably would have suffered defeat.

It is a mistake to assume that in the fight over ratification there emerged a simple and clear-cut division between the rich and the poor, the wellborn and the humble, the mighty and the lowly. The Lees in Virginia and Elbridge Gerry in Massachusetts, dedicated foes of the Constitution, were men of wealth; Alexander Hamilton and John Marshall, who defended it, were not. All sorts of considerations entered into the taking of sides, some political, some sectional, some personal.

The Federalists possessed the larger vision: they saw for America a growing role in international affairs, an expanding territory and economy, a nation which could obtain the respect of its citizens only as its instrumentalities of government had integrity and vigor. The Antifederalists were much narrower in outlook and interest; they were states' men who could see liberty defended and rights maintained only as government was sharply limited in its powers; they were suspicious of Britain and indifferent to commerce; they deprecated change. On the one side there were those who feared disunion and collapse, if not the end of the Republic. On the other—as in Virginia, New York, and Pennsylvania, which managed their own internal affairs well—there was satisfaction with the little that the Confederation was doing.

To leave out the self-interest of men would be idle and unrealistic. Hamilton saw this as well as anyone. Writing in September, 1787, just after the close of the Convention, he noted that these were the forces in favor of the Constitution: [11]

...the good will of the commercial interest throughout the States, which will give all its efforts to the establishment of a government capable of regulating, protecting and extending the commerce of the

Union. The good will of most men of property in the several States, who wish a government of the Union able to protect them against domestic violence, and the depredations which the democratic spirit is apt to make on property, and who are besides anxious for the respectability of the nation. The hopes of the creditors of the United States, that a general government possessing the means of doing it, will pay the debt of the Union.

And, in opposition, there were these forces:

... the disinclination of the people to taxes, and of course to a strong government; the opposition of all men much in debt, who will not wish to see a government established, one object of which is to restrain the means of cheating creditors; the democratical jealousy of the people...; and the influence of some foreign powers who...will not wish to see an energetic government established throughout the States.

So it turned out to be. those regions of states associated with commerce supported the Constitution; while the back country generally was opposed. The contest was waged at length in the press, by pamphlets, in the legislatures, the election campaigns, and on the floors of the ratifying conventions. The friends of the Constitution were winning the day. Delaware was the first to ratify on December 7, 1787: its vote was unanimous. Pennsylvania and New Jersey followed in the same month, Georgia and Connecticut, in the next. In Massachusetts—where a long struggle was carried on behind the scenes—ratification took place in February, the majority being but nine out of 355 delegates. Maryland ratified in April, South Carolina in May, and New Hampshire in June. In not much more than seven months, the required nine states had given their approval: the Constitution of the United States of America was adopted.

The two great states of Virginia and New York had not yet made their decisions: without their assent, the Constitution would remain only a paper frame of government, perhaps never to be installed. In Virginia, impressive talents were gathered on both sides. Against the Constitution were Patrick Henry, Richard Henry Lee (author of the persuasive *Letters of a Federal Farmer*), and George Mason. For it, were George Washington, James Madison, and John Marshall. Thomas Jefferson, away in France representing the United States, was of mixed mind. He could see reasons for being opposed: because he believed the Articles of Confederation could be changed by a few amendments; because he was afraid the proposed government might be too "energetic"; because there was no harm in rebellion—the uprising of Shays and his friends was a good thing. But he could accept the Constitution if amendments, notably those incorporating a Bill of Rights, were carried along with ratification. Ultimately, this latter was the line he followed. On June 25, after prolonged debate, the Virginia convention, too, gave its approval; the majority was only 10 in a total of 168 votes. As in the case of Massachusetts, the Convention submitted a group of amendments.

New York remained. (Rhode Island refused to call a convention; and, when North Carolina did, in August, 1788, it rejected the Constitution.) Alexander Hamilton at once entered the lists for the Constitution, in New York. As early as October, 1787, he and Governor Clinton had crossed swords and they continued to be the leaders of the opposing forces until ratification was finally won on July 26, 1788. In New York City newspapers, with Clinton signing himself "Cato" and Hamilton "Caesar," the discussion was begun, and the wide attention given the exchange of statements encouraged Hamilton to undertake the writing of the famous *The Federalist* papers. The first letter of *The Federalist* —addressed to the "People of the State of New York"—appeared in the New York *Independent Journal* of October 27, 1787, and it bore the signature "Publius." Between that date and August 15, 1788, in various New York newspapers, 85 letters in all appeared; they were reprinted in other cities, and their favorable reception encouraged Hamilton to put them together in book form. Volume one, containing the first 36 letters, was published March 22, 1788;

volume two, containing numbers 37 to 77 (already printed) plus eight others, made its appearance May 28, 1788. Hamilton was the principal but not the sole author, for he had the aid of James Madison and John Jay in the enterprise. Hamilton wrote 51 letters, Madison 26, an additional three were probably written jointly; Jay wrote only 5, and these were entirely on foreign affairs.

The Federalist—even though it was written so hastily and as a joint product—is a remarkable document; beyond question, it continues to remain America's outstanding work in politics. What is impressive about it is how the authors, to achieve a purpose to which they were so deeply devoted, suppressed their own personal doubts and, almost, their differences. We read it as a brief; three lawyers were pleading a cause in terms of the charges made against their plan by their contemporaries. We read it as a defense of republican government, which, the authors argue, will create responsible political institutions in America. Good government was their interest and their passion; and the outstanding characteristics of good government were energy, stability, and justice.

In the first number, Hamilton declared, *The Federalist* would discuss these topics: The utility of the Union to America's political prosperity—The inadequacies of the Confederation—The necessity of a strong government to attain Union—The Constitution and its conformity to the true principles of republican government—Its analogy to the New York State Constitution—and the security its adoption will give to republican institutions, to liberty, and to property. This scheme was generally adhered to.

But *The Federalist* can be examined in other ways. According to Vernon L. Parrington, for example, politically, it stressed these four ideas: "The necessity for taking effective action in view of the self-confessed failures of the Articles of Confederation; the urgent need of a sovereign, unitary state, to avoid the horrors which must follow from 'the political monster of an *imperium in imperio*'; the necessity of providing that justice shall prevail over the majority will; and the adaptability of the republican form to a great extent of territory and divergent interests." [12]

The argument for a unitary state, "a general government completely sovereign," was largely developed by Hamilton; that for a system of justice, was the work of Madison. Both accepted a seventeenth-century view of human nature rather than an eighteenth-century, a conservative approach and not a liberal; for both viewed men as swayed by passion and not reason, by caprices and wickedness, rather than by "policy, utility and justice." [13] They saw therefore the necessity for a "coercive" sovereignty. Only so could justice be made to prevail, as restraints were imposed upon the majority as well as the minority. Unless government could make its presence felt, factions—special interests which challenge the rights of other citizens or those of the whole community—by their hostilities would dissolve government. For Madison says, in the tenth paper:

Complaints are everywhere heard from our most considerate and virtuous citizens, equally the friends of public and private faith, and of public and personal liberty, that our governments are too unstable, that the public good is disregarded in the conflict of rival parties, and that measures are too often decided, not according to the rules of justice and the rights of the minor party, but by the superior force of an interested and overbearing majority.

Madison declared that property is "the most common and durable source of faction" and that, in a regime of liberty, inequality of property is inevitable. But a limited republican government, a "compound republic," based upon the representative principle, would reconcile such conflicting interests to assure justice.

Hamilton agreed, but he went further: only a "firm union," a national government with coercive powers can repress "domestic factions and insurrections." [14] And in the fifteenth paper, he sets out his nationalist credo: [15]

But if we are unwilling to be placed in this perilous situation; if we still adhere to the design of a national government, or, which is the same thing, of a superintending power, under the direction of a common council, we must resolve to incorporate in our plan those ingredients which may be considered as forming the characteristic differences between a league and a government; we must extend the authority of the union to the persons of the citizens—the only proper objects of government.

Where shall the ultimate power lie? In the people, of course. Madison, however, is prepared [16]

...to refine and enlarge the public views, by passing them through the medium of a chosen body of citizens, whose wisdom may best discern the true interest of their country, and whose patriotism and love of justice will be least likely to sacrifice it to temporary or partial considerations.

Again Hamilton, less ambivalent than his coadjutor, is ready to place his trust in the Republic's servants. In papers, 70, 71, 76, and 78 he comes back again and again to the idea of stewardship, the aristocratic principle of noblesse oblige: [17]

The republican principle demands that the deliberate sense of the community should govern the conduct of those to whom they intrust the management of their affairs.

Energy in the Executive is a leading character in the definition of good government. It is essential...to the security of liberty against the enterprises and assaults of ambition, of faction, and of anarchy.

Notably a judiciary, holding office during good behavior, develops "impartiality" and the "requisite integrity" fundamental to government.[18]

The independence of the judges is equally requisite to guard the Constitution and the rights of individuals from the effects of those ill humors, which the arts of designing men, or the influence of particular conjunctures, sometimes disseminate among the people themselves, and which...have a tendency...to occasion dangerous innovations in the government, and serious oppressions of the minor party in the community.

BEFORE LONG, THE DIFFERENCES BETWEEN HAMILTON AND MADISON were to become unbridgeable chasms. But Hamilton, not deterred by the opposition of the Antifederalists, was to go ahead with his great program for the reform of the country's public credit: he had that "deliberate sense of the community" that republican government could develop in its servants.

This was later. In 1788, the New York convention was still to be won. New York had been willing to go no further than revision of the Articles of Confederation. The proposition to send delegates to Philadelphia had been but narrowly carried. All free white males of proper age were allowed to vote for delegates to the ratifying convention, but enthusiasms were not high: for the vote cast here was not very much larger than at the regular elections where suffrage was restricted. Of the 65 delegates who were chosen, 46 were known opponents of the Constitution.

The convention met June 17 at Poughkeepsie with Governor Clinton, Hamilton's old foe, in the chair. The Antifederalists were powerfully led; but so were the Federalists, for Hamilton had been picked as a delegate. The convention debated the question for more than a month; at the same time, it delayed final action, waiting to see how Virginia would go. And Hamilton—as he kept in constant touch with Virginia—talked, argued, cajoled, appealed with "exquisite skill" to his fellow delegates. No doubt, news of Virginia's ratification had an effect; but there can be no question that Hamilton was chiefly responsible for the day being carried. He did not know it, but this was to be his last appearance in a popular assembly as an advocate. He shone. To one young spectator he displayed a "magnanimous candor," a "temper spirited but courteous," as he made "pathetic and powerful appeals to the moral sense and patriotism, the fears and hopes of the assembly." [19]

Melancton Smith was Hamilton's leading opponent: on Smith he turned all his attention, him he sought to win over. They engaged in duel after duel; nothing displays better Hamilton's great ability in debate—his capacity to find a chink in his foe's armor, his skill in pressing the advantage, and yet his reasonableness and courtesy as he did so—than these exchanges.

At one point, Smith had said, in discussing the representation clause in the Constitution, that it was ambiguous. Representation ought to be large enough to include all classes; otherwise government would fall into the hands of a "natural aristocracy." Such a government would be oppressive, for it would be out of sympathy with the masses; and it could be easily corrupted, because it was small.

Hamilton replied: "Sir, the general sense of the people will regulate the conduct of their representatives." And he went on: [20]

After all, sir, we must submit to this idea, that the true principle of a republic is, that the people should choose whom they please to govern them. Representation is imperfect in proportion as the current of popular favor is checked. This great source of free government, popular election, should be perfectly pure, and the most unbounded liberty allowed. Where this principle is adhered to; where in the organization of the government, the legislative, executive, and judicial branches are rendered distinct; where, again, the legislature is divided into separate houses, and the operations of each are controlled by various checks and balances, and, above all, by the vigilance and weight of the State governments, to talk of tyranny, and the subversion of our liberties, is to speak the language of enthusiasm.

In another speech, once again Hamilton turned to the key role of the people in a republican form of government. His breadth of historical understanding and his ability to generalize brilliantly, are at the same time displayed here. "The great desiderata [of government] are free representation and mutual checks." Could the proposed national government ever try to abrogate the people's liberties? [21]

Certainly it would be for ever impracticable. This has been sufficiently demonstrated by reason and experience. It has been proved, that the members of republics have been, and ever will be, stronger than the head. Let us attend to one general historical example.... The history of the feudal wars exhibits little more than a series of successful encroachments on the prerogatives of monarchy. Here is one great proof of the superiority which the members in limited governments possess over their head. As long as the barons enjoyed the confidence and attachment of the people, they had the strength of the country on their side, and were irresistible. [The barons in turn began to oppress their vassals.] As commerce enlarged, and as wealth and civilization increased, the people began to feel their own weight and consequence; they grew tired of their oppressions; united their strength with that of the prince; and threw off the yoke of aristocracy. These very instances prove what I contend for. They prove that in whatever direction the popular weight leans, the current of power will flow. Whatever the popular attachments be, there will rest the political superiority.

It was not until July 23 that Melancton Smith finally yielded and joined Hamilton; its principal champion lost to it, the opposition gave in. The Antifederalists had hoped to tie ratification to the acceptance of amendments to the Constitution by a second convention. This they now gave up. On July 26 the vote was taken, and ratification was carried by a majority of three, 30 voting for and 27 against. The Antifederalists were conciliated when the convention adopted unanimously a circular letter to all the states, urging another convention to take up the amendments New York, Virginia, Massachusetts, and others, were seeking.

New York was in the new Union. Its chief city, for some time at any rate, would be the residence of the federal government, for the Continental Congress had been sitting in New York City since 1785.

Secretary of the Treasury

ALEXANDER HAMILTON SOON WAS TO HAVE THE OPPORTUNITY TO TEST his ideas, for with George Washington's election as President of the United States, Hamilton was the first Washington turned to when he came to make up his official family. Hamilton was then thirty-four years old. The business of organizing a government proceeded slowly. Washington was not actually inaugurated until April 30, 1789; Congress had to authorize the departments of government; a revenue had to be provided. It was not until September that Washington found it possible to pick his formal advisers, and then he named four. Alexander Hamilton was to be the Secretary of the Treasury, Henry Knox the Secretary of War, Thomas Jefferson the Secretary of State (he was not to return from France until March 21, 1790), and Edmund Randolph, the Attorney General.

The problems facing the new government would have taxed even stouter hearts than those who assembled in New York. The contest over the Constitution's ratification had created animosities that never were put to rest: every step of the Administration was followed by a critical press and a hostile minority in Congress; while many of the states looked on the efforts to form the federal government with either indifference or resentment.

Certainly the Administration's inheritance was meager. There was a staggering burden of debt, almost no revenue, and literally no credit at all. The foreign office was manned by a handful of clerks: its relations with foreign powers were at a standstill. The army had 840 men; there was no force to keep in check the Indian forays which constantly kept the frontiers in a state of alarm. Yet within five years wonders were performed.

North Carolina and Rhode Island ratified the Constitution and joined the Union. Vermont and Kentucky were added to the company of states. Ten Amendments to the Constitution were adopted and ratified, incorporating that Bill of Rights whose absence from the original document had fed so much of the opposition to it in the states. The State Department was functioning, with a diplomatic and consular service stationed abroad. An army was in being, and it was augmented and strengthened by 15,000 militiamen. The Post Office had expanded its operations. A judicial system had been erected and federal courts, attorneys, and marshals were at work enforcing the laws of the United States.

The greatest miracle of all was to be found in the state of the national finances. On July 4, President Washington signed Congress' first important piece of legislation: an act which, in effect, gave sanction at last to the impost of 1783. Even here there had been delays and sectional quarrels. Madison, in the House, had introduced the bill April 8. After seven weeks of debate, a law emerged that incorporated both specific and ad valorem duties on over thirty kinds of commodities; ad valorem duties ran from 5 to 10 per cent; the average rate of duties was 8½ per cent. Iron was to pay 7½ per cent; linens, woolen and cotton fabrics, 5 per cent; glassware, 10 per cent. Certain enumerated raw materials—cotton, wool, hides—were exempt from duties, and all other articles not mentioned in the law were to pay 5 per cent. Goods imported in ships built or owned by Americans were allowed a drawback of 10 per cent; while a tonnage tax of fifty cents a ton was placed on foreign vessels using American ports. The over-all purpose of the law was not to impose restraints on foreign goods and ships but to produce a revenue; and this was accomplished.

Alexander Hamilton was to say in 1792, "Most of the important measures of every government are connected with the Treasury." [1] This simple yet profound axiom he had come to as a result of his reflections on the nature of statecraft and the obligations of government. Installed in office, he had accepted this as his guiding principle.

The basic nature of public finance to assure stability and promote welfare has been alluded to in these observations again and again. A government that keeps its own house in order both attracts and creates confidence: to the financing of its own obligations and for the support of those business ventures, or enterprises, without which a society cannot create employment and wealth.

Confidence had been destroyed under the Congress and the Confederation; and to its restoration Hamilton set to work at once. In less than three years, as the Secretary of the Treasury, as the result of a series of masterly reports all but one of which ended in legislation, Hamilton laid the basis of the financial integrity of the United States. His brilliant mind ranged over every aspect of the government's needs.

He concerned himself with the debt—its assumption, consolidation, funding, and management and redemption; he watched the revenue inflow—recommending and obtaining new sources when government outlays increased; he pressed for and obtained the creation of a national bank—to act as a government depository and lender and to safeguard the money supply of the nation; he established a mint—thereby fixing the gold-silver ratio and assuring a bimetallic standard for the United States; he worked ceaselessly to attract foreign capital into the United States—to provide the funds for private banking institutions, public works projects, even manufacturing.

The Treasury at once became the largest and the leading office of the government. Its interests ramified into the whole economic life of the nation: through the customs service, it was intimately associated with commerce and shipping; through the bank, with the commercial banks of the nation; through the excise, with a large part of the country's farming community. It bought the army's supplies, it sold the nation's public lands, it negotiated with foreign governments. This was not usurpation: for Congress, in establishing the Treasury Department, had given it wide powers independent of the Executive. Hamilton was simply utilizing his opportunities.

Hamilton was, in the European sense, the head of the government: his was the chief portfolio; from his office went out those policies with which the Administration was identified. This Washington accepted; and the two men were now on excellent terms. They wrote to each other constantly; on every major point Hamilton was consulted; and when he replied, he subscribed himself "with high respect and the most affectionate attachment."

All this did not fail to create unease and then dissent. Madison, originally the Administration's spokesman in the House of Representatives, left Hamilton's side in the battle over the assumption of the state debts. Jefferson, who at the start had expressed his satisfaction with the Constitution and Hamilton's funding proposals, more and more saw their differences in terms of power: an energetic government could become an irresponsible, and therefore a dangerous, one. By the spring of 1792, there was an organized opposition to the Administration with Hamilton the chief focus of distrust.

The charges against Hamilton ran the whole gamut from truth to falsity. His hand was too obviously revealed in all the departments of government; and this was so. He was not respectful enough of Congress' prerogatives; and this was equally the case. He sought to subordinate the legislative function and the authority of the states before the leadership of the Executive; again, his opponents were right.

But, it was also being said, he was consistently the friend of a speculative interest, he unduly favored commerce and finance at the expense of agriculture, he himself was personally involved in questionable practices. He was subverting democracy; he was preparing the way for a monarchy. These charges were both unkind and untrue.

Hamilton was indignant at accusations directed against his personal rectitude; and he had every right to be. If there was a public servant in all of America's annals who conducted himself with exact propriety, it was he. From the vast operations in the public funds, neither he nor his family ever benefited; and he quit his post after more than five years in office a poor man. In one of his letters to Washington, he cried out against his detractors: "I have not fortitude enough always to hear with calmness calumnies which necessarily include me. . . . I trust I shall always be able to bear, as I ought, imputations of errors of judgment; but I acknowledge that I cannot be entirely patient under charges which impeach the integrity of my public motives or conduct." [2]

As for seeking to undermine democracy, it again must be noted that Hamilton was distrustful of democracy only in its equalitarian sense. He was not convinced of the equality of talents among men; he was realistic concerning their motives and knew how quickly they could be encouraged to yield to passion and rancor. He believed in government by the people, but on the representative principle, and he was prepared to accept the guidance of leaders as long as they regarded office as a public trust. This was republicanism in its pure and proper form, and while it recognized rule by men of capacity it had nothing to do with an hereditary concept. The charge that he was a monarchist was a political one designed to embarrass him; it never had any foundation in fact.

ON SEPTEMBER 21, 1789, CONGRESS REQUESTED HAMILTON TO INFORM it on the status of the American debt and the possibilities of its assumption and funding by the new government. On January 14, 1790, he submitted his first great public document, the *Report on the Public Credit*. Here he called for the recognition and consolidation of all elements of the debt—the foreign debt, the domestic debt, and the state debt. He asked for the payment of the defaulted interest on the first two. He proposed refunding through new public issues. And he requested that specific revenues be earmarked for interest payments and debt retirement; and that a machinery be set up to engage in open-market operations to prevent the securities from declining in value.

These were Hamilton's proposals for the fiscal management of the nation. But the report was more than this, of course. It was a ringing statement of faith in the public credit and an appeal to the business community for its support in order to quicken the sluggish economic life of America. "States, like individuals," said Hamilton, "who observe their engagements, are respected and trusted; while the reverse is the fate of those who pursue an opposite conduct." [3]

Hamilton calculated the public debt, as of December, 1789, as follows: [4]

Foreign debt		
	Principal	$10,070,307
	Arrears of interest	1,640,072
	Total	$11,710,379
Domestic debt		
	Principal	$27,383,917
	Arrears of interest	13,030,168
	Total	$40,414,085
State debt		
	Ascertained	$18,201,206
	Estimated balance	6,798,794
	Total	$25,000,000
	Total public debt	$77,124,464

Hamilton started out, as he had before, with the simple assertion that the maintenance of the public credit was the first requirement of good government. For: [5]

While the observance of that good faith, which is the basis of public credit, is recommended by the strongest inducements of political expedience, it is enforced by considerations of even greater authority. There are arguments for it, which rest on the immutable principles of moral obligation. And in proportion, as the mind is disposed to contemplate, in the order of Providence, an intimate connection between public virtue and public happiness, will be its repugnancy to a violation of these principles.

A country must be prepared to borrow, particularly a country like the United States which "is possessed of little active wealth, or ... little monied capital." Borrow from whom? From "the most enlightened friends of good government." [6]

To justify and preserve their confidence; to promote the increasing respectability of the American name; to answer the calls of justice; to restore landed property to its due value; to furnish new resources both to agriculture and commerce; to cement more closely the union of the states; to add to their security against foreign attacks; to establish public order on the basis of an upright and liberal policy—

such are the ends to be secured from a support of the public credit.

These were general benefits. But every part of the community would gain. The public creditors, now holding the debt, would profit. The increase of money in circulation—for the debt, when properly funded, would serve that purpose—would help trade, agriculture, and manufactures. Interest rates would drop, for these were affected by the quantity and the circulation of money. "And from the combination of these effects, additional aids will be furnished to labor, to industry, and to arts of every kind." [7]

Hamilton made an especial appeal to agriculture, for land values, since the Revolution, had fallen from 25 to 50 per cent. This decrease could be attributed to the scarcity of money. "Consequently, whatever produces an augmentation of the moneyed capital [by which Hamilton meant the quantity and circulation of currency] must have a proportional effect in raising that value. The beneficial tendency of a funded debt, in this respect, has been manifested by the most decisive experience in Great Britain." [8]

So much for the broad considerations guiding policy. But what specific steps should the Congress take? It should provide for the payment of the foreign debt "according to the precise terms of the contracts relating to it." [9] It should fund the domestic debt, both principal and interest. It should recognize the claims of current holders. And it should assume the state debts.

From the first and second propositions there could be no dissent. The debt was incurred in the waging of war. "It was the price of liberty. The faith of America has been repeatedly pledged for it, and with solemnities that give peculiar force to the obligation." [10] The third presented more complex problems. It involved these questions: "Whether a discrimination ought not to be made between original holders of the public securities, and present possessors, by purchase?" [11] And if a discrimination, should the original holders receive full payment, the present possessors only what their purchase prices had been, with the difference going to the first purchaser?

Hamilton cut through this tangle boldly: he was against any kind of discrimination; the debt was to be purchased from those now in possession at full value. In the handling of a problem like this, Hamilton was at his best: he knew how to marshal arguments tellingly and present them simply. The carrying out of the details of a plan based on discrimination would be immense, the difficulties insurmountable. Further, discrimination was unconstitutional; it ran counter to the position of Congress, expressed as early as 1783. Most important of all: [12]

The impolicy of a discrimination results from two considerations: one, that it proceeds upon a principle destructive of that quality of the public debt, or the stock of the nation, which is essential to its capacity for answering the purposes of money—that is, the security of transfer; the other, that, as well on this account as because it includes a breach of faith, it renders property in the funds less valuable, consequently it induces lenders to demand a higher premium for what they lend, and produces every other inconvenience of a bad state of public credit.

As for the assumption of the state debts, they would have to be paid in any case: why not do so under one general plan, where "competition for resources" [13] would be avoided? In this argument, the subtilties of his mind manifested themselves. The states, deprived of their most important support, their import duties, would cast about for new sources of revenue to meet their obligations. They would adopt different schemes of taxation; and these would create a wide confusion at the same time burdening industry. Again, assumption was a way of attracting loyalty to the federal government, thus once more demonstrating that a national debt was a national blessing.[14]

If all the public creditors receive their dues from one source, distributed with an equal hand, their interest will be the same. And having the same interests, they will unite in the support of the fiscal arrangements of the government—as these, too, can be made with more convenience where there is no competition. These circumstances combined will insure to the revenue laws a more ready and more satisfactory execution.

Finally, it was unrealistic to differentiate among public creditors: all the debts were incurred in the financing of the war. "And it is most equitable that there should be the same measure of retribution for all." [15]

Hamilton then went into great detail on a number of technical matters: how the state debts were to be assumed; the different methods of funding; what sources of revenue could be tapped for interest payments and debt service. In connection with the last, he proposed to set aside receipts from duties on imports and tonnage, and impose new taxes on wines, spirits (including those distilled within the United States), teas and coffee. He had some interesting observations to make concerning an excise on spirits: [16]

The consumption of ardent spirits, particularly no doubt very much on account of their cheapness, is carried to an extreme which is truly to be regretted, as well in regard to the health and morals as to the economy of the community. Should the increase of duties tend to a decrease of the consumption of these articles, the effect would be in every respect desirable.

To the two questions of debt retirement and open-market purchases Hamilton then turned. He favored the first, even though he accepted the dictum "that the proper funding of the present debt will render it a national blessing." [17]

It will be recalled that he had used the phrase once before, in his letter to Robert Morris in 1781. He had immediately followed it with the words: "It will be a powerful cement of our Union." That is, Hamilton was thinking politically. He was no irresponsible inflationist; he feared fiscal prodigality—it was "liable to dangerous abuse." [18] Indeed, in this report, and again in the *Report on Manufactures*, he called for immediate measures for debt retirement. In the former he said that "he ardently wished to see it incorporated as a fundamental maxim in the system of public credit of the United States, that the creation of debt should always be accompanied with the means of extinguishment. This he regarded as the true secret for rendering public credit immortal." [19] And in the *Report on Manufactures*, he said, "There ought to be in every government, a perpetual, anxious and unceasing effort to reduce that [debt] which at any time exists, as fast as shall be practicable, consistently with integrity and good faith." [20]

He was a realist, however; emergencies might appear when the government might have to postpone meeting its regular obligations. Yet such a breach of its good faith was a serious decision and required the most scrupulous examination of needs and consequences. He said: [21]

When such a necessity does truly exist, the evils of it are only to be palliated by a scrupulous attention, on the part of the government, to carry the violation no further than the necessity absolutely requires, and to manifest, if the nature of the case admit of it, a sincere disposition to make reparation whenever circumstances shall permit. But, with every possible mitigation, credit must suffer, and numerous mischiefs ensue. It is, therefore, highly important, when an appearance of necessity seems to press upon the public councils, that they should examine well its reality, and be perfectly assured that there is no method of escaping from it, before they yield to its suggestions.

As for the second problem, open-market purchases, Hamilton proposed a machinery under which a government agency would buy up in the market federal securities that had fallen below par. And he ended by again asserting—as it had been his position from the very start of his preoccupation with public policy —that the only relief the country could have from "individual and national embarrassments" was the establishment of the public credit "by a satisfactory provision for the public debt." [22]

EVERY RECOMMENDATION HAMILTON MADE WAS CARRIED OUT, almost in exact detail; but it took Congress more than seven months to do it. Representatives and senators were cool or indifferent, uncomprehending or openly antagonistic. To Senator Maclay of Pennsylvania, Hamilton's proposals were absurd and dangerous; Hamilton himself had "a very boyish, giddy, manner, and Scotch-Irish people could well call him a 'skite.'" [23]

The opposition in the House of Representatives struck out in every direction. It did not like the speculators in public securities who would profit heavily from Hamilton's plans. It could not see why funding should take place at face value: many of the states had wholly or partially repudiated, why not the federal government? It would have no part of Hamilton's proposal that no discrimination between original and current holders be exercised. It was opposed to the assumption of the state debts.

The act setting up the Treasury Department had taken particular pains to deny the Secretary direct access to Congress (he was not to "*report* plans for the improvement and management of the revenue" but to "digest and *prepare* plans"); [24] Hamilton therefore could not guide the discussion. It was, in consequence, in large part discursive and trivial; in other instances, as in the case of Madison's proposals on discrimination, so impracticable that the debate inevitably ended in confusion. Hamilton could only hope, the hostility to his proposals having finally spent itself, that anxiety over the fundamental interests of the nation would ultimately prevail.

The four major concerns of the lower house were with speculation, repudiation, discrimination, and assumption. Something of the acrimony that entered into the contest, on both sides, may be gathered from the following brief quotations.

The anti-Hamilton position on speculation was thus presented by James Jackson of Georgia: [25]

Since this report has been read in this House, a spirit of havoc, speculation, and ruin, has arisen, and has been cherished by people who had an access to the information the report contained, that would have made a Hastings blush to have been connected with, though long inured to preying on the vitals of his fellow men. Three vessels, sir, have sailed within a fortnight from this port, freighted for speculation; they are intended to purchase up the state and other securities in the hands of the uninformed, though honest citizens of North Carolina, South Carolina, and Georgia. My soul rises indignant at the avaricious and immoral turpitude which so vile a conduct displays.

Samuel Livermore of New Hampshire had this to say on repudiation: [26]

It is well known, that a large proportion of this domestic debt was incurred for paper money lent. To be sure Congress acknowledged its value equal to its name; but this was done on a principle of policy, in order to prevent the rapid depreciation which was taking place. But money lent in this depreciated and depreciating state can hardly be said to be lent from a spirit of patriotism; it was a mere speculation in public securities.

James Madison spoke for the first time on February 11, 1790; and he returned to the attack several times thereafter. It was the beginning of the break with Hamilton; he presented this argument on discrimination: [27]

Here, then, was a debt [to the original holders] acknowledged to have been once due, and which was never discharged; because the payment was forced and defective. The balance consequently, is still due, and is of as sacred a nature as the claims of the purchasing holder can be; and if both are not to be paid in the whole, is equally entitled to payment in part.... It was a great and an extraordinary case; it ought to be decided on the great and fundamental principles of justice. He had been animadverted upon for appealing to the heart as well as the head; he would be bold, nevertheless, to repeat, that in great and unusual questions of morality, the heart is the best judge.

And Madison came back to the charge on the question of assumption: [28]

If during the war, she [Virginia] has made as great exertions, and has suffered as much as any of the states; if she has, since the peace, paid her full proportion of the supplies to the federal government, at the same time exerting herself to the utmost to discharge her state debt, and if, finally, she will probably be found to be in advance of the union, and would, therefore, if justice could at once be done, be now entitled to a reimbursement—what must be said by the citizens of that state, if, instead of reimbursement, they are called upon to make further advances?

To all these there were replies. On the matter of speculation, the pro-Hamilton answer was: It was true such had taken place, particularly after the program of assumption had been announced. But buyers and sellers were on equal ground; both were speculating. This was notably so because not until the last moment could anyone have any assurance that assumption would carry. The only way to prevent similar speculation in the future was to give the public funds stability as soon as possible.

Concerning repudiation, it was pointed out that the scaling down of debt would subvert every principle on which public contracts were founded. Said Fisher Ames of Massachusetts: [29]

Must every transaction that took place, during the course of the last war, be ripped up? ... If this is the case, what kind of rights will the people have in their property? None but the will of the Government. And will this tend to the establishment of public credit? What security will they derive from a new promise? None. They will know that this can be set aside equally with the other, provided it is deemed expedient. What mischief will follow this idea? The public faith destroyed, our future credit will be a mere vapor. . . .

Against discrimination, it was declared that the proposition (to effect a composition between original and current creditors, as Madison proposed) was unjust, impolitic, and impracticable. Property rights had been exchanged by buyers and sellers, for, by act of Congress, the securities were transferable. Into these transactions both parties had entered knowingly; there was, in consequence, no seizure of property by force. But once a legislative body intervenes, justice is forfeited.[30]

Now [said William L. Smith of South Carolina], the plain line of conduct is, to do justice, such as is enforced in judicial tribunals, between man and man, in a similar case. The debtor is bound to pay the debt to the holder of the security; the contract, between the giver of the bond and the person to whom it was given, is done away the moment the latter assigns it to another person.

And as for assumption: Neither section contributed more to the support of the war than the other. It was a continental war, and all citizens were involved. Actually, because the war was largely carried on in the North, that section furnished more men, supplies, and credit to the government than did the South. The real point was the political consequences of assumption, and there could be no doubt that greater ties of union would be created by it.

On the floor of the House, with Madison now leading the antifunding forces, attack particularly was directed against Hamilton's requests for nondiscrimination and assumption. Madison, as a countermeasure to the first, submitted his amendment for the effecting of a composition to compensate both original and current creditors. This was argued back and forth for eleven days; and it was decisively defeated on February 22, 1790, by a vote of 36 to 13.

The question of assumption now took the floor. Madison had showed the way: he presented the position against assumption in terms of the putative losses to his own state. So narrow was the adherence to state loyalties that again and again, others followed Madison's lead, weighing out gains and losses with an apothecary's scales. Livermore, representing New Hampshire, which the war had never touched, went so far as to say, "I conceive that the debt of South Carolina, or Massachusetts, or of an individual, has nothing to do with our deliberations. If they have involved themselves in debt, it is their misfortune, and they must extricate themselves as well as they can." [31] And Stone of Maryland, also from a state removed from the areas of combat, unfeelingly declared, "... however inconvenient it may be to Massachusetts or South Carolina to make a bold exertion, and nobly bear the burdens of their present debt, I believe in the end it would be found to conduce greatly to their advantage." [32]

To this, Burke of South Carolina replied: [33]

Was Maryland like South Carolina constantly grappling with the enemy during the whole war? There is not a road in the state but has witnessed the ravages of war; plantations were destroyed, and the skeletons of houses, to this day, point out to the traveler the route of the British army; her citizens were exposed to every violence, their capital taken, and their country almost overrun by the enemy; men, women, and children murdered by the Indians and Tories; all the personal property consumed, and now is it to be wondered at that she is not able to make exertions equal with other states, who have been generally in an undisturbed condition?

FINALLY, ON APRIL 12, THE HOUSE DEFEATED ASSUMPTION BY 31 TO 29. Senator Maclay, inveterate foe of funding, was pleased to note in his diary that it was a telling blow struck at Hamilton's "gladiators." [34] Hamilton's armory was not empty, however: he was highly skilled in the art of negotiation. He had had many opportunities to learn—in the courts, legislative assemblies, the New York ratifying convention—that accommodations could be effected if one was prepared to yield elsewhere, sometimes on a wholly extraneous matter. The Southerners wanted something badly that had nothing to do with assumption. They were distrustful of cities, where, presumably, powerful mercantile interests played too large a role in the affairs of government: put the capital of the new government, therefore, in a distant sylvan retreat. But it should be on the banks of a river, of course, for some access to the outside world was desirable. Virginians, favored the Potomac River as the residence of the government; and then Pennsylvanians began to push their claims. Hamilton talked to the Pennsylvanians—perhaps not too seriously; and he listened to the Virginians.

One wonders a little today over the insignificance of a concern that preoccupied the minds of so many of the young America's leaders for so many months. Their correspondence and journals would seem to indicate that this matter of the capital's site surpassed all other public issues in importance. Madison was full of it; Jefferson, at once on his return, was drawn into the discussions, plans, and counterplans. Hamilton was detached, even uninterested: he has been taken to task for this. Did it not show a want of real patriotism—possibly even a lack of identification with his adopted country—that he should regard such a question so lightly? Madison and Jefferson were good Virginians; therefore, they were good Americans. Hamilton was not a good New Yorker; therefore, he was a West Indian, or an Englishman, or a continentalist, without roots, and hence all cold, calculating head and no heart.

The charge is an amusing and an irrelevant one. Hamilton was deeply attached to both the state and the city of New York and all his adult life he closely linked his own interests with theirs. Here was his home: here he loved to return. He served as legislator and spokesman for New York again and again; he participated in its civic causes. New York knew this: it honored him not once but many times, by making him a freeman of the city, granting him an honorary degree, designating him a regent of the University of the State of New York, naming an academy after him.

The heart of the matter is, Hamilton was a good New Yorker exactly because he linked the future of his state with the stability and well-being of the nation. In a time of great crisis and momentous decision, unerringly he chose the superior, the transcendent interest. To gain his funding bill and assure the country's public credit once and for all, he would have put the capital on the Susquehanna or the Potomac or even the Chattahoochee.

Jefferson sent a message to Hamilton: would Madison and Hamilton dine with him? At the dinner the affair was completed. The Virginians would support assumption if Hamilton would marshal enough votes to put the residence on the Potomac. A bill, creating the District of Columbia, accordingly was drawn up and passed July 24. The Funding Act of 1790 (including assumption) was approved by the President, August 4.

Years later, Jefferson expressed regret over his part in the bargain. He was unfamiliar with what really was going on; it therefore was not difficult for him to be imposed upon: he "was most ignorantly and innocently made to hold the candle" to Hamilton's "game." [35] But on June 20, Jefferson had written to Monroe that unless the controversy over assumption and the site was settled "there will be no funding agreed to, our credit will burst and vanish, and the States separate, to take care, every one of itself." [36] Two years later, not only was Jefferson wholly in disagreement, but he was seeking a fundamental basis for his rejection of the Hamilton scheme. In 1792, the break between the two great men no longer was a secret, and Jefferson was writing to Washington that Hamilton's system "flowed from principles adverse to liberty"; it was "calculated to undermine and demolish the republic, by creating an influence of his department over the membership of the legislature." [37]

THE FUNDING ACT OF 1790 AUTHORIZED THE TREASURY TO MAKE a series of loans to refund the old foreign, domestic, and state debts. The government was to obtain immediate relief from the heavy burden of interest payments by being permitted to carry only a portion of the new bonds at 6 per cent interest at once. Other parts were to pay 3 per cent; and still others no interest until 1800, and then 6 per cent.

The national revenues were pledged to pay the interest on the domestic loans. Provision for a sinking fund also was included: the proceeds of sales of western lands could be used for debt redemption. This fund was to be managed by a board made up of the President, the Chief Justice of the Supreme Court, the Secretary of State, the Secretary of the Treasury, and the Attorney General. The fund, also, was to be used to protect the price of government bonds by open-market purchases.

The Funding Act of 1790 did not give Hamilton the additional revenues the Treasury needed; and to this question he came back, and on March 3, 1791, Congress yielded. To the imposts of 1789, it added taxes on spirits, notably on rum and whiskey. This was the beginning of an excise: and from this source sprang a good deal of the hostility to the government. The Whiskey Insurrection of 1794 will be discussed later; it is enough here to note that the tax on whiskey did not produce the anticipated revenues. New excises were then added, the law of 1794 including taxes on carriages, the sales of certain liquors, the manufacture of snuff and the refining of sugar, and on auction sales.

These complicated fiscal affairs Hamilton managed with his customary orderliness and energy. He built up an excellent staff in all the Treasury's offices and maintained it at a high morale. His general rules and circulars of instruction to his customs collectors and loan commissioners were models of simplicity and clarity. He required frequent and regular reports from his field workers and insisted upon prompt financial settlements. Favoritism he would not tolerate; delinquencies he punished. But he was quick to praise and to push the claims of subordinates before Congress. He had every right to say, as he did in a letter to King in October, 1798, that "the business of government" was "widely different from the speculation of it" and "energy of imagination dealing in general propositions [different] from that of *execution* in *detail*." [38] Hamilton was a great administrator; one of the greatest of all time. He was more, too, of course, for his "speculation" on government had both an immediate and a permanent consequence.

There was no doubt that the Treasury's achievements were impressive. The elaborate business of opening books for subscriptions to the new funds and exchanging state debts for federal issues was handled with great success; within a few years the whole operation was completed. At the same time, Hamilton set to work to unravel the tangle of foreign obligations. Congress was not always prompt in voting the revenues he needed; he turned, therefore, to Dutch bankers—in 1790, 1791, and 1792 —for loans to meet outstanding commitments. Interest was promptly paid; a part of the principal due France and all of that due Spain were retired; a portion of the moneys voted to the foreign officers who had joined the Continental army was provided. To the end of 1790, arrears in interest alone on the French and Spanish debt, totaling almost $2 millions, were met. He also began negotiations with France to convert the outstanding French loans into domestic loans; this his successor in the Treasury, Oliver Wolcott, achieved in 1795. Nor was debt redemption forgotten. By 1800, Hamilton and Wolcott had retired $3,215,000 of the old Confederation funded debt.

The ordinary fiscal affairs of government were regularized and improved. In 1791, the government's total ordinary receipts came to $4.4 millions; in 1795, to $6.1 millions; and in 1801, to $13 millions. While customs duties furnished the major part during the period, internal revenues were contributing a growing share. In 1792, these were only $209,000; but by 1801, $1.6 millions. Expenditures, however, were heavy, not only because of interest on the public debt (this was between $2 millions and $3 millions annually) but because of the unforeseen extraordinary requirements the Treasury had to meet. The government was called upon to finance the Indian War of 1790 and the Whiskey Insurrection of 1794, the payment of an indemnity to Algiers in 1795, and the costs of the undeclared war against France in 1798–1799. The establishment and upkeep of the army and navy, in consequence, became the country's heaviest charge. Nevertheless, gross debt increased by only $7 millions from 1791 to 1800 (the years of the Federalist administrations); and, in the same period, Treasury receipts were only fractionally short of Treasury expenditures.[39]

Public finance was thus on a sound footing; even better, private international transactions steadily improved. Exports began to mount, foreign capital poured into the United States for investment, the country was probably moving toward a favorable balance of payments. The rehabilitation of the public credit of the United States meant that not only could the government borrow but private enterprise could confidently expand.

If "speculation" on government by political leaders has, as its first requirement, the creation of a public policy that will achieve and advance welfare within a climate of liberty, then in addition to being a great administrator Alexander Hamilton was a great statesman.

The National Bank

THE "CREDIT AND HONOR" OF A NATION, HAMILTON HAD SAID, WAS linked with the scrupulous fulfillment of its engagements. Its prosperity, through the efforts of private undertakers, could not be assured and protected unless facilities for private credit also were made available. Banks performed this function; but banks should be quasi-public agencies. Hamilton, in fact, was always subordinating the creations of government, whether they were public or private corporations, to the common good.

He knew the risks of private enterprise; no one has ever phrased the question of power, as it arises from individual accumulation, better than he. Yet he approached the problem boldly and frankly. In a letter to Robert Morris he had written: [1]

I am aware of all the objections that have been made to public banks; and that they are not without enlightened and respectable opponents. But all that has been said against them only tends to prove that, like all other good things, they are subject to abuse, and, when abused, become pernicious.... Great power, commerce, and riches, or, in other words, great national prosperity, may ... be denominated evils; for they lead to insolence, an inordinate ambition, a vicious luxury, licentiousness of morals, and all those vices which corrupt government, enslave the people, and precipitate the ruin of a nation. But no wise statesman will reject the good from an apprehension of the ill. The truth is, in human affairs there is no good, pure and unmixed;

every advantage has two sides; and wisdom consists in availing themselves of the good, and guarding as much as possible against the bad.

One of the ways of attaining such an end was by the wise intervention of government: not always, not consistently, but at those
times when its guidance was imperative. This was particularly so
when private corporations were being authorized. So, Hamilton
had this to say about banks, which had to be chartered: [2]

Public utility is more truly the object of public banks than private
profit. And it is the business of government to constitute them on such
principles that, while the latter will result in a sufficient degree to afford competent motives to engage in them, the former be not made
subservient to it.

Hamilton concerned himself with banking for the same reasons
that he endlessly devoted himself to the matter of public credit:
both would make his country secure and prosperous. He was
constantly weaving together in an intricate and seamless fabric
public policy and private striving, the good of the whole community and the benefits accruing from enterprise. So, he said in
his *Report on a National Bank*, banks were important "not only
in relation to the administration of finances but in the general
system of the political economy." With banks, the United States
would overcome these instabilities that were so characteristic
of the 1780s. But everything else would contribute: the nature
of the government, the funding of debt, the increase in the country's circulating medium. His confidence was never shaken.
There is this typical statement in the same report: [3]

These evils have either ceased or been greatly mitigated. Their more
complete extinction may be looked for from that additional security
to property which the Constitution of the United States happily gives
(a circumstance of prodigious moment in the scale both of public
and private prosperity); from the attraction of foreign capital, under
the auspices of that security, to be employed upon objects and in enterprises for which the state of this country opens a wide and inviting
field; from the consistency and stability which the public debt is fast
acquiring, as well in the public opinion at home and abroad, as in
fact; from the augmentation of capital which that circumstance and

the quarter-yearly payment of interest will afford; and from the more copious circulation which will be likely to be created by a well-constituted national bank.

It was to this matter of a national bank that Hamilton turned in his second public paper, the *Report on a National Bank,* which went to the Congress on December 14, 1790. This was as carefully drawn as were his other communications. He presented a soundly and cogently argued theoretical analysis of the pros and cons of banking; and he offered a specific program that was to serve as the basis for legislation. As always, Hamilton thought of his country's welfare, for he sought to come to grips with fundamental questions like the following. How would a national bank facilitate the operations of government by providing for its normal monetary needs and also rendering extraordinary aid in times of emergency? How would it help trade and industry, through stimulating credit and easing the circulating medium, to add to the wealth, or productive powers of the nation? How would such an agency attract foreign capital to America? How would a bank, in conjunction with government, regularize the country's money supply and, therefore, its credit flow? To all of these he had answers; and when an opposition developed, it took its position not on economic grounds but on constitutional ones.

Hamilton had been giving his attention to banking as far back as 1780, as we have seen. He had been a prime mover in the creation of the Bank of New York. There were now commercial banks in existence, one in Philadelphia, one in New York, one in Boston. Another one, in Baltimore, was in process of being set up at the very time Hamilton was placing his report before Congress. But they were small: their combined capital was in the neighborhood of two millions; they had no branches; and their notes were not legal tender for government payments. An enlarged circulation medium, convertible into specie on demand, was sorely required, for both public and private purposes. The government, dependent as it was upon a meager supply of gold and silver, notably felt the lack of currency for its daily needs and to transfer about the country.

The first function he saw such a bank rendering was "the augmentation of the active or productive capital of the country." He was not confusing currency with capital, as has been charged against him. Not only had Hamilton familiarized himself with the history of banking, particularly that of the Bank of England, but he knew his Adam Smith so well and leaned on him so closely —in both the *Report on a National Bank* and the *Report on Manufactures*—that often he used Smith's pattern of thought and sometimes Smith's very words.

Smith had said, in Book II, Chapter ii of *The Wealth of Nations:* [4]

> It is not by augmenting the capital of the country, but by rendering a greater part of that capital active and productive than would otherwise be so, that the most judicious operations of banking can increase the industry of the country. That part of his capital which a dealer is obliged to keep by him unemployed, and in ready money for answering occasional demands, is so much dead stock, which, so long as it remains in this situation, produces nothing either to him or to his country.... The gold and silver money which circulates in any country ... is, in the same manner as the ready money of the dealer, all dead stock.... The judicious operations of banking, by substituting paper in the room of a great part of this gold and silver, enables the country to convert a great part of this dead stock into active and productive stock; into stock which produces something to the country.

Hamilton paraphrased the passage in this way in the *Report on a National Bank:* [5]

> [Among the principal advantages of a bank is the] augmentation of the active or productive capital of a country. Gold and silver, when they are employed merely as the instruments of exchange and alienation, have not been improperly denominated dead stock; but when deposited in banks, to become the basis of a paper circulation, which takes their character and place, as the signs or representatives of value, they then acquire life, or, in other words, an active and productive quality.

And in the *Report on Manufactures* he said explicitly, when he insisted that public "stock" (government bonds) added to the nation's money supply: [6]

... it is important to distinguish between an absolute increase of capital, or an accession of real wealth, and an artifical increase of capital, as an engine of business, or as an instrument of industry and commerce. In the first sense, a funded debt has no pretensions to being deemed an increase of capital; in the last, it has pretensions which are not easy to be controverted. Of a similar nature is bank credit; and, in an inferior degree, every species of private credit.

Hamilton then went on to argue that when bank notes are issued they are "indefinitely suspended in circulation"; that through banks large sums are transferred by check without the intervention of coin; that deposits for safekeeping as well as for accommodation form an "effective fund" for their use, for, even if they are withdrawn, they are speedily replaced, because money "much oftener changes proprietors than place." Thus, not only is the quantity of money increased, but its circulation is "quickened." Without notes, coin must be remitted from place to place with "trouble, delay, expense, and risk." Bank notes, on the other hand, can be transmitted by post or other forms of conveyance. With their use, therefore, the metals are "not suspended from their usual functions during this process of vibration from place to place," but "continue in activity." [7]

A national bank would serve the government, "especially in sudden emergencies"; as well, in facilitating the payment of taxes. "There is, in the nature of things...an intimate connection of interest between the government and the bank of a nation." [8] And as for taxes, banks make possible loans for their payment and their facilities ease collection.

Hamilton then enumerated the most common charges against banks: that they encouraged usury; that they tended to prevent other kinds of lending; that they furnished temptations to over-trading; that they afforded aid to ignorant adventurers, or enterprisers; that they gave to bankrupt and fraudulent trades a fictitious credit; and that they tended to banish gold and silver from the country. Hamilton examined all these statements and proceeded to answer them.

On enterprise, he had some judicious observations to make: [9]

Credit of every kind ... must be, in different degrees, chargeable with the same inconvenience [encourage overtrading]. It is even applicable to gold and silver, when they abound in circulation. But would it be wise, on this account, to decry the precious metals, to root out credit, or to proscribe the means of that enterprise which is the main-spring of trade, and a principal source of national wealth, because it now and then runs into excesses, of which overtrading is one?

When it came to the contention that bank notes would drive the precious metals out of the country, Hamilton is at his best. He is no mercantilist with an erroneous understanding of the roles of gold and silver; in fact, he talks in straightforward Smithian terms: [10]

... the intrinsic wealth of a nation is to be measured not by the abundance of the precious metals contained in it, but by the quantity of the productions of its labor and industry.... Hence, the state of its agriculture and manufactures, the quantity and quality of its labor and industry, must, in the main, influence and determine the increase or decrease of its gold and silver.

In two places, he alludes to the beneficent role of foreign capital in the economy of a new and still underdeveloped country. Foreigners would buy the stock of the bank (a sound prediction; they did), thus increasing the gold and silver of the country. True, they would withdraw their dividends. "But as this rent arises from the employment of the capital by our own citizens, it is probable that it is more than replaced by the profits of that employment. It is also likely that a part of it is, in the course of trade, converted into the products of our own country...." [11]

Hamilton, opposing the issue of paper by government and supporting that of bank notes payable in coin, then shows that none of the three existing banks can be converted into a national bank. He goes into details only concerning the Bank of North America in Philadelphia. Now a state bank, its capital has been sharply reduced by its new charter. This charter does not provide for rotation in the board of directors; it permits each shareholder a single vote; it does not prohibit foreigners from becoming directors or voting by proxy. Most important, there are limitations upon the expansion of the bank's capital, thus subordinating the interests of the public to those of the stockholders.

Hamilton proceeds to lay out the broad lines upon which a national bank is to be organized. It should have branches. It should not lend on land. It should be under private direction; but government should be a minor stockholder. Government, however, should reserve to itself the right of inspection. And these details: The capital stock was to be $10 millions, with shares at $400. Subscriptions were to be one-fourth in specie and the other three-fourths in the government's new 6 per cent bonds. The bank's liabilities (excluding deposits) were not to exceed its capital. The bank was to deal only in bills of exchange, gold and silver bullion, and goods pledged for loans; 6 per cent was to be the maximum interest rate on its loans and discounts. The bills and notes of the bank were to be payable, on demand, in gold and silver coin; and they were to be legal tender in all payments to the United States.

As for the bank's board of directors, they should be chosen by stockholders with restricted powers of voting to prevent "a combination between a few principal stockholders of the bank, to monopolize the power and benefits of the bank, too easy." [12] There was to be one vote for one to two shares; another vote for every two shares above two and not exceeding ten; and so on, up to an additional single vote for every ten shares above one hundred. But "no person, copartnership, or body politic was to have more than thirty votes." [13] Foreigners could not sit on the board of directors, nor could they vote by proxy. The government of the United States could subscribe up to $2 millions of the bank's stock; and it could borrow for this purpose from the bank an equal sum. For ordinary purposes of government, the bank could lend to the United States up to $100,000, and to states up to $50,000; but it could not lend to foreign powers without specific Congressional authorization.

A BILL, ALMOST ENTIRELY FOLLOWING THESE SUGGESTIONS (THERE were minor changes having to do with the methods of limited voting), was introduced in the Senate on December 23, 1790. The bill fixed the charter for a period of twenty years; during this time no other bank was to be established by the United States. The debate was not very searching; and the measure was passed January 20, 1791. In the House, with Madison taking the lead, the opposition, however, was great. Southerners generally lined up against the bill, while Northerners supported it. Madison knew little about banking and he paid no attention to Hamilton's requests for measures to develop the country's trade and industry. The bank was unconstitutional: for there was nothing in the Constitution to authorize Congress to grant charters of incorporation. Madison called attention to the fact that this question of incorporation had come up when the Bank of North America had been created by the Confederation; and he sought to prove that the Constitutional Convention had considered and refused to give Congress that power.

An aside here is in order. Madison was in error, or his memory had failed him. The fact is, the Constitutional Convention discussed, on two different occasions, the granting to Congress of the right of incorporation. On August 18, 1789, it was Madison himself who raised the point, when he submitted a resolution that Congress be empowered "To grant charters of incorporation in cases where the public good may require them, and the authority of a single State may be incompetent." [14] Charles Pinckney of South Carolina offered a similar suggestion; both were carried unanimously and submitted to the committee on detail.

On September 14 the subject came up again, when Franklin asked that in addition to furnishing post roads, the federal government be authorized to build canals. Madison then availed himself of the opportunity to produce once more his request for a broad power of incorporation. The debate narrowed itself down to the single matter of canals; and on this a vote was taken and the motion was lost. The wider proposition was not brought up and the Constitution remained silent on the whole matter.

Hamilton, with his customary fairness, when he came to discuss the bank's constitutionality, called attention to the fact that the only vote taken concerned canals; and then went on to say that there were many different and contradictory recollections of the incident and the motives for rejecting Madison's resolution. All this, however, had nothing to do with the real merits of the question. And he ended: "The Secretary of State will not deny that, whatever may have been the intention of the framers of a constitution or of a law, that intention is to be sought for in the instrument itself, according to the usual and established rules of construction." [15]

Finally, on February 8, 1791, the House passed the bill by a vote of 39 to 20. The measure was presented to Washington on February 14. He was troubled by the debate and he sought counsel, turning to Randolph, Jefferson, and Hamilton. Randolph and Jefferson advised the President to veto the bill on the grounds of constitutionality; Hamilton advised that he sign. Washington was so persuaded by Hamilton's arguments that he signed the bill February 25, 1791.

WASHINGTON HAD WRITTEN TO HAMILTON ON FEBRUARY 16; ON February 23, Hamilton sent to him one of America's great public documents. The difference between his and Jefferson's statement was startling. Jefferson's was a bare outline; Hamilton's a full and closely reasoned argument. Jefferson discussed the question almost exclusively in constitutional terms; Hamilton, while not disregarding the wording and intention of the Constitution, concentrated on the immediate exigencies of the situation. Jefferson's position was as follows: He was opposed to giving the bank monopoly powers; he feared that its incorporation would "prostrate" the fundamental laws of the states. He took his stand not on the "welfare" clause of the Constitution (which he read narrowly), but on the "necessary and proper" clause, and he sought to differentiate between "necessary" and "convenient." A bank was a matter of convenience and not necessity; in consequence, the President could be guided only by the enumerated powers in the Constitution. "It [the Constitution] was intended to lace them up straitly and within the enumerated powers, and those without which, as means, these powers could not be carried into effect." Of course, Congress had passed the bill; and Jefferson declared that—unless Washington was certain of its unconstitutionality—the Executive must have "a just respect for the wisdom of the legislature." And then he observed, somewhat gratuitously, that Congress had been "misled by error, ambition, or interest." [16]

Hamilton seized the opportunity thus presented to him. Prepared in a week, his opinion on the constitutionality of the bank —actually, his replies to Jefferson and Randolph—was even longer than his original report. He came to grips at once with the immediate question Jefferson was raising: was it possible for any government to survive within the straitjacket in which Jefferson wished to confine it? And as for Jefferson's contention that the creation of the bank violated the rule against monopoly, it was true, was it not, that all states could charter banks?

But Hamilton did more than this: his was a striking defense of governmental sovereignty, a broad, theoretical declaration of the powers of the state devoted to the common weal. What are the nature and objects of government? "The means by which national exigencies are to be provided for, national inconveniences obviated, national prosperity promoted, are of such infinite variety, extent, and complexity, that there must of necessity be great latitude of discretion in the selection and application of those means." [17]

Within such general outlines, needless to say, the American government has been able to function: to acquire new territory, to make possible the building of railroads, to protect agriculture, and to pass social legislation. The Supreme Court again and again has recognized the relevance of Hamilton's doctrine of implied powers not only to permit the bank to function but to allow the government to regulate corporations and put on the statute books laws of the widest general consequence. Hamilton called such a principle of government "essential to the preservation of the social order"; [18] in the long run, the verdict of American history has been overwhelmingly on his side.

Said Hamilton: [19]

Now it appears to the Secretary of the Treasury that this *general principle* is inherent in the very *definition* of government, and essential to every step of the progress to be made by that of the United States, namely: That every power vested in a government is in its nature *sovereign*, and includes, by *force* of the *term*, a right to employ all the *means* requisite and fairly applicable to the attainment of the *ends* of such power, and which are not precluded by restrictions and exceptions specified in the Constitution, or not immoral, or not contrary to the *essential ends* of political society. [Italics original.]

The power to erect corporations was an incident of sovereign power, with this difference: "Where the authority of the government is general, it can create corporations in *all cases;* where it is confined to certain branches of legislation, it can create corporations *only* in those cases." There is a constitutional statement of the powers of the federal government: it is to have all those functions delegated to it. Nevertheless the question of delegation is one of fact "to be made out by fair reasoning and construction, upon the particular provisions of the Constitution, taking as guides the general principles and general ends of governments." [20]

And then this bold and ringing declaration: [21]

It is not denied that there are *implied*, as well as *express powers*, and that the *former* are as effectually delegated as the *latter*.... Then it follows, that as a power of erecting a corporation may as well be *implied* as any other thing, it may as well be employed as an *instrument* or *means* of carrying into execution any of the specified powers, as any other *instrument* or *means* whatever.... Thus a corporation may not be erected by Congress for superintending the police of the city of Philadelphia, because they are not authorized to *regulate* the *police* of that city. But one may be erected in relation to the collection of taxes, or to the trade with foreign countries, or to the trade between the States, or with the Indian tribes; because it is the province of the Federal Government to *regulate* these objects, and because it is incident to a general *sovereign* or *legislative* power to *regulate* a thing, to employ all the means which relate to its regulation to the best and greatest advantage. [Italics original.]

Jefferson's argument about "necessity" was brilliantly handled. Did Jefferson interpret the word to mean "absolutely or indispensably"? [22] If so, "There are few measures of any government which would stand so severe a test. To insist upon it, would be to make the criterion of the exercise of any implied power, a *case of extreme necessity;* which is rather a rule to justify the overleaping of the bounds of constitutional authority, than to govern the ordinary exercise of it." And again: "The *relation* between the *measure* and the *end;* between the *nature* of the *means* employed towards the execution of a power, and the object of that power, must be the criterion of constitutionality, not the more or less of *necessity* or *utility*." (Italics original.) [23]

Hamilton then went on, in great detail, to show how, even under the enumerated powers, a bank would serve the requirements of government: in the collection of taxes, to facilitate government borrowing, in the regulation of trade between the states, and the like. His imagination ranged still more widely: he could see how the government could create corporations, if need be, to advance foreign trade. Hamilton, in fact, anticipated all those strong American political leaders, who, when confronted by dire emergency, used the powers and devices he advocated either to enlist business in the public need or expanded government's activities into countless areas of enterprise. Needless to say, the publicly chartered corporation—sometimes working with private, sometimes with state funds—has been widely employed in the United States.

THE STOCK OF THE BANK OF THE UNITED STATES—AS IT WAS NAMED —was quickly subscribed, businessmen in every important city in the country participating, so that in December, 1791, the main office opened in Philadelphia. In time, eight branches were set up, in Boston, New York, Baltimore, Washington, Norfolk, Charleston, Savannah, and New Orleans. The bank established friendly relations with the state-chartered banks, extending credit to them and handling their notes. Here it played an important and salutary role: it was, in effect, a primitive form of central bank. The bank accepted its public responsibility, as Hamilton had predicted and, as early as the 1790s, was seeking to check the speculative activities of the state banks by restricting the circulation of their notes.

The bank rendered yeoman assistance to the government. It lent the Treasury the $2 millions to make possible the government's subscription. It supplemented this aid by other loans, not only in anticipation of tax collections, but when emergencies arose. In May, 1792, to meet the expenses of one of its Indian wars, the Treasury borrowed $400,000. In December, 1794, Congress authorized a loan of $1 million, and another of the same amount in March, 1795. At the end of its first year, the bank had loaned the Treasury over $2.5 millions; by January 31, 1795, when Hamilton resigned, the total loans outstanding were $4.7 millions. At the end of the year, the sum was $6.2 millions. This was going too far, of course; the bank's services to trade and industry were being severely restricted, as was its ability to handle the government's short-term needs. The bank therefore requested that the loans already due be taken up. Ultimately, during 1796–1797, the government parted with a portion of its bank stock in order to reduce its obligations; in 1802, the remainder was disposed of in London.

Despite the earlier misgivings of Madison and Jefferson, the government profited handsomely from its relations with the bank. The government paid 5 and 6 per cent on its loans; the annual dividends it received from the bank were 8 per cent and better. Total dividends to the government amounted to more than a million dollars, while premiums realized on the sale of its bank stock came to almost another million.

The bank aided the government in other ways. It handled its foreign-exchange operations; it was a depository of public funds; it helped importers to pay their customs duties; it transferred the public moneys from place to place; it assured the successful establishment of the Mint for, from it, came the chief source of bullion supply for the country's coinage.

The bank was more than a government agency, of course: it was a bank for deposit and discount. In the latter connection, it had the right of note issue and this it exercised sparingly. The total amount in circulation never exceeded $6 millions; and their movement was limited, for these could be accepted only by the issuing branches. The bank, as a commercial institution, was governed with great discretion and outstanding success. Its financial statement, as of January, 1811, for example, showed that among its resources were $2.7 millions in government bonds, $5 millions in specie, and $14.5 millions in loans and discounts. And among its liabilities were $5 millions in circulating notes outstanding, $5.9 millions in private deposits, and $1.9 millions in government deposits. Undivided profits came to half a million. Albert Gallatin, at that time the Secretary of the Treasury, in submitting the statement to Congress, declared, "The affairs of the Bank, considered as a moneyed institution, have been wisely and skillfully managed." [24]

Jefferson's opposition to the bank continued to the end; Gallatin, his Secretary of the Treasury, on the other hand, always remained the bank's supporter. Jefferson never passed up the opportunity to tax the bank with playing politics: its directors and stockholders in Congress, he said, "could always make the Federal vote that of the majority." [25] But when he became President, the course he followed was no better. He proposed the dispersion of the government's deposits among the state banks, although many of these, notably those in the South and the West, were insecurely established and already involved in wildcat note issues. In supporting one such bank's plea, Jefferson could write to Gallatin, "The consideration is very weighty that it is held by citizens, while the stock of the United States Bank is held in so great a proportion by foreigners." [26] And in another letter he declared, quite coolly, "I am decidedly in favor of making all the banks Republican by sharing deposits among them in proportion to the dispositions they show." [27]

How little Hamilton's contemporaries, particularly those who opposed him politically, understood about banking, John Adams proved. In a letter to John Taylor of Caroline, that complete and perfect agrarian, Adams said: [28]

I have never had but one opinion concerning banking, from the institution of the first, in Philadelphia . . . , and that opinion has uniformly been that banks have done more injury to the religion, morality, tranquility, and even wealth of the nation, than they can have done or ever will do good. They are like party spirit, a delusion of the many for the interest of the few.

And to Benjamin Rush, as late as 1811 Adams said: [29]

Our whole banking system I ever abhorred, I continue to abhor, and shall die abhorring . . . every bank of discount, every bank by which interest is to be paid or profit of any kind to be made by the deponent, is downright corruption. It is taxing the public for the benefit and profit of individuals; it is worse than old tenor, continental currency, or any other paper money.

Jefferson was much of the same mind, for when a Pennsylvania bank ran into trouble in 1802 and called upon the government for help, he wrote to Gallatin about banks generally, "Between such parties the less we meddle the better." Hamilton said, on the other hand, in 1792 to the cashier of the Bank of New York, when it was being pressed, "I consider the public interest as materially involved in aiding a valuable institution like yours to withstand the attacks of a confederated host of frantic and, I fear in too many instances, unprincipled gamblers." [30]

To declare that this concern on Hamilton's part expressed a limited class interest in other words, to fail to realize, as he did, that a secure government and a progressive economy are linked at a hundred and one different places by fiscal policy—is to miss helplessly and hopelessly the very essence of statecraft. Hamilton realized—long in advance of his time—the combined roles of the Treasury and a national bank, the coordination of the money and the credit functions, as great stabilizing agencies. He was setting up the beginnings of a central banking system; only within the last two decades, in America, have we—through joint action by the Treasury and the Federal Reserve System—been moving toward the effective accomplishment of those purposes Hamilton was able to envision.

THE REGULARIZATION OF THE COUNTRY'S COINAGE WAS PART OF THE same program; and to this Hamilton turned in his *Report on the Establishment of a Mint* of January 28, 1791. The money supply of the country was in the greatest confusion. The gold and silver coins of most of the European nations were circulating: English guineas, crowns, and shillings; French guineas, pistoles, and crowns; Spanish doubloons and pistoles; Portuguese johannes and moidores—with no real authority in existence to give them uniform values. The Spanish milled dollar (from Havana) was employed in the country's money transactions; but it had depreciated by 5 per cent of its original value. This was a matter of concern to Hamilton, for it affected his national pride, always a strong factor with him. A depreciated and fluctuating coin had an undesirable effect on contracts and prices; the United States, too, should not be at the mercy of a foreign mint and the value of the property of its citizens "change with the changes in the regulation of a foreign sovereign." [31]

There were other inconveniences. The same coins were given unequal values in different places; many were defective; there were wide dissimilarities in the moneys of account. All these required a national coinage; but many complex questions arose in this connection. To these Hamilton addressed himself with his customary thoroughness and skill.

He proposed that both gold and silver coins be minted and that their ratio be 15 to 1, which were the existing bullion values in Great Britain and Holland. American trade and financial transactions were largely tied to these countries; this was another way of assuring stability. The monetary unit should consist of 24¾ grains of pure gold or 371¼ grains of pure silver, with the basis a coin somewhat similar to the Spanish dollar. (Actually, it was a little lighter than the Spanish "piece of eight.") He further recommended the coinage of ten-dollar and one-dollar gold pieces, one-dollar and ten-cent silver pieces, and one-cent and one-half cent copper pieces.

The Mint Act of April 2, 1792, carried out these suggestions, after the customary prolonged debate. Congress worried over the cost of maintaining a mint and the increase in the number of federal officeholders because of it; and it regarded with suspicion (and rejected) Hamilton's proposal that the coins carry the head of the President of the United States. Nor did it want to see the Mint under the direction of the Treasury. It was put into the State Department; later, however, it was transferred to the Treasury.

Hamilton was giving thought to the stabilization of commercial transactions and the psychological effects upon the country as a consequence of the creation of its own coinage. And here, too, he was right. Slowly, American coins began to make their appearance. By the end of the century, there were some $2 millions in circulation; by 1809, about $8 millions. As one of the curiosities of American development, it may be noted that foreign coins continued as legal tender in the United States almost up to the outbreak of the Civil War.

9

The Report on Manufactures

THE REAL HAMILTON NOW BEGINS TO EMERGE. HE IS NO AUTHORI-
tarian, constantly possessed by the need for building a powerful
central state because he is distrustful of the normal political
processes. He is no antipopulist and no monarchist, committed
to the elimination of the people from the franchise and office.
A tradition of service to the public well-being must be developed
if government is to survive; why not base office on good behavior? He is not the dedicated and unreasoning partisan of a
moneyed class, seeking only to advance their cause at the expense of the general community. Private striving must remain un-
hampered if material progress is to be the lot of the entire nation.
Decisions must be made and therefore risks taken: but because
a government moves ahead, there is never a time when recon-
siderations cannot occur or new avenues be explored. Security,
stability, and honor must ever be the keynotes to public policy.

And what of welfare? What are to be the relations between
the state and enterprise? Hamilton is the complete libertarian
devoted to a "system of perfect liberty," in which men make
free choices and nations survive and prosper in a climate of free
exchanges because they cultivate those "peculiar advantages"

which natural resources, habits, and skills have helped develop. Internationally, such a system does not exist; it is therefore the duty of the statesman to accommodate himself to an imperfect world. Only because of this is Hamilton an interventionist: American trade labors under discriminations; the defense of the country, still young and weak, necessitates the artificial stimulation of manufactures. But intervention must be temporary and abandoned when it has served its purpose or the world without has improved. Only in such a broad context can Hamilton's *Report on Manufactures* be read.

Hamilton is a libertarian, then, and not a mercantilist. He had seen the havoc mercantilist policy had wrought in British West India and in the British mainland possessions. Mercantilism—with its basic assumptions of full government intervention to achieve national self-sufficiency and the subordination of colonial plantation wares to the trade and manufacturing of the metropolis; and with its confusion of wealth with bullion stocks or money, and its addiction to a favorable trade balance—Hamilton rejects again and again in all his famous reports. It is true that in 1782, in the fifth essay of *The Continentalist* he talked in mercantilist terms. At that time he said: [1]

To preserve the balance of trade in favor of a nation ought to be a leading aim of its policy. The avarice of individuals may frequently find its account in pursuing channels of traffic prejudicial to that balance, to which the government may be able to oppose effectual impediments. There may, on the other hand, be a possibility of opening new sources. . . . The undertaking may often exceed the influence and capital of individuals, and may require no small assistance, as well from the revenue as from the authority of the state.

But in 1791, in the *Report on Manufactures,* he was declaring that the efforts to achieve self-sufficiency had been carried "to an injudicious extreme." [2] One of the unfortunate consequences of such action had been the creation of barriers to exchanges among nations, so that "the manufacturing nations abridge the natural advantages of their situation, through an unwillingness to permit the agricultural countries to enjoy the advantages of theirs, and sacrifice the interests of a mutually beneficial intercourse to the vain project of selling everything and buying nothing." [3]

And there follows that clear clarion call for the creation of an international community based on "perfect liberty." Here is the mature Hamilton expressing his confidence in a world founded on free enterprise: [4]

If the system of perfect liberty to industry and commerce were the prevailing system of nations, the arguments which dissuade a country, in the predicament of the United States, from the zealous pursuit of manufactures, would doubtless have great force. It will not be affirmed that they might not be permitted, with few exceptions, to serve as a rule of national conduct. In such a state of things, each country would have the full benefit of its peculiar advantages to compensate for its deficiencies or disadvantages.

Unhappily, such a state of affairs is yet to be established, for nations are regularly interfering with the unrestricted entry of American goods. The United States, in consequence, cannot exchange with Europe on equal terms. If the United States adopted free trade, it would stand alone, compelled to pay high prices for its finished goods and confronted by uncertain markets for its staples. America therefore must render itself "least dependent on the combinations, right or wrong, of foreign policy." Only because of these considerations are "the incitement and patronage of government" required. [5]

The defense of his country is never absent from Hamilton's mind. One of the arguments for the Bank of the United States was that it could make loans available for such a purpose, pending the creation of new sources of income derived from taxation. The soundness of the public credit, he was to write in 1795, made possible the securing of the country's frontiers. And, in the *Report on Manufactures*, he saw the wealth, independence, and security of the United States connected with the "prosperity of manufactures." And he went on: [6]

The possession of these is necessary to the perfection of the body politic; to the safety as well as to the welfare of the society. The want of either is the want of an important organ of political life and motion; and in the various crises which await a state, it must severely feel the effects of any such deficiency. The extreme embarrassments of the United States during the late war, from an incapacity of supplying themselves, are still matters of keen recollection; a future war might be expected again to exemplify the mischiefs and dangers of a situation to which that incapacity is still, in too great a degree, applicable, unless changed by timely and vigorous exertion. To effect this change, as fast as shall be prudent, merits all the attention and all the zeal of our public councils: 'tis the next great work to be accomplished.

It should now come as no surprise how heavily Alexander Hamilton leans on Adam Smith; in fact, the spirit of *The Wealth of Nations* informs all the great reports. The basic assumptions of Smith are all here. The world is an orderly one and is guided by law: government, in consequence, must keep hands off the economic processes, for the self-interest that prompts men undoubtedly improves the welfare of all. The key to national wealth and well-being is production; this is advanced by the division of labor; and the proper rewards spread to the whole of society. All this leads to "an increase of national industry and wealth," an augmentation of "revenue and capital." The welfare of the people—in greater employment, a more diversified industry, a prosperous agriculture, higher standards of living—results. The heart of the matter is, the individual must be free in a "system of natural liberty": only in this way is progress realizable.

Again and again, Hamilton uses Smith to buttress an argument, or to round out an exposition. Notably in three places, the Smithian analysis and even terminology are employed. These have to do with the criticism of physiocratic doctrine, the presentation of the concept of the division of labor, and the necessity for the development of internal improvements as an aid to manufactures.

There is no point here in presenting the discussion of physiocratic doctrine at length. Hamilton was concerned with a point of
view common to his times—and long since abandoned—that had
to do with a belief in the sterility of manufactures; only agriculture was productive. In Book IV, Chapter ix, of *The Wealth of
Nations*, Smith examines in detail the claims and fallacies of that
"system which represents the produce of land as the sole source of
the revenue and wealth of every country." [7] Smith marshals five
reasons for rejecting the physiocratic position; Hamilton presents
three, copying Smith's statements almost word for word. As an
example, Smith's fourth observation starts: [8]

Fourthly, farmers and country laborers can no more augment, without parsimony, the real revenue, the annual produce of the land and
labor of this society, than artificers, manufacturers, and mechanics.
The annual produce of the land and labor of any society can be augmented only in two ways; either, first, by some improvement in the
productive powers of the useful labor actually maintained within it;
or, secondly, by some increase in the quantity of that labor.

While Hamilton's third observation starts: [9]

That the annual produce of the land and labor of a country can only
be increased in two ways—by some improvement in the productive
powers of the useful labor which actually exists within it, or by some
increase in the quantity of such labor.

In his treatment of the division of labor, Hamilton again uses
Smith, not only taking over the concept but even repeating Smith's
enumeration of the advantages of the technical division of labor. In
Book I, Chapter i, Smith gives the advantages as three: the improved dexterity of the worker, the saving of time, and the larger
use of machinery. And so does Hamilton, employing almost
Smith's words.

In a third connection, Hamilton directly quotes Smith (with no
reference to the source). Hamilton, in his discussion of bounties,
is calling upon the national government to lay out a comprehensive
scheme of internal improvements. Again, he is far in advance of

his times when he says, "This is one of those improvements which could be prosecuted with more efficacy by the whole than by any part or parts of the Union." [10] And he cites Smith, Book I, Chapter XI, in the passage beginning, "Good roads, canals, and navigable rivers, by diminishing the expense of carriage, put the remote parts of a country more nearly upon a level with those in the neighborhood of the town." [11]

Such is the broad and general background against which the *Report on Manufactures* is to be read. It is not narrowly an inventory of the then existing industrial resources of the country; nor is it exclusively a defense of a high protective system of tariffs. These are only incidental to Hamilton's leading purpose, which was to make his country secure and prosperous.

ON JANUARY 15, 1790, A RESOLUTION OF THE HOUSE OF REPRESENTA-tives requested Hamilton to report to it a "proper plan or plans . . . for the encouragement and promotion of such manufactories as will tend to render the United States independent of other nations for essential, particularly for military supplies." This was the origin of the *Report on Manufactures* of December 5, 1791. It was both the longest and most complex of the public documents Hamilton drew up at this time; it was also his whole statement of his hopes for and his faith in the future of the United States.

Hamilton wanted men of affairs—adventurers, enterprisers, the capitalist class, in short—to rally to the support of the new government. They were to buy its "stock," strengthen its financial fabric, expand its commercial relations with other nations. In a climate of confidence and safety, accumulation could occur: and these savings, as the result of "parsimony," were to be invested in a diversified and increasingly industrialized economy. For the same reasons, foreign capital would flow into the United States. With what consequences? Notably the position of the country's agriculture would be strengthened, employment opportunities for artisans would increase, a large European emigration could be supported—the "general interest" of the nation, the general welfare of the whole American people, would benefit.

In an imperfect world, government intervention to encourage manufactures was necessary. It was undesirable, it should be temporary; but it was required for political and psychological reasons. This was the background of Hamilton's thinking when he sat down to comply with Congress' request. It at once becomes apparent how much farther than Congress he was prepared to range.

The report is divided into two parts, the first of which is by far the more important. It is a theoretical analysis of the role of the manufacturing industries in the economy, the reasons why they should be encouraged, and the means to be followed toward this end. The second part is made up of the results of an investigation of the then existing state of manufactures. This was carried on by his agents during the summer of 1791. It was quite comprehensive in the sense that it revealed the reasons for the backward state of the industrial arts in the United States: enterprise, in short, had many obstacles to overcome of both an organizational and psychological character. Workers were unskilled or careless; machinery was imperfect; capital was lacking and interest rates were high; employees generally were burdened with direct taxes and militia duties. The competition of foreign countries had to be met and overcome; for these were using "bounties, premiums, and other artificial encouragements" which "second the exertions of their own citizens in the branches in which they are to be rivalled." [12] Not least among the difficulties to be cleared away were the attitudes of Americans: "The strong influence of habit and the spirit of imitation; the fear of want to success in untried enterprises;... apprehension of failing in new attempts." [13]

All these findings were helpful—but at certain points not too informing. The modern reader will look in vain for statistics of costs, wages, and prices. He will find no recitals of actual accomplishments in terms of production and profits; and no accounts of the state of progress in foreign countries.

One does not turn to the report for such information, however. One reads it—as the generation after the Civil War did—for the wisest counsel one can find anywhere to justify the conversion of an agricultural economy into an industrial one. The first part of the report was a defense of the acquisitive principle, a call for innovation, enterprise, and risk-taking; and it was a text for protectionists. Its argument ran as follows.

The expediency of encouraging manufactures in the United States was already generally admitted, especially because of the damages done by the restrictions on foreign trade. It was necessary, therefore, to widen the domestic market; and this went hand in hand with the expansion of manufacturing enterprise, equally so important to the "national independence and safety." [14]

Reasons were being offered against such a change and these were to be found in the importance of agriculture in the American economy, the danger of giving industries artificial stimulation, the lack of skilled workers, the dearness of labor, the greater attraction of the wild lands of the country, and the dearth of capital. Governmental encouragement would create monopolies and raise prices. "It is far preferable, that these persons should be engaged in the cultivation of the earth, and that we should procure, in exchange for its products, the commodities with which foreigners are able to supply us in greater perfection and upon better terms." [15] Thus Hamilton, ever reasonable, presented the position of a world system where the rule of comparative costs is generally recognized, and there are neither impediments to universal free trade nor national necessities to interfere with it.

But nations are not being guided by such doctrine; and there are, too, certain errors in the position advanced. Granted the great and even primary importance of agriculture, for the production of foods and fibers, as creating "a state most favorable to the freedom and independence of the human mind." [16] Yet it is not wise to give it exclusive preference, nor would its real interests be sacrificed even if other industries were introduced. Hamilton, in other words, was meeting the contention of the physiocrats—that only agriculture was productive—directly, and refuting the analysis point by point.

In fact, he goes on, manufacturing will not only increase the country's wealth; for this purpose, it is superior to agriculture. Manufactures will allow a large application of the division of labor; they permit a wider use of machinery; they offer additional employment for classes of the community not fully or customarily utilized; they stimulate emigration from foreign countries; they furnish a vast field for the exercise of human ingenuity, and a wider scope for enterprise; they create a new and—more important—a certain and constant demand for agriculture's surplus products. The home market, as it expands and specializes, will sustain the economy.

On the division of labor, he says: [17]

It has justly been observed that there is scarcely anything of greater moment in the economy of a nation than the proper division of labor. The separation of occupations causes each to be carried to a much greater perfection than it could possibly acquire if they were blended.

As to the extension of machinery, he declares: [18]

It is an artificial force brought in aid of the natural force of man; and, to all the purposes of labor, is an increase of hands, an accession of strength, unencumbered too by the expense of maintaining the laborer. May it not, therefore, be fairly inferred, that those occupations which give greatest scope to the use of this auxiliary, contribute most to the general stock of industrious effort, and, in consequence, to the general product of industry?

Hamilton is eloquent on the stimulation manufactures will give to emigration to the United States. Workers and enterprisers, coming over, will get a better price for their fabrics or their labor; they will find lower costs for food and raw materials; they will be relieved from "the chief part of the taxes, burdens, and restraints which they endure in the Old World." [19] And could there be a greater tribute to his own adopted country than this? Emigrants would find "greater personal independence and consequence, under the operation of a more equal government, and of what is far more precious than mere religious toleration, a perfect equality of religious privileges." [20]

As to encouraging enterprise, he had this to say: "To cherish and stimulate the activity of the human mind, by multiplying the objects of enterprise, is not among the least considerable of the expedients by which the wealth of a nation may be promoted. . . . The spirit of enterprise, useful and prolific as it is, must necessarily be contracted or expanded, in proportion to the simplicity or variety of the occupations and productions which are to be found in a society." [21]

Yet it must be noted that foreign demand for agricultural products is uncertain and inconstant; it is wiser to rely on an extensive, domestic market. This manufactures will supply. And here Hamilton pauses to summarize his argument to this point: [22]

The foregoing considerations seem sufficient to establish, as general propositions, that it is in the interest of nations to diversify the industrious pursuits of the individuals who compose them; that the establishment of manufactures is calculated not only to increase the general stock of useful and productive labor, [and, in the same connection, he says elsewhere, "to an augmentation of revenue and capital"] but even to improve the state of agriculture in particular,—certainly to advance the interests of those who are engaged in it.

Hamilton then takes up three specific objections being offered to the establishment of manufactures in the United States—the scarcity of hands, the dearness of labor, and the want of capital.

As to the scarcity of hands: Women and children can be employed; machinery will replace human labor; part-time workers can be utilized; foreign emigrants will be attracted.

As to the dearness of labor: In part, this is true; country laborers, in particular, receive higher wages in America. But high labor costs can be reduced by the introduction of machinery. Hamilton, says simply and wisely, "This circumstance is worthy of the most particular attention. It diminishes immensely one of the objections most strenuously urged against the success of manufactures in the United States." [23]

As to the want of capital, Hamilton is sanguine that capital for both credit and investment will be found for manufactures as it has been for commerce. Here he repeats and amplifies his discussions on the same subject to be found in the *Report on the Public Credit* and the *Report on a National Bank.*

Money and credit—moneyed capital, active capital—will be created, extended and expanded by the establishment of banks. (Elsewhere—in his unpublished defense of the funding system— Hamilton further amplified his meaning: "All property is capital; that which can quickly and at all times be converted into money is active capital." [24]). Active capital, from abroad, has helped in the financing of American foreign trade.

Foreign capital, notably, can be counted on for investment purposes as "an augmentation of real wealth." Hamilton knows why international capital transfers take place: there is "a deficiency of employment" at home or rates of interest and profit are higher abroad. He says: [25]

Both these causes operate to produce a transfer of foreign capital to the United States. It is certain, that various objects in this country hold out advantages, which are with difficulty to be equalled elsewhere; and under the increasingly favorable impressions which are entertained of our government, the attractions will become more and more strong. These impressions will prove a rich mine of prosperity to the country, if they are confirmed and strengthened by the progress of our affairs. And, to secure this advantage, little more is now necessary than to foster industry, and cultivate order and tranquillity at home and abroad.

Hamilton is both nationalist and internationalist, desirous of enhancing the "revenue and capital" of his own country yet willing to employ whatever foreign assistance can be found available. Hostility to foreign capital is an "unreasonable jealousy." "Instead of being viewed as a rival, it ought to be considered as a most valuable auxiliary, conducing to put in motion a greater quantity of productive labor, and a greater portion of useful enterprise, than could exist without it. It is at least evident that ... every farthing of foreign capital which is laid out in internal meliorations, and in industrial establishments, of a permanent nature, is a precious acquisition." [26]

Hamilton then reverts to a favorite theme: that the funded debt of the United States acts as a "species of capital," that is, as active capital, or money. As has already been said, Hamilton knows the difference between money and wealth; and he does not confuse them. "But though a funded debt is not ... an absolute increase of capital, or an augmentation of real wealth, yet, by serving as a new power in the operations of industry, it has within certain bounds, a tendency to increase the real wealth of a community." [27] Therefore, government "stocks" are both income bearers and an acceptable circulating medium; they act as security for loans, they are liquid assets, and their holders are in a ready position—certainly more so than are the owners of real estate—to invest in new undertakings. All this was true in the 1790s as it is in the 1950s; it is unnecessary to comment on the important role of the public debt in the money and credit operations of modern banking and industry.

Many arguments have been brought forth, Hamilton goes on, to prove the impracticability of establishing manufactures in the United States; but how can Americans close their eyes to their own successes? Hamilton enumerates seventeen industries which already flourish in America of which the more important have to do with the fabrication of leather, iron, wood, flax, and hemp. These do not include household manufactures, to be found all over the United States.

But what of the contention that the encouragement of manufactures will give a monopoly to particular classes, at the expense of the rest of the community, and will raise prices? For a short time, it is true, prices will increase; but the reverse ultimately will take place. Domestic manufacture does not have to pay the heavy costs of oceanic transport; and "the internal competition which takes place soon does away with everything like monopoly, and by degrees reduces the price of the article to the minimum of a reasonable profit on the capital employed." [28]

Having thus disposed of the objections commonly made to the expediency of encouraging and to the probability of success of manufacturing in the United States, Hamilton makes some additional observations. He insists that the trade of a country, where both manufacturing and agriculture flourish, is more lucrative than that of one wholly dependent upon agriculture. Further, economic stagnation is likely to affect more quickly countries whose economies are based on agricultural staples rather than on a diversified industry. In consequence, those nations possessing both manufactures and agriculture (as, parenthetically, it should be said, the United States did after 1865) are more likely to have a favorable balance of trade and "to possess more pecuniary wealth, or money, than those of the latter." [29]

Finally, the promotion of manufactures will not benefit the Northern states alone and harm the Southern states, as has been charged. "Ideas of a contrariety of interests between the northern and southern regions of the Union are, in the main, as unfounded as they are mischievous." [30] For: "Mutual wants constitute one of the strongest links of political connection; and the extent of these bears a natural proportion to the diversity in the means of mutual supply." Indeed "every thing tending to establish substantial and permanent order in the affairs of a country, to increase the total mass of industry and opulence, is ultimately beneficial to every part of it." [31]

How NOW TO GO ABOUT THE BUSINESS OF PROMOTING MANUFACtures in the United States? Examining the practices of other nations, Hamilton finds that the following devices have been employed with success: protective duties on imports; prohibition of and prohibitive duties on rival articles; prohibition of the export of raw materials; bounties; premiums; the exemption of raw materials from duty; drawbacks on raw materials from which manufactured articles are to be exported; the encouragement of new inventions; and government assistance to internal improvements.

At this point, Hamilton the statesman and political economist —the leader of affairs utilizing economic analysis as a key to public policy—emerges in full splendor. One does not find a Hamilton of narrow protectionist, or high tariff, interests, or an interventionist employing government to serve only a single class, or a pleader of special causes, or an enemy of agriculture: in fact, there never was such a Hamilton. If only these passages were read, by admirers as well as detractors, there would be a more general appreciation of his wisdom and devotion. For the very devices Hamilton was advocating in 1791 are those the United States is turning to today; and the reasons he offered for government intervention—in the short run, always—are still sound to develop infant industries and to protect those that are necessary for the national defense.

Hamilton does not accept protectionism without qualification. At every point there are reservations. Indeed, he contends, the most desirable form of assistance is to be found in the use of bounties. He presents these reasons:

1. Bounties furnish direct, positive, and immediate encouragement.

2. Bounties will not increase prices, or only slightly, "either by making no addition to the charges on the rival foreign article, as in the case of protecting duties, or by making a smaller addition." The fact is, paying a bounty will lead to a fall in prices, "because, without laying any new charge on the foreign article, it serves to introduce a competition with it, and to increase the total quantity of the article in the market." [32]

3. Bounties, unlike high protective duties, will not produce

scarcity. Protective duties ultimately lead to higher prices; in the short run, they discourage importations.

4. Bounties are not only the best but the only proper expedient for uniting a new agricultural activity with a new one in manufactures. "It is the interest of the farmer to have the production of the raw material promoted by counteracting the interference of the raw material of the same kind. It is the interest of the manufacturer to have material abundant and cheap." A protective duty is the wrong way of going about serving both: it destroys the supply of the raw material, or raises its price too high for "the conductor of an infant manufacture." [33] The new industry is abandoned; the farmer has no market for his product. Bounties, therefore, are equally effective in the stimulation of both agriculture and industry.

Again, unlike protective duties, bounties will promote exports too. The former only succeeded in giving protected industries advantages in the home market; they can have no "influence upon the advantageous sale of the article produced, in foreign markets." [34]

If the United States is to have manufacturing "pecuniary bounties are, in most cases, indispensable to the introduction of a new branch." Hamilton wants such support; it is essential if we wish to overcome the "obstacles which arise from the competitions of superior skill and maturity elsewhere." [35] Bounties, then, by all means, but bounties only for infant industries! These reservations are significant; to Hamilton, government aid was only a temporary device. He says: [36]

The continuance of bounties on manufactures long established must almost always be of questionable policy; because a presumption would arise, in every such case, that there were natural and inherent impediments to success. But, in new undertakings, they are as justifiable as they are sometimes necessary.

And again, in defending bounties as serving the general welfare: [37]

But it is the interest of the society, in each case, to submit to the temporary expense—which is more than compensated by an increase of industry and wealth, by an augmentation of resources and independence, and by the circumstance of eventual cheapness. . . .

In support of government intervention, Hamilton comes back again and again to the absence of reciprocity; this compels the United States to undertake reprisals. If it did not do so, "the want of reciprocity would render them the victim of a system which should induce them to confine their views to agriculture, and refrain from manufactures. A constant and increasing necessity on their part for the commodities of Europe, and only a partial and occasional demand for their own in return, could not but expose them to a state of impoverishment, compared with the opulence to which their political and natural advantages authorize them to aspire." [38]

Intervention, then, is caused by imperfect political institutions; equally, it is justifiable as preparation against war. As we have seen, Hamilton eloquently defends his country and regards, as the first charge upon its leaders, the taking of measures to protect it. America must produce all those commodities it would require should war once more break out. This, again, is intervention for reasons of policy; and Hamilton's position was as justifiable then as is our current concern over the scarcity of key raw materials and the protection of native industries that serve sensitive military requirements.

Intervention, thus, is a matter of necessity and opportunity. Public policy should be variable and sensitive: it must adjust to changing circumstances and it must be moderate. To Hamilton, protectionism is no ideal and isolation no virtue. If protection—as an expedient—will help undertakers, or the capitalist class, if it will attract foreign capital to the United States, the results will redound to the benefit of the whole community in the increase of its "revenue and capital."

A diversified economy, where both manufactures and agriculture have the benefits of mechanization, is more stable: it creates higher standards of living. Greater "revenue and capital," fuller employment, domestic markets for staples and finished goods, a larger population: these, then, are economic reasons for intervention. Hamilton, here, has hit upon an economic truth of the first importance: that as a nation ascends to higher levels of production—from the creation of raw materials alone to agriculture and from agriculture to manufactures—its standards of living mount. Combine agriculture and manufactures, and an important step in this direction has been taken.

Hamilton is not unmindful of agriculture's uncertain and insecure position; for this there are artificial causes—the absence of reciprocity—but there are natural causes as well. He says: [39]

Independently likewise of the artificial impediments which are created by the policy in question, there are natural causes tending to render the external demand for the surplus of agricultural nations a precarious reliance. The differences of seasons in the countries which are the consumers make immense differences in the produce of their own soils in different years, and consequently in the degrees of their necessity for foreign supply. Plentiful harvests for them, especially if similar ones occur at the same time in the countries which are the furnishers, occasion of course a glut in the market of the latter.

Finally, there are psychological reasons justifying intervention: and here is to be found the heart of the protectionist argument. Infant industries will not be launched, indeed will not survive, without government's fostering care. It has been held by the opponents of government encouragement, that manufactures "will grow up as soon and as fast as the natural state of things and the interest of the community will require." Hamilton disagrees; there are very cogent reasons why this is not so.[40] He writes:

These have relation to the strong influence of habit and the spirit of imitation; the fear of want of success in untried enterprises; the intrinsic difficulties incident to first essays towards a competition with those who have previously attained to perfection in the business to be attempted; the bounties, premiums, and other artificial encouragements with which foreign nations second the exertions of their own citizens, in the branches in which they are to be rivalled.

Experience teaches, that men are often so much governed by what they are accustomed to see and practice, that the simplest and most obvious improvements, in the most ordinary occupations, are adopted with hesitation, reluctance, and by slow gradations. The spontaneous transition to new pursuits, in a community long habituated to different ones, may be expected to be attended with proportionately greater difficulty. When former occupations ceased to yield a profit... changes would ensue; but these changes would be likely to be more tardy than might consist with the interest either of individuals or of the society. In many cases they would not happen, while a bare support could be insured by adherence to ancient courses, though a resort to a more profitable employment might be practicable. To produce the desirable changes as early as may be expedient may therefore require the incitement and patronage of government.

The apprehension of failing in new attempts is, perhaps, a more serious impediment. There are dispositions apt to be attracted by the mere novelty of an undertaking; but these are not always the best calculated to give it success. To this it is of importance that the confidence of cautious, sagacious capitalists, both citizens and foreigners, should be excited. And to inspire this description of persons with confidence, it is essential that they should be made to see in any project which is new—and for that reason alone, if for no other, precarious —the prospect of such a degree of countenance and support from governments, as may be capable of overcoming the obstacles inseparable from first experiments.

The superiority antecedently enjoyed by nations who have preoccupied and perfected a branch of industry, constitutes a more formidable obstacle...to the introduction of the same branch into a country in which it did not before exist. To maintain, between the recent establishments of one country, and the long-matured establishments of another country, a competition upon equal terms, both as to quality and price, is, in most cases, impracticable. The disparity, in the one, or in the other, or in both, must necessarily be so considerable, as to forbid a successful rivalship, without the extraordinary aid and protection of government. ...

And then there is a bow to Adam Smith:

Whatever room there may be for an expectation that the industry of a people, under the direction of private interest, will, upon equal terms, find out the most beneficial employment for itself, there is none for a reliance that it will struggle against the force of unequal terms, or will, of itself, surmount all the adventitious barriers to a successful competition which may have been erected, either by the advantages naturally acquired from practice and previous possession of the ground, or by these which may have sprung from positive regulations and an artificial policy.

This statement has been the protectionist's vade mecum, the very pith and marrow of the argument presented by tariff leagues all over the world. It carries great weight; and it is sound, up to a point, as Hamilton himself understood. Young and underdeveloped countries—bound to the production of staples because of a scarcity of capital and the timidity among enterprisers to which Hamilton justly refers—will be doomed to uncertainties of the world market and unequal terms of trade; they will be unable to initiate, develop, and expand production with attendant rises in standards of living, unless government promotes, expedites, incites. It should do so as long as the country is unequal to the race and its industries need assistance.

Hamilton, at this stage only, urges protection—for he is aware of its shortcomings and its dangers. Protective tariffs raise prices; they create scarcities; they build up special interests; they breed isolation. To Hamilton, the maker of policy, the patriot concerned with the welfare of the American people in an expanding and free world, protection is a weapon and not a principle, and because it is a sharp and dangerous sword—used to compel equal opportunities in all markets—it must be sheathed at once with the accomplishment of its purpose. Rather than protective duties, bounties and premiums are by far the more desirable governmental device. They have none of the faults of a protective tariff system; they have the great virtue of being positive and direct—and they can be quickly terminated. There can be no escape from the finality of this observation: "The continuance of bounties on manufactures long established must almost always be of questionable policy."

THIS IS THE ARGUMENT FOR A DIVERSIFIED ECONOMY, THE STIMU-
lation of manufactures, and the short-run intervention of government in a world not yet prepared to live in a "system of perfect
liberty." It is one of the most impressive pieces of writing in
political economy (i.e., economics applied to statecraft) in our
literature. It has, curiously enough, more to say to us today than
it did to its readers in 1791. *The Report on Manufactures* was put
aside by his contemporaries; in the 1830s and the 1860s, that portion having to do with protectionism was eagerly studied.

Today the whole statement needs reading and pondering over
again, not only in the United States, where the limits of government intervention require such careful definitions, but particularly in those new and underdeveloped countries, all over the
world, which see the necessity for conversion to industrialization
but which only faintly comprehend the key roles of the integrity
of the public credit and the safeguarding of the investment function (native as well as foreign) in such a process.

In one sense, however, Hamilton's policies met with immediate and amazing success. He could lay plans for future generations; yet he could create a house of order for his own times.
Beginning with 1790, and continuing for a quarter-century, the
United States was launched on an extraordinary period of expansion and prosperity, its first and perhaps even its greatest.
Wholesale prices, by the spring of 1789, began to mount slowly;
and by 1790 a boom was in progress that, with the customary short
cycles of recession and recovery, lasted up to 1814. Taking 1910–
1914 as the base period, or 100, the indices of wholesale prices
were 86 in 1789, 90 in 1790, 146 in 1796, and 182 in 1814. The
tonnage of American ships in the foreign trade increased from
123,893 tons in 1789 to 981,019 tons in 1810: by that time, the
United States had the largest neutral mercantile fleet in the world.
Looking back upon this era, the Earl of Liverpool told the House
of Lords in 1820 that "America increased in *wealth*, in *commerce*,
in *arts* [industry], in *population*, in *strength* more rapidly than

any nation ever before increased in the history of the world." [41]

The exports of the country were worth $19,012,000 in 1791; in 1801, they stood at $93,021,000, an increase of 400 per cent. At the same time, the gap between imports and exports narrowed, with imports for the two years $29,200,000 and $111,363,000 respectively, an increase of 280 per cent. Presumably, for the eleven years 1790 through 1800, there was an import balance against the United States of $127,000,000; in the same period, also, $2,500,-000 was paid off on the principal of the federal foreign debt and from $15,000,000 to $20,000,000 was paid abroad in interest and profits on federal "stock" and investments in American companies held by Europeans. The balance of international payments appeared to be heavily against the United States.

On the credit side, however, were these factors: imports were overvalued (frequently they included transportation costs); at the same time, annually, from one-third to one-half of total imports were not paid for because of the willingness of European merchants to extend as much as fifteen months' credit to American buyers. The American merchant marine, in the years in question, may have earned $50,000,000. In the same period, a minimum of $35,000,000 in new European capital came into the United States. The figures are fragmentary and many are guesses: but there are two pieces of evidence to encourage one to speculate that perhaps the balance of payments was really in favor of the country. The first was that sterling exchange during the greater part of the period was selling at a discount in New York and Philadelphia. The second was the doubling of specie circulation in the United States. In 1790, American specie circulation amounted to $9,000,000; by 1801, this had risen to between $15,000,000 and $20,000,000. The United States may, during this early period, have been a creditor nation: this status was not to be achieved or possibly to be re-achieved until a whole century later as a result of World War I.

How thoroughly justified Hamilton was in looking to foreign

capital for aid, the following figures show. (The estimates are from a contemporary source, Samuel Blodget's *Economica*, published in 1806. The figures are as of June 30, 1803.) Federal "stock" outstanding at that time came to $81,325,000, of which $43,369,000, or 53 per cent, was owned abroad. The shares of American corporations (banks, insurance companies, turnpike and canal companies) were worth $48,400,000; of this $15,880,000, or 33 per cent, was owned abroad. The Bank of the United States (included in the above) was capitalized at $10,000,000; and $6,200,000, or 62 per cent, was owned abroad. Never again in its annals were American government and enterprise to be so heavily dependent upon European funds; what is significant is that when, in the first and crucial decade of its history, help was needed, it came so readily.

Jefferson's initial indifference and then growing opposition to the whole Hamilton program has been noted. It is amusing to record that when Jefferson embarked on his greatest enterprise, the purchase of Louisiana from Napoleon in 1803, he turned to foreign money markets for his financing. The price of the territory was fixed at $15,000,000; $3,750,000 of this made up claims of American citizens against the French government and were met out of revenues. The balance, $11,250,000, was raised by issuing 6 per cent bonds payable in four installments during the years 1818–1821. So good was the public credit of the United States that the whole issue was taken up at once in Europe, the English subscribing $9,250,000, the French, $1,500,000, and other European nationals, $500,000.

The decade of the 1790s was to see an enormous increase in company promotions, as a result of the voting of business corporation charters by the states. During the 1780s, only 33 charters were granted; during the 1790s, 295. As a result, by 1800 there were 34 banks in the United States, of which 27 were established after 1789; and 33 insurance companies (marine and fire), of which 30 were created after 1789. Other private corporations obtaining approval—most of these were actually established—were inland navigation, turnpike and toll bridge companies; water supply and dock companies; and manufacturing and mining companies.

The banks and insurance companies did very well. They all earned profits and with some the dividends were so high that their stock sold well above par. The Bank of North America (established in 1781) averaged dividends of 10.2 per cent during 1782–1800; the Bank of New York (1783), paid 8.8 per cent; the Bank of Massachusetts (1783), 10.6 per cent; the Bank of Maryland (1790), 12 per cent; the Bank of the United States (1791), 8.3 per cent. The turnpike companies, begun late in the decade, were already being financed and some were earnings profits. The same was true of the bridge companies and water supply companies. The canal and navigation companies—whose technical problems were much more complex—had got off to a poor start. In all, eight manufacturing companies had been incorporated; but none was a real success, in part due to the want of skills in early America, in part to the superior attractions commerce, banking, and transport held out for capital.

One of these manufacturing corporations, with whose launching Alexander Hamilton was closely associated (as its prime mover) was "The Society for establishing Useful Manufactures" (S.U.M.), which the New Jersey legislature chartered on November 22, 1791. Its prospectus was phrased in the most sanguine terms. It began: [42]

The establishment of manufactures in the United States when maturely considered will be found to be of the highest importance to their prosperity. It seems an almost self-evident proposition that communities which can most perfectly supply their own wants are in a state of the highest political perfection. And both theory and experience conspire to prove that a nation ... cannot possess much active wealth but as a result of extensive manufactures—

The undertakers proposed the raising of an initial capital of $500,000; that a charter be sought in New York, Pennsylvania, or New Jersey; and that machinery and skilled workers be obtained from abroad. How large were the expectations of the founders one notes from their plans. They would manufacture paper and paper products, sail cloth and other linen cloths, stockings, ribbons, thread, blankets, carpets, "Chip Hats," women's shoes, pottery and earthenware, brass and iron ware, and print cotton and linen goods. A town was to be erected. Even the right to establish a lottery was to be sought.

The charter, when finally granted, was a sweeping one. The company was to raise funds—the authorized capital stock was to be $1,000,000—"for the purpose of introducing and establishing useful Manufactures"; all its workers were to be exempt from poll and capitation taxes and from militia duty; its property was to be tax-free for 10 years; it could raise as much as $100,000 from a lottery. The Society was given the right to "open and clear" rivers and other waters and to build canals to aid the transport of its materials and wares; and, to facilitate this, the power of eminent domain was granted. Finally, the erection of a new city— the corporation and town of Paterson—as the principal seat "of their said manufactories" was approved.

New Jersey could not have been more generous (here, in fact, was the origin of its liberal attitude toward corporations); and in a short time, $625,000 was subscribed. In all the preliminary discussions, the drawing up of the company's statements, the maneuvers in New Jersey, Hamilton participated. His correspondence indicates that the preparation of his *Report on Manufactures* and the inception of the S.U.M. went hand in hand; the company in fact, was to be a gigantic demonstration of his belief that Americans had the desire and the capacities to begin manufacturing enterprises at once.

Hamilton was too hopeful. All sorts of blunders and extravagances were committed; all manner of obstacles—scarcely to be anticipated by promoters who had no actual experience with industrial operations—arose. There were problems involving engineering, the organization and management of a labor force, the financing of construction, and the acquisition of machinery and raw materials. Finally, and at too great a cost, a cotton mill was erected and the printing of cotton goods was also begun. At the end of five years, the Society had received and disbursed $250,000 from its stockholders toward their subscriptions; other than land, buildings and machinery—largely unused—the company had little to show for this vast but ill-starred effort. In 1796, the works were shut down.

Some of the reasons for the Society's collapse were apparent: management was not yet skilled enough in the United States to handle such intricate operations. Contemporaries listed others: the high cost of labor, the heavy costs of installation and operation of waterworks and mills, the inexpertness of the artisans. A local newspaper made an observation that throws a good deal of light on prevailing attitudes: [43]

But it may reasonably be questioned, whether manufactures of the kind mentioned, can succeed in this country for many years to come; Between countries very populous, where no wealthy lands invite the inhabitants to remove from manufacturing towns, and this with millions of acres, unoccupied and purchased at a low price, present the industrious man with an independent estate for a little labor.

Hamilton played a large part in getting the Society started and his labors—in the handling of technical details, employing managers and skilled workers, advising on construction and the use of water power—were prodigious. His relations with the Society, on financial matters, were impeccable. He did not solicit potential shareholders or seek business for the company; he was always ready to advise and was very generous with his time; but he never sought to influence stockholders or directors. By 1793, he had withdrawn from the scene; by then, apparently, he was already reconciled to the Society's failure.

EXCEPT, THEN, FOR MANUFACTURES ON A CORPORATE BASIS, THE whole American prospect was pleasing. In these words, written in May, 1791, a contemporary of Hamilton's thus paid tribute, in effect, to the Secretary of the Treasury's towering accomplishments: [44]

In general, our affairs are proceeding in a train of unparalleled prosperity. This arises from the unbounded confidence reposed in it by the people, their zeal to support it, and their conviction that a solid Union is the best rock of their safety, from the favorable seasons which for some years past have co-operated with a fertile soil and a genial climate to increase the productions of agriculture, and from the growth of industry, economy and domestic manufactures; so that I believe I may say with truth, that there is not a nation under the sun enjoying more present prosperity, nor with more in prospect.

These observations were to be found in a letter sent by Thomas Jefferson to C. W. F. Dumas. Just sixty years later, the historian Richard Hildreth, in his *History of the United States of America*, put his finger on the same key factor: "The great secret of the beneficial operation of the funding system was the re-establishment of confidence.... By the restoration of confidence in the nation, confidence in the States, and confidence in individuals, the funding system actually added to the labor, land, and capital of the country a much greater value than the amount of the debt thereby charged upon it." [45]

Defense of Policy
& Defense of Country

By 1792, THERE WAS AN ORGANIZED OPPOSITION TO THE HAMILTON program and while it never succeeded, in a single important particular, in disturbing the grand plan to which Hamilton was dedicating himself, the Republicans (as they called themselves) ended by turning the victory into a bitter fruit. Hamilton prevailed; yet Jefferson and his friends, in a curious and ironic sense, won. Hamilton and his followers, from 1789 to 1800, left their indelible mark upon the American nation, and then, in a brief twelve years, they had run their course and were done. The Federalists literally disappeared without trace, as far as the national scene was concerned. This was an extraordinary failure.

Hamilton had sought to attract the "wise, the good, and the rich" to the service of government. The Federalists regarded the conduct of public affairs as a sacred personal trust: this has always been a conservative idea and ideal. Individuals succeeded each other in office as policies changed; but because there was no personal stake in government and no specific class interest to defend, organization to assure election was unnecessary, indeed it was undesirable. George Washington in his "Farewell Address" of September 17, 1796 (in whose composition Alexander Hamilton played such a large part), reverted to this theme again and again.

Washington said, alluding to party organization and partisan discussion and opposition, "All obstructions to the execution of the laws, all combinations and associations under whatever plausible character, with the real design to direct, control, counteract, or awe the regular deliberations and action of the constituted authorities, are destructive of this fundamental principle, and of fatal tendency." Again, "Let me now take a more comprehensive view, and warn you in the most solemn manner against the baneful effects of the spirit of party generally." And again, "There is an opinion that parties in free countries are useful checks upon the administration of the government, and serve to keep alive the spirit of liberty. . . . But in those of the popular character, in governments purely elective, it is a spirit not to be encouraged." [1]

This was a fatal misunderstanding. And because of it, the Federalists failed to build organizations from the grass roots up— in every ward and town, in every county, city and state—and they neglected to develop the arts of consultation, persuasion, and discipline. They made another prime mistake, and this followed from their faulty analysis. They did not address themselves to the whole American people nor did they prepare, ironically enough—for their intention was the preservation and strengthening of the Union—a national program. A conservative party, notably, requires popular support, for it seeks to draw upon all those enduring influences of the past—love of country, devotion to religion, a common welfare, human dignity, the rule of law— that bind a people together. It accepts change, of course, but change which is an orderly progress and yet is ever linked with the proved experience of the past.

If Hamilton and his colleagues had brought such a message to the American people, engaged, in short, in the constant process of education with which democratic institutions must always be associated, if they had pointed out their great commitments to responsibility and order and to tranquility and welfare within a dynamic system of change, they would have endured.

It was not until Henry Clay appeared, a whole thirty years later, that the Whigs, the successors of the Federalists, repaired this error: they built their party on a broad social base. The Whigs called their program "The American System" and as such, it spoke consciously to the high and the low, enterprisers in the cities and farmers on the land, workers in factories and pioneers seeking to create productive farms on the country's frontier. A national transportation network would open up the whole nation's resources and markets. The protection of infant industries, in the South as well as in the North, would engage American capital, create work for artisans and the unskilled, and raise standards of living. (The later Republican party of the post–Civil War era, not unjustly, called this program "a working-man's tariff.") A sound banking system would protect the nation's currency and assure the orderly flow of capital into yet undeveloped regions.

Hamilton was not insensible to the fact that he and his Federalist friends had failed. Early in 1799, writing to Jonathan Dayton, he confessed: the country has been remarkably successful in its domestic and foreign policies; yet "public opinion has not been ameliorated: sentiments dangerous to social happiness have not been diminished; on the contrary, there are symptoms which warrant the apprehension that among the most numerous class of citizens, errors of a very pernicious tendency have not only preserved but have extended their empire." [2] Should not a wider program be laid out, one that "will extend the influence and promote the popularity of government?" Among other things he proposed a national system of turnpikes, the building of canals from public funds, and devices to encourage and improve agriculture; but, in 1799, he was too late.

The Federalists had been made synonymous with "favoritism,

influence and monopoly"; against them were juxtaposed "the industrious mechanic, the laborious farmer and the poorer classes generally." [3] That faction, or party spirit, which both Madison and Hamilton, in 1789, had hoped would be never introduced in American political life, now made its appearance; and bitter and unseemly wrangling confused every issue and made every decision difficult.

The stakes in play were immense; nothing less than the survival of the American nation was involved. Alexander Hamilton had dedicated all his powers to the building of a united and strong people. And yet, even that accomplishment is held lightly in many quarters today. Indeed, it is fashionable to deride the idea of nationality. Nationality, it is said, is restrictive and possessive; it disregards the greater claims of the whole of humanity; it possesses no moral consciousness; it makes men quarrelsome and it breeds wars. The nation builders, who summon their fellow men to consecrate their lives to glory, only too frequently lead out their legions to destruction.

This is an unhappy half-truth. There is nothing wrong about the possession or the inculcation of a sense of a belonging, whether in one's family, working or professional association, or country. Indeed loyalty and devotion to country are fine things, for there is a common sharing of heritage, experiences, and sacrifice. Men learn—despite differences of birth, education, and capacities—that in the nation they have a unifying core of accomplishment as well as a common destiny. The democratic political process of discussion, deliberation, and agreement makes this living, national tradition realizable and workable.

What encourages men to strive? Personal recognition, self-realization, provision for one's family, a sense of accomplishment: these are strong human motivations, but no less powerful is the desire to merge oneself in the common interest and identify oneself with one's times. Patriotism requires and means a compelling sense of community. Alexander Hamilton had that. And because of his attachment to the United States, he wanted to see it virtuous, tranquil, and prosperous. He was a great administrator and a great statesman: his public life one of sacrifice and rectitude, he labored unceasingly to establish the integrity of the government, to assure the welfare of the American people, and to guarantee the endurance of republican institutions.

In 1796, he wrote to Rufus King, saying simply what his all-encompassing hope was: "We are laboring hard to establish in this country principles more and more *national* and free from all foreign ingredients, so that we may be neither 'Greeks nor Trojans,' but truly Americans." [4] And two years later, writing again to King, in the midst of a European war that for the second time was threatening to engulf the United States, he was able to express his confidence in his country's future: "I anticipate with you that this country will, ere long, assume an attitude correspondent with its great destinies—majestic, efficient, and operative of great things. A noble career lies before it." [5]

One does not dismiss such a man simply by saying he was ambitious. George Washington, who learned to lean so heavily on Hamilton, knew Hamilton for an ambitious man, yet he called him, in 1798, "enterprising, quick in his perceptions, and his judgment intuitively great." [6] And as for his ambitions, said Washington, "it is of that laudable kind which prompts a man to excel in whatever he takes in hand." That is a sound judgment; by such standards all public servants might well be tested.

ALEXANDER HAMILTON, TOO, DID SOMETHING ELSE TO PRESERVE American nationality; he sought to give its foreign policy a national interest, as its only real protection. America, from 1792 to 1800, was beset by danger from without and by confusion from within. What was the United States to do as war began to rage all over Europe and approach closer its own shores? What was it to do in the face of an alliance that was threatening republican

France, a France that had raised the banner of equality and humanity? Did a nation commit itself to a broad moral principle and sally forth in all directions in its defense—as we are told by some we must today—or did it try to preserve its own integrity and in so doing maintain its strength and its freedom of action?

Hamilton's clear answer in favor of self-interest as against a crusading zeal, of narrow and clearly defined objectives as against broad principle, has stood America in good stead throughout its history when dealing with foreign nations. Only when it has strayed from this narrow path has it got into difficulties and, despite its good intentions, sown suspicion everywhere.

Such a choice came in 1792; and Hamilton showed the way Americans were to pursue as they faced foreign involvement and even war.

Hamilton had never had any illusions about the French Revolution; he had sensed its dangers a whole year before Edmund Burke sought to sound the alarm. Thus, in October, 1789, he wrote to his close friend Lafayette: [7]

I have seen, with a mixture of pleasure and apprehension, the progress of events which have lately taken place in your country. As a friend to mankind and to liberty, I rejoice in the efforts which you are making to establish it, while I fear much for the final success of the attempts . . . and for the danger, in case of success, of innovations greater than will consist with the real felicity of your nation.

. . . I dread the vehement character of your people, whom I fear you may find it more easy to bring on, than to keep within proper bounds after you have put them in motion. . . . And I dread the reveries of your philosophic politicians, who appear in the moment to have great influence, and who, being mere speculatists, may aim at more refinement than suits either with human nature or the composition of your nation.

Hamilton watched the unfolding events with growing concern, as the French Revolution moved from democratic debate and settlement to dictatorship and violence. Louis XVI was dethroned and executed; the French Republic was proclaimed and the Jacobins seized power; they installed the Terror, declared war against

Great Britain and Holland, and proceeded to expand the French Empire in Europe and rebuild it overseas. The Revolution could be made secure only when France was ringed around by a company of satellite nations.

In a fragment he wrote on the French Revolution, Hamilton saw the threat to liberty and order in the new doctrine, the "artificial and false morality," being preached. And the same concern he had expressed about the nature of man in *The Federalist*, he voiced here. "Theories of government unsuited to the nature of man, miscalculating the force of his passions, disregarding the lessons of experimental wisdom, have been projected and recommended. These have everywhere attracted sectaries, and everywhere the fabric of government has been in different degrees undermined." [8]

The full force of the Jacobin terror he realized: it was "a despotism unlimited and uncontrolled," it left "to a deluded, an abused, a plundered, a scourged, and an oppressed people, not even the shadow of liberty to console them for a long train of substantial misfortunes, of bitter suffering." [9]

France was at war; and France had claims on America, sentimental ties, claims of gratitude for earlier aid, the bonds of alliance and amity. The treaties of 1778 had been two. One was a treaty of alliance; it guaranteed the territorial integrity of both "forever against all powers." The other was a treaty of amity and commerce which, among other things, permitted each country to use the ports of the other for the anchorage of warships and for privateers and their prizes. On these France was prepared to stand when war broke out in Europe in 1792.

The Administration was in a difficult position. It had a treaty of peace with Great Britain and a treaty of alliance with France; it was not unmindful of the fact that the newly arrived French minister Edmund Genêt was fomenting disorders everywhere; it also knew of the broad popular sympathies the French cause had invoked in America. But the country teetered on the edge of involvement when privateers, which Genêt had sent out, came sailing back into American ports with their prizes and seized cargoes. A declaration of neutrality was the least the Administration could do and a proclamation to this effect was issued April 22, 1793.

It was in defense of the Proclamation of Neutrality that Hamilton laid out in detail the concept of national interest as the basis of foreign policy. Between June 29 and July 20, 1793, he wrote seven brief newspaper essays, signed "Pacificus," in which he addressed himself to the question being so heatedly debated. Did the President have authority to issue the Proclamation of Neutrality? Did it contravene the treaties with France? Was it contrary to the gratitude we owed France? Was it untimely and unnecessary?

About the right of the President to take such summary action, without Congressional consultation, Hamilton had no doubts. He said, "The legislative department is not the organ of intercourse between the United States and foreign nations. It is charged neither with *making* nor *interpreting* treaties. It is therefore not naturally that member of the government which is to pronounce on the existing condition of the nation with regard to foreign powers, or to admonish the citizens of their obligations and duties in consequence...." [10] (Italics original.)

On gratitude or even moral principle as the basis of policy, Hamilton was frankness itself. Gratitude he rejected; it was the business of a nation to look after its own welfare: [11]

Self-preservation is the first duty of a nation; and though in the performances of stipulations relating to war, good faith requires that its ordinary hazards should be fairly met, because they are directly contemplated by such stipulations, yet it does not require that extraordinary and extreme hazards should be run....

The basis of gratitude is a benefit received or intended which there was no right to claim, originating in a regard to the interest or advantage of the party on which the benefit is, or is meant to be, conferred. If a service is rendered from views relative to the immediate interest of the party who performs it, and is productive of reciprocal advantages, there seems scarcely, in such a case, to be an adequate basis for a sentiment like that of gratitude.... It may be affirmed as a general principle, that the predominant motive of good offices from one nation to another, is the interest or advantage of the nation which performs them.

Indeed, the rule of morality in this respect is not precisely the same between nations as between individuals. The duty of making its own welfare the guide of its actions, is much stronger upon the former than upon the latter; in proportion to the greater magnitude and importance of national compared with individual happiness, and to the greater permanency of the effects of national than of individual conduct.

These discourses and another newspaper series Hamilton wrote about Genêt's tampering with our neutrality—they were signed, significantly, "No Jacobin"—had a mounting effect. Hamilton could appeal to the national pride when he characterized Genêt's flouting of the government—he had sent out a converted British prize as an armed privateer when expressly forbidden to do so— as the "height of arrogance on the one side and the depths of humiliation on the other." [12] Madison, among others, sought to answer Hamilton, but Genêt's conduct was indefensible. The French minister's recall was finally asked for; and the danger of American involvement in war was averted. Hardheaded sense had triumphed over sentiment. And as Europe sank deeper in the abyss, the young American nation was able to proceed unmolested to consolidate its nationality and build up its own strengths.

IT SHOULD NOT BE ASSUMED THAT HAMILTON WENT UNCHALLENGED. The years 1789–1795 were stormy ones in American politics. At virtually every point, almost from the beginning, Jefferson faced Hamilton, and out of these differences the Republican (later Democratic) party was born. Hamilton and Jefferson had met briefly in 1783, when both were in Philadelphia sitting in the Continental Congress; and then, the year following, Jefferson had gone to France where he had represented the United States until 1790. Jefferson remained in the Cabinet until the end of 1793, Hamilton until the beginning of 1795. Around Jefferson, the opposition to the Hamilton program—on the public credit, the bank, tax policy, foreign affairs—began to form.

These two great men, who contributed so much to the shaping of the American tradition, should have complemented each other. It is true that their intellectual habits, temperaments, and interests were diametrically opposed. But they were both devoted to a free and prosperous America. Yet they clashed; and the bitterness of their strife gave that peculiar flavor of partisanship and irresponsibility to American party politics that has always been one of its weaknesses. The opposition in the United States—unlike its position under parliamentary government—will use every device to undermine the authority of the Administration; it will openly exacerbate class suspicions; it will make disingenuous and impossible promises of reform; it will talk of the personal corruption and even treason of its opponents. And then, as like as not, once itself installed in office, it will calmly continue the policies it has inherited. It must, of course; for in a democracy, if it is to survive, change must be orderly and popular consent is imperative. In fact, once in office, Jefferson realized this, for despite all his talk of the Revolution of 1800, in no significant particular was the Hamiltonian program disturbed. Even, ironically enough, the doctrine of implied powers, which Jefferson had so completely rejected, was utilized by him to justify his purchase of Louisiana.

Every now and then an age throws up a man with an insatiable curiosity; he wishes to encompass all the knowledge of his time. Aristotle, Bacon, and Voltaire were such men; Jefferson was another. His speculations were universal; he sought full release for the human mind; he yearned for perfect liberty. Power he was distrustful of, whether it was the power of large agglomerations of wealth, the invisible power of finance, or the power of government. His political credo he summed up in these words: "I owe I am not a friend to a very energetic government. It is always oppressive." [13] This concern we must recognize as a fundamental truth. For government, with great power, can be abused, it does not always necessarily function in the public interest, public leaders are not always selfless and dedicated men. One exception must be taken from Jefferson's dictum: in times of emergency, extraordinary energy on the part of government is in order. Jefferson refused to recognize the 1790s as such a time; Hamilton's whole plan of action was based on that belief.

Hamilton did not become the leading spokesman of the Washington Administration by deceit. Madison and Jefferson, both fellow Virginians, were closer personally to Washington than Hamilton was. To this extent, Hamilton was always the outsider, perhaps even the arrivist. Hamilton had an understanding of what needed to be done; he was aware of how, to the most minute detail, the program was to be carried out; he was clear and forthright and decisive. Washington was forced to accept Hamilton's proposals because he had no alternative: for Jefferson knew how to oppose but he did not know how to act. He debated; he hesitated; he temporized. Nothing proves this better than Jefferson's confidence in Genêt; ultimately he had to admit that Genêt's instructions from the very start were to embroil the United States in the European war. But Hamilton's immediate and successful defense of the Proclamation of Neutrality had checked the mischief before it had spread too far.

Jefferson had come out of the back country of Virginia. The son of a pioneer, his sympathies were always with the men of the western waters. He had become a great planter—he owned 150 slaves—but his politics and economics were those of the frontier communities. His *Notes on Virginia*, written in 1781, reveal his universe. It was a moral one; free men, guided by intelligence, lived in an easy, equalitarian society, whose public hand was lightly felt; and when government acted, it did so discreetly and virtuously. Here was the high glow of the Age of Reason actually realized; here in America, the selfishness of men and the oppression of power did not exist.

Whether true or not, such an early and happy era cannot be

permanently fixed in time. And yet Jefferson sought to do so; it
was the very heart and substance of his opposition to the Hamiltonian scheme and the basis of his own economics. This was the
world Jefferson dreamed of; the passage is from the *Notes on
Virginia:* [14]

Generally speaking, the proportion which the aggregate of the other
classes of citizens bears in any state to that of its husbandmen, is the
proportion of its unsound to its healthy parts, and is a good enough
barometer whereby to measure its degree of corruption. While we
have land to labor then, let us never wish our citizens occupied at a
work-bench or twirling a distaff. Carpenters, masons, smiths, are want-
ing in husbandry; but, for the general operation of manufacture, let
our workshops remain in Europe. It is better to carry provisions and
materials to workmen there, than to bring them to the provisions and
materials, and with them, their manners and principles. The loss by
the transportation of commodities across the Atlantic will be made up
in the happiness and permanence of government. The mobs of great
cities add just so much to the support of pure government, as sores do
to the strength of the human body. It is the manner and spirit of a
people which preserve a republic in vigor. A degeneracy in these is a
canker which soon eats to the heart of its laws and constitution.

Thus conditioned and committed, Jefferson and Hamilton developed differences almost daily, about small things and about
large. Jefferson advocated tying the country's money to the metric
system; Hamilton proposed the Spanish dollar and the pound
sterling. Hamilton, fearing for the country's neutrality and smarting under the insults of the Algerine pirates, wanted to see a navy
established; Jefferson was opposed. They took opposite sides on
the creation of a military academy, the fortification of harbors,
and the taxing of whiskey. Again and again—bitterly and frequently in unseemly dispute—they crossed swords on Treasury
policy and the relations of the United States with Britain and
France. As a result of Hamilton's prevailing in every instance, the
government's right to tax was established, when the Whiskey
Rebellion was sternly checked; a navy was begun so that, while
tribute was paid to Algiers, a few years later Stephen Decatur was

able to defy Tripoli successfully; the United States was not drawn into the imperialist designs of France; and a treaty of commerce was finally written with Great Britain, under which at the same time the northern boundary and the western country of the United States were at last made secure.

BY 1792, JEFFERSON WAS OPENLY IN OPPOSITION IN THE CABINET. In May of that year he addressed a long letter to Washington in which he filled out in detail his bill of particulars. Hamilton had built up an artificial debt which far exceeded the country's ability ever to discharge it. An excise tax had been saddled on the country: it was odious. The interest rate being paid by government "stock" was excessive. The paper notes of the bank would drive the meager amount of coins still in circulation out of the country. There was a "corrupt squadron" of speculators and stock jobbers in Congress always ready to carry out Hamilton's mandates. Hamilton was seeking to establish a monarchy in the United States! [15]

The very same month, Hamilton was writing to his Virginia friend Colonel Edward Carrington, seeking to explain Jefferson's hostility; the two letters need reading side by side.[16] They account for many things and point up the strength and weaknesses of the two great antagonists: that Jefferson possessed slight economic understanding but had extraordinary political skills; and that Hamilton had much of the former and little of the latter, and therefore disdained the use of accommodation.

What was behind Jefferson's opposition, as Hamilton sought to analyze it? He took up the Republican position, point by point. There was the question of funding: Jefferson disapproved; indeed, he seemed to question the need of funding a debt at all. "I do not mean that he advocates directly the undoing of what had been done, but he censures the whole, on principles which, if they should become general, could not but end in the subversion of the system." But the followers of Jefferson were less discreet; in fact, they had openly declared that "a Legislature had no right to fund the debt by mortgaging permanently the public revenues, because they had no right to bind posterity. The inference is that what has been unlawfully done may be undone."

In foreign politics, the position taken by the Jeffersonians was "equally unsound and dangerous." [17]

> They have a womanish attachment to France and a womanish resentment against Great Britain. They would draw us into the closest embrace of the former, and involve us in all the consequences of her politics; and they would risk the peace of the country in their endeavors to keep us at the greatest possible distance from the latter. . . . Various circumstances prove to me that if these gentlemen were left to pursue their own course, there would be, in less than 6 months, an open war between the United States and Great Britain.

To France, Hamilton was eminently fair: [18]

> I trust I have a due sense of the conduct of France towards this country in the late revolution; and that I shall always be among the foremost in making her every suitable return; but there is a wide difference between this and implicating ourselves in all her politics; between bearing good-will to her and hating and wrangling with all those whom she hates. The neutral and the pacific policy appears to me to mark the true path to the United States.

On the other hand, he saw what lay at the basis of Jefferson's emotional commitments to France: [19]

> In France, he [Jefferson] saw government only on the side of its abuses. He drank freely of the French philosophy, in religion, in science, in politics. He came from France in the moment of a fermentation, which he had a share in exciting, and in the passions and feelings of which he shared both from temperament and situation. . . . He came, electrified with attachment to France, and with the project of knitting together the two countries in the closest political bands.

The Republicans were playing dangerous politics in their effort to discredit the Administration: [20]

> In such a state of mind both these gentlemen [Jefferson and Madison] are prepared to hazard a great deal to effect a change. Most of the important measures of every government are connected with the treasury. To subvert the present head of it, they deem it expedient

to risk rendering the government itself odious; perhaps foolishly thinking that they can easily recover the lost affections and confidence of the people, and not appreciating, as they ought to do, the natural resistance to government, which in every community results from the human passions ... and the infinite danger that the national government, once rendered odious, will be kept so by these powerful and indefatigable enemies.

Hamilton finally came to the astounding charge being made by the Republicans that there had sprung up "a monarchical party meditating the destruction of State and republican government." Hamilton says, for himself: [21]

As to my own political creed, I give it to you with the utmost sincerity. I am affectionately attached to the republican theory. I desire above all things to see the equality of political rights, exclusive of all hereditary distinction, firmly established by a practical demonstration of its being consistent with the order and happiness of society.

What republican institutions really have to fear is "the spirit of faction and anarchy." And there follow these acute remarks on how a dictatorship begins its work of fomenting discontent and creating uneasiness in order to capture power: [22]

If I were disposed to promote monarchy and overthrow State governments, I would mount the hobbyhorse of popularity; I would cry out "usurpation," "danger to liberty," etc., etc. I would endeavor to prostrate the national government, raise a ferment, and then "ride in the whirlwind, and direct the storm."

Three months later, in writing to Washington in reply to Jefferson's charges, Hamilton embroidered further on this fascinating theme of the seizure of power: [23]

When a man, unprincipled in private life, desperate in his fortune, bold in his temper, possessed of considerable talents, having the advantage of military habits, despotic in his ordinary demeanor, known to have scoffed in private at the principles of liberty; when such a man is seen to mount the hobby-horse of popularity, to join in the cry of danger to liberty, to take every opportunity of embarrassing the general government and bringing it under suspicion, to flatter and fall in with all the nonsense of the zealots of the day, it may justly be suspected that his object is to throw things into fusion, that he may "ride the storm and direct the whirlwind."

The effort to alarm Washington, and thus force the ousting of Hamilton, proved unavailing; but the pressures on the President and the open bickering compelled him to cry out against "internal dissensions" which were so harrowing and "tearing our vitals." He consented to run for a second term only as a result of the pleadings of both men. Yet the quarrel continued; worse still, it became public, as both adversaries resorted to the use of newspapers.

Here it took an ugly turn; Hamilton and Jefferson both were involved and the reputations of both have always suffered, in consequence. In 1789, John Fenno set up the *Gazette of the United States*, which supported the Hamiltonian program and received part of the government printing. In 1791, Jefferson, with the agreement of Madison, decided that Hamilton's opponents needed their own organ; and Madison brought Philip Freneau, the poet of the Revolution, to Philadelphia to publish the *National Gazette*. Freneau at the same time was made a translating clerk in the Secretary of State's office.

Freneau was clever and his thrusts began to hurt. He proclaimed his devotion to the great principles of the American Revolution; he talked of corruption in Congress; he saw monarchists and aristocrats undermining the Republic. Fenno was not his equal; and Hamilton—unwisely—took up his pen in his own behalf. He wrote pseudonymously to Fenno's *Gazette* to hint that Freneau was really being subsidized by Jefferson. Freneau replied virtuously and with a show of great indignation; Hamilton sank deeper into the bog. In a series of letters, published over various names, and appearing in Fenno's *Gazette* during July–December, 1792, he named Jefferson as the inspirer of the campaign of calumny. It was Jefferson who was leading the opposition to almost everything with which the Administration was associated; he was the promoter of "national disunion, national insignificance, public disorder and discredit"; the circulation of "foul and pestilent whispers" was his work; he was "cautious and sly, wrapped up in impenetrable mystery." [24]

These were stinging phrases and they should not have come from the Secretary of the Treasury; Jefferson, personally, refused to reply. But his friends did, and, also writing pseudonymously, James Madison, George Tucker, and James Monroe entered the lists to keep the quarrel going. Jefferson did seek to defend Freneau privately to Washington, saying that he was ready to assume that Freneau would want to give "free place to pieces written against the aristocratic and monarchical principles." [25] This wretched spectacle was over by the end of 1792; but out of it was born the Jeffersonian Republican party.

THE REPUBLICAN PARTY WAS BUILT ON HOSTILITY TO "ARISTOCRATIC and monarchical principles." Its purpose was the defeat of the Administration's domestic and foreign policies. It was not too difficult to rally an opposition to its standards.

The country was prospering; it was at peace, although it was a precarious one; there were real probabilities that the differences with Spain and Great Britain were on the way to settlement. A steady flow of settlers was moving across the Appalachians to carve out farms and erect homes in the territories north and south of the Ohio River. But talk of corruption in high places and aristocratic pretensions could be heady: particularly when the French Revolution had released such a flood with its dedication to the Rights of Man and its apostrophes to the Goddess of Reason.

It is hard to believe, today, what a profound effect the French Revolution and Jacobinism, despite its violence, had on America. In America freedom reigned; in France, Jacobinism, in the presumable interests of equalitarianism, suppressed it. Yet, beginning with 1793, secret political clubs, usually called Democratic Societies, sprang up virtually all over the Union, committing them-

selves to the defense of France; the new Republican party built
up a part of its constituency among these clubs.

These clubs suspected the Administration, expressed their concern over the growth of its power, and proclaimed their hatred
of England and their devotion to France, our "magnanimous
ally." The "Circular Letter" sent out by the Pennsylvania Society
rang the changes on all those fears and anxieties on which dema-
goguery knows so well how to play.[26]

Every mind capable of reflection must perceive that the present crisis
in the politics of nations is peculiarly interesting to America. The
European Confederacy, transcendent in power, and unparalleled in
iniquity, menaces the very existence of freedom. Already its baneful
operation may be traced in the tyrannical destruction of the constitution, and the rapacious partition of the territory of Poland; and
should the generous efforts of France be eventually defeated, we have
reason to presume that, for the consummation of monarchical ambition, and the security of its establishment, this country, the only remaining depository of liberty, will not long be permitted to enjoy in
peace the honors of an independent and the happiness of a republican
government.

Nor are the dangers arising from a foreign source the only causes,
at this time, of apprehension and solicitude. The seeds of luxury appear
to have given root in our domestic soil; and the jealous eye of patriotism already regards the spirit of freedom and equality as eclipsed by
the pride of wealth, and the arrogance of power.

In the face of such profound hostilities, the Federalists had no
defense. And the Republican party ended by attracting the great
masses of the humble folk of America—the backwoodsmen and
small farmers, the city laborers, and the skilled mechanics. That
it could gain power and hold it, through much of the first half of
the nineteenth century, by allying these with the planter-slave lords
of the Southern tidewater (so that it could be radical and reac-
tionary at the same time) is the measure of the magic and the
success of the Republican striving. John Taylor of Caroline,
that foe of government generally; Aaron Burr, aristocrat and gentleman and soon to be the head of New York's Sons of Tammany;
Willie Jones of Halifax, North Carolina, great patrician slave

and land owner—these were members of the Republican coalition. And their prototypes have always continued to be participants in the successors of Jefferson's anti-"aristocratic and monarchical" party.

The Republicans organized, mobilized, and drilled; Jefferson himself was an indefatigable correspondent; and soon their clubs and groups covered the country. Fisher Ames, a Hamiltonian Federalist, expressed the wonder and despair of the Administration men when he said, "The discipline of the party is as severe as the Prussian and deserters are not spared." [27] In the November elections of 1792, so swiftly did the Republicans work, Governor George Clinton of New York, Hamilton's ancient antagonist, received 50 votes in the electoral college. All those of Virginia, New York, North Carolina, and Georgia went to him. And when the Third Congress met, on December 2, 1793—Jefferson was still Secretary of State—the Republicans organized the House of Representatives and elected its Speaker.

IT WAS UNDERSTANDABLE THAT THE FIGHT ON HAMILTON SHOULD now have its center in the House more than ever before. A new leader of the opposition appeared: this was William Branch Giles of Virginia. In January, 1793, with the assistance of Madison and Jefferson, Giles introduced a series of resolutions which requested, in effect, a full accounting of all the Treasury's acts from the beginning until the end of 1792. Hamilton had wanted to resign in 1793: he had neglected his family needs too long in order to serve the Administration. But he could not quit under fire; so he stayed on, to meet the challenges which came again and again in 1793 and 1794.

Hamilton answered the House's request for information almost at once, so good were the records the Treasury was keeping. Giles was prepared to continue pressing; and on February 27, another set of resolutions was presented which openly charged

Hamilton with derelictions of duty and irregularities in office. In almost so many words, the Republicans were seeking the impeachment of the Secretary of the Treasury. Hamilton was not called on to appear, however, and he had to defend himself through friends. They handled themselves with competence, so that charge after charge vanished in thin air; and the resolutions were defeated by mounting majorities. At the last, only seven Congressmen stood by Giles, and Madison was one of them.

The Third Congress, assembling in December, 1793, returned to the attack. Giles once more threw out the accusation of abuse of authority by Hamilton. This time Hamilton insisted upon a formal inquiry by the House and he could not be denied. He appeared before a House committee in April, 1794, and deported himself so well—he was able to prove that all his official acts were with the knowledge and consent of the President—that the Giles resolutions were buried in committee.

Another challenge was to appear in 1794; this one involved the fundamental one of the ability of the government to survive if its right to tax was questioned. Hamilton, as we have seen, realizing the danger of depending entirely on customs duties for the public revenue, had pressed for the passage of excise laws. Here he had been successful; and, in 1791, taxes had been put on domestic distilled liquors and domestic stills. The law had become unpopular in the back country and particularly in Virginia, North Carolina, and western Pennsylvania, where a good part of the harvested grain—because of difficulties of transportation—could be moved only in the form of whiskey. Jefferson, called this excise "of odious character with the people"; and, disregarding that the government's inherent and necessary power to tax was involved, went on to say of the law that it was "partial in its operation, unproductive unless enforced by arbitrary and vexatious means, and committing the authority of the government, in parts where resistance is most probable and coercion least practicable." [28]

Hamilton, writing to Washington on August 18, 1792, replied with his customary patience and good sense. An excise is no more partial in its operation "than any other tax on a consumable commodity. . . . The consumer, in the main, pays the tax; and if some parts of the United States consume more domestic spirits, others consume more foreign, and both are taxed." The law was not being "enforced by any arbitrary or vexatious means," for "collection of the tax will not appear in that light but to men who regard all taxes, and all the means of enforcing them, as arbitrary and vexatious." Of course "the authority of the government was being committed." It could not be otherwise: there is always a risk; "but if there were motives sufficiently cogent for it, it was wisely run. It does not follow that a measure is bad because it is attended with a degree of danger." [29]

There is no doubt that in a pioneering country, such a tax, particularly if it had to be paid in coin or notes (not too easy to obtain), would cause some hardship. It was easy to link—as the Republicans were quick to do—the drainage of currency with the government's payments of high interest rates to eastern stock jobbers and speculators. Jacobin ideas, too, became involved; and absurd things were said. Thus, a protest meeting in Pittsburgh, said in a memorial, "Our minds feel this with so much indignancy, that we are almost ready to wish for a state of revolution and the guillotine of France, for a short space, in order to inflict punishment on the miscreants that enervate and disgrace our government." [30]

With passions so inflamed, it was not hard for resistance and violence to follow. Western Pennsylvania became the seat of disaffection. Here, stills paying taxes were destroyed; Treasury agents, trying to collect the excise were assaulted, and local police and judicial authorities refused to move against rioters. Washington issued a proclamation in September, 1792, calling upon the recalcitrant Pennsylvania farmers to cease and desist; it was unheeded, and matters drifted from bad to worse. How this local protest over an unpopular tax was being blown up into general opposition to the government was revealed when federal commissioners came into the region to confer with Pennsylvanians. They regarded the law, these said, as "unequal and oppressive"; and they also complained against militia duty and the government's inability to force the British to evacuate the Western posts, put a stop to Indian attacks, and open the Mississippi to free navigation. By the summer of 1794 western Pennsylvania was actually in a state of open defiance: the Whiskey Rebellion had begun.

Risking great unpopularity, for troops were necessary, Hamilton called upon Washington to use every means possible "to suppress the insurrection and support the civil authority." [31] The very existence of government itself was at stake. The whole Cabinet, except for Randolph, agreed; and Washington proceeded to call upon the governors of Pennsylvania, New Jersey, Maryland, and Virginia for militia. A troop of some 15,000 men was assembled; all the details of their movement and supply were put in Hamilton's hands; and the march into the west—across difficult country, in the midst of a hostile population—was begun. There was no resistance, and discipline among the raw troops was maintained with a firmness and understanding that promised well for future law enforcement. By November, 1794, Pittsburgh having been reached, government offices once more were open and the excises were being paid: and a great victory had been won, for the central government's right to tax was upheld.

IN HIS MESSAGE TO CONGRESS OF NOVEMBER, 1794, WASHINGTON gave an account of his dealing with the uprising, and blamed it largely on the activities of the Democratic Societies. These "self-created societies" had "assumed the tone of condemnation" of the government's measures, hoping "by a more formal consort" to defeat its operations.[32] Nor was this all. The Democratic Societies were bitterly anti-English, and their hostility made a settle-

ment with Great Britain—indeed, the ordering of all foreign relations—increasingly difficult.

The fact is, America's position in the company of nations was
still very insecure. Nothing proved better how lightly it was held
than the defiance of the Algerine pirates. These sea marauders had
been preying on American ships in the Mediterranean and enslav-
ing American seamen while Algiers held them for ransom. There
had been Americans languishing in North African dungeons since
1785. Protests from the United States were unavailing; only a
show of force, it was apparent, could assure American ships
and men the right to navigate in the Mediterranean. A navy was
required; and this the Administration's opposition rejected, Madison and Giles once again being its spokesmen.

A bill to create a navy was brought up in January, 1794: the
building of four frigates and two smaller ships was to be authorized. To Madison, all considerations other than expense were
irrelevant; peace with Algiers could be had for "less money than
the armament would cost." [33] He was willing, then, to buy off the
pirates, as Jefferson had in 1787; this failing—astounding proposal!—he was prepared to hire protection for American shipping from one or another of the European powers. A bitter
wrangle ensued and the navy bill did not pass in the House until
March, the vote being 50 to 39. In the Senate, the lines for and
against were so closely drawn that the vote was a tie, and only
Vice-President Adams's vote in its favor carried the measure. Even
then the navy bill turned out to be a sad compromise: the ships
were to be laid down, but building on them was to cease at once
if a "peace" with Algiers was arranged.

Such an understanding was worked out in September, 1795. The
United States consented to pay both ransom for the prisoners
and annual tribute to the rulers of Algiers; even more humiliat-
ing, a ship for Algiers was to be built at American expense. The
total cost of this "peace" treaty was in the neighborhood of
$1,000,000; the uncompleted frigates remained in their yards;

and piracy, for the time being, was checked for "less money."

This was the time also to push for a settlement with Spain: for Spain, as one of France's foes, now realized that its American possessions were constantly in danger. In 1794, Thomas Pinckney was sent to Madrid; and in October, 1795, a treaty with Spain was finally written. It fixed the American southern boundary roughly at the thirty-first parallel of latitude, which is where the United States wanted it; each country promised not to meddle with Indian relations in the territory of the other; and both were to share in the free navigation of the Mississippi. Americans, for three years, were to have the right of deposit at New Orleans; thereafter, either New Orleans or "an equivalent establishment" was to be placed at the disposal of American ships and merchants "without paying any other duty than a fair price for the hire of the stores."

A complete understanding with Britain still remained; with it was linked the very substance of all of Hamilton's striving from the first hour of his assumption of public office—the survival of the United States. There were many points at which tensions and short tempers, in the relations between the two countries, had developed. America had no commercial treaty with Britain and her merchants therefore were not assured of equality of treatment—in fact, they were subjected to unjust discriminations—in British ports all over the world. The British not only continued to hold the Western posts, but they were seeking to establish new ones and were constantly at work among the Indians encouraging if not inciting them to resistance. There was wrangling over prewar claims: the British insisted they continued to find difficulties collecting pre-Revolutionary mercantile debts; the Americans demanded compensation for the some 3,000 Negro slaves British troops had carried off and freed. The Northern boundary remained unsettled, particularly troublesome being the location of the headwaters for the Mississippi River; with this was linked the question of the river's navigation.

And when, beginning with 1793, as the European war expanded, the British began to challenge the rights of the United States as a neutral, to seize ships and cargoes, and impress American seamen, friendly relations were strained almost to the breaking point. Most American public opinion was hostile to Great Britain, just as it was devoted to France. To seek a settlement at such a time required deep understanding, the utmost tact, and great courage. This Hamilton—in fact as early as 1789, when he established contact with the British agent, Lieutenant Colonel George Beckwith, in America—set himself to accomplish. The Jay Treaty of 1794 was really his work.

Hamilton was not buying peace at the expense of the national honor. Subsequent events have clearly demonstrated that the idea of neutral rights—when a world war rages—is largely a fiction. One temporizes with the power holding control of the seas, waiting for a postwar settlement, or one fights it. Certainly in 1793–1794, because America had no navy, its growing commerce was in great jeopardy. The British fleet was "the shield of the republic" to a greater extent in these years than in the whole of the nineteenth century. There was even a more important reason why an understanding, arrived at amicably, with Britain was imperative. The national existence depended upon Anglo-American trade. Fully 90 per cent of American imports came from Britain; in 1792, 60 per cent of all the goods carried between the two nations was in American bottoms (and by 1800, 95 per cent). In view of the fact that the national revenue was almost entirely derived from the duties on imports, and the refunding program and the stability of the national credit were tied in with the country's ability to obtain regular annual receipts, any disordering of the foreign trade struck at the vitals of America's "revenue and wealth."

This Hamilton knew: and this the Republicans refused to comprehend. They proposed, as a retaliatory measure, reprisals against British investors who held the government "stock" or owned private American securities. They also talked nonintercourse and, in fact, the House carried a bill to this effect, April 25, 1794, by a vote of 58 to 34. In the Senate, the vote was tied, and the bill was defeated only by Vice-President Adams's adverse vote. The Republicans persisted, trying to accomplish the same end by a joint resolution; this, too, was voted down, with Madison continuing as the leading advocate to the very end. It was in such a climate and with such high stakes involved that John Jay, Chief Justice of the United States Supreme Court, left America in May, 1794, to negotiate directly with Lord Grenville, the British Secretary of State for Foreign Affairs. Jay was Hamilton's appointee; his instructions were largely drawn up by Hamilton; the indignation and denunciation which greeted Jay, upon his return, he was compelled to share with Hamilton.

The treaty Jay brought back in 1794 was not a good treaty; but it was a treaty which prevented war and recognized the existence of American nationality, and to this extent Admiral Mahan surely was right when he characterized it as an event of "epochal significance." [34] The treaty was silent on impressments and was obscure, and perhaps worthless, on American neutral rights. The United States in effect recognized the British command of the seas and the British writing and reading of maritime law. The treaty made no provision for compensation for the Negro slaves. It virtually kept the West Indian trade closed to the United States.

On the other hand, this treaty of "amity and commerce" extended American trade full reciprocal rights ("a reciprocal and perfect liberty of commerce and navigation") in the British European territories. The East Indian ports were opened up to American ships. It created the peaceful machinery of joint commissions to settle the debt claims of the British merchants against Americans and the spoliation claims (as a result of British seizures of ships and cargoes) of Americans against Britain. And the United States achieved notable triumphs in the Northwest. The

Western posts were to be evacuated by June 1, 1796; there were to be reciprocal trading privileges for Americans and British in the northwestern territories of both countries; and a joint commission was provided to settle the northern boundary and look into the source of the Mississippi. (On this last, the boundary, as finally laid, was definitely favorable to America, as was the question of the Mississippi River.)

At only one point did Jay blunder, and this was in the case of the British West India trade. By Article 12 of the Treaty, only American vessels of limited tonnage might bring American wares into the islands; but they were denied the right to carry out of the islands, molasses, sugar, coffee, cocoa, or cotton; in fact, the United States surrendered any participation in the re-export of these tropical commodities. It is amusing, at this time, to note the presence of cotton on the list; Jay was unaware, apparently, of the beginnings of cotton culture in the United States. In any case, the opposition to the treaty was bitter and long-drawn-out; never did the Administration stand so low in the regard of Americans. Finally, however, the Republicans yielded and the Senate ratified the Jay Treaty, in June, 1795; but it struck out Article 12.

How well Hamilton knew what was at stake is revealed in a letter he wrote to Washington in 1794. He said then: If war "should extend to the total prohibition of her [Britain's] commodities, however brought, it deprives us of a supply for which no substitute can be found elsewhere—a supply necessary to us in peace, and more necessary to us if we are to go to war. It gives a sudden and violent blow to our revenue, which cannot easily, if at all, be repaired from other sources. It will be so great an interruption to commerce as may very possibly interfere with the payment of duties which have hitherto accrued, and bring the Treasury to an absolute stoppage of payment—an event which would *cut up credit* by the roots." [35]

On January 31, 1795, at last yielding to the pleadings of his friends, but with his great work completed, Alexander Hamilton left the Treasury. He was then forty years old. He wrote a final report, *The Second Report on the Public Credit*, which he addressed to the Senate on January 16 and January 20, 1795. In many ways, it is his outstanding public paper; for it is a record of lofty accomplishment, a statesman's handbook, and a text and guide for all fiscal officers thereafter. In his statement to Washington of August, 1792, Hamilton had used a phrase which he might have quoted as the motto of the report; it also sums up his achievement and his heritage to the American people. He had strived, he said, "to revive and establish credit, the palladium of public safety." [36]

The report presented in the greatest detail the history of the Treasury's work: the revenues which had been established; the provisions for funding the debt and for the payments of its interest; and the program pursued for debt retirement. None had more reason for self-congratulation; none a better right to advise his fellow citizens. He wrote: "And it is a matter of solid consolation that the result, presenting a state of our finances prosperous beyond expectation, solicits the public councils to enter, with zeal and decision, upon measures commensurate with the greatness of the interests to be promoted." [37]

He could afford to be discursive. He warned his countrymen that the imposition of taxes would always be unpopular; and that there always would be political leaders ready to expand the services of government but reluctant to make provisions for their financing. He called for debt extinguishment. He denominated credit, public and private, a country's "invigorating principle." Credit had sustained the country's economy from the beginning; it had assured the successful outcome of the Revolution; it was at the foundation of the country's "increase of national and individual welfare." Credit was necessary in war; it was of particular importance "to a young country, with moderate pecuniary capital, and not a very various industry." He asked his countrymen to consider long before imposing taxes on income derived from the public "stock"; and solemnly appealed to them to safeguard jealously the property rights of foreigners who had invested in America. In this latter connection, he wisely pointed out: "The security of each creditor is inseparable from the security of all creditors. The boundary between foreigner and citizen would not be deemed a sufficient barrier against extending the precedent of an invasion of the rights of the former to the latter."

And these were his closing remarks—and his valedictory: [38]

It is wisdom, in every case, to cherish whatever is useful and to guard against its abuse. It will be the truest policy of the United States to give all possible energy to the public credit, by a firm adherence to its strictest maxims; and yet to avoid the ills of an excessive employment of it by true economy and system in the public expenditures; by steadily cultivating peace; and by using sincere, efficient and persevering endeavors to diminish present debts, prevent the accumulation of new, and secure the discharge, within a reasonable period, of such as it may be at any time matter of necessity to contract. It will be wise to cultivate and foster private credit by an exemplary observance of the principles of public credit, and to guard against the misuse of the former by a speedy and vigorous administration of justice, and by taking away every temptation to run in debt, founded in the hope of evading the just claims of creditors.

Critical Years, 1795-1800

AT THE END OF JANUARY, 1795, ALEXANDER HAMILTON QUIT PHILA-delphia to return to New York to repair his private fortunes. The Hamilton family was a large one, and it continued to grow. When the Hamiltons went to Albany for a short stay, while they were hunting for a house in New York, Philip, the eldest child, was thirteen and Angelica was eleven. In addition, there were Alexander, who was nine, James Alexander, seven, and John Church, three. William Stephen was born in 1797 and Eliza in 1799. There are a few glimpses remaining to us of a close family circle. James Alexander, writing when he was grown man, remembered the daily scene at the breakfast table with Eliza Hamilton behind the coffee service buttering bread, as the younger children recited their lessons. When Hamilton and the older boys came down, the youngsters scampered off, leaving the dining room to their elders. Hamilton liked children, and he and his wife took a friend's daughter into their home and brought her up along with their own.

The eighteenth century kept a proper distance between parents and children; Hamilton's letters to his youngsters are more austere than fond in expression. When nine-year-old Angelica went off to school in 1793, her father told her how pleased he was that she had begun studying French. She should always apologize if she knew herself in the wrong, but she should act with "so much politeness, good manners and circumspection" [1] that she would have no need to ask for forgiveness. But the affection and humor crept through. A rather formal letter to Philip, then nine, ends "A good night to my darling son." [2] James asked Hamilton to draft a speech the young man was to deliver at a Columbia College public exercise. The manuscript went off, and with it a note: "My dear James—I have prepared for you a Thesis on Discretion. You may need it. . . ." [3]

Philip, the eldest, was the center of the household, and Hamilton was deeply attached to him. Philip was bright and high-spirited; Hamilton, following the pattern of eighteenth-century fathers, sought to guide his footsteps. When the young man graduated from Columbia College, he drew up a set of rules for his governance. From the first of April to the first of October "Mr. Philip Hamilton" was to rise not later than six o'clock; the rest of the year not later than seven. "If earlier, he will deserve commendation." Bedtime was at ten. From rising until nine, he was to read law; he was then to proceed to the office where he would write and read law until dinner. After that, he was to return to his lawbooks until five. From five to seven, he might do as he chose. From seven until ten, he might read or study what he liked. After twelve on Saturday, he was "at liberty to amuse himself." On Sunday, after attendance at morning church, he might give the rest of the day to "innocent recreations." And Hamilton ended, "He must not depart from any of these rules without my permission." [4]

This promising young man's life was over when he was less than twenty. At a theater he quarreled over politics with a partisan of Aaron Burr; a challenge followed and Philip was killed on the dueling ground at Weehawken. The parents were grief-stricken, and to commemorate his memory, their youngest child, born in 1802, was also named Philip.

Hamilton was very close to his wife's parents, the Schuylers, and to one of her sisters, Angelica, who married John Barker Church. Hamilton corresponded frequently with Angelica Church and he and Church were associated in many business enterprises. (Reference to Church's connection with the Bank of New York has already been made.) When Hamilton drafted his will, in July, 1795, he expressed the hope that Church, who was his principal creditor, would relieve the others of loss. With Mrs. Church, Hamilton was on terms of affectionate friendship. Of him Angelica Church wrote to her sister, "Ah! Bess! You were a lucky girl to get so clever and so good a companion." [5] And in another letter, she sent her love "to Alexander the good, and the amiable." [6] When Hamilton resigned as Secretary of the Treasury, he wrote to Mrs. Church not to worry: public affairs were in a good train; he had determined to take some thought for his own, therefore, and to "indulge in my domestic happiness the more freely." [7]

Church, who was one of the wealthy men of the day, had as many interests in England as in America; and the Churches were frequently crossing the ocean, although for a considerable length of time they lived in London. At the end of 1799, they were residing in America; and we catch a picture of Mrs. Church and Hamilton, in the correspondence of Harrison Gray Otis. (True, Otis's tone is nasty; but the gayety shows through the innuendo.) The occasion was a dinner in the home of Mr. Samuel Breck, in his handsome suburban residence outside of Philadelphia, where Hamilton had gone on the business of the army. Mrs. Church, reports Otis, who was a "mirror of affectation," dropped her shoe-bow. Her sister, "a young wild flirt" picked it up and put it into Hamilton's buttonhole, saying, "There, brother, I have made you a knight." Mrs. Church wanted to know of what order, "he can't be a knight of the garter in this country." "True, sister," said the girl, "but he would be if you would let him." [8]

Hamilton liked the society of women and he shone in their

company. Of that same dinner, Otis wrote that he was "very trifling in his conversation with ladies." Otis was in a carping mood; but "trifling" was undoubtedly the correct word. A man as busy as Hamilton, and as closely observed by friends and enemies alike in a period given to letter writing and ill-natured gossip, scarcely has the leisure for the elaborate intrigue which women of his own social standing in the eighteenth century expected and engaged in.

Once he did become involved, with a Maria Reynolds, who appealed to him for financial help—her husband had deserted her—and who ended by becoming his mistress. The affair had taken place in Philadelphia in 1791; Mrs. Reynolds had been given money; and before long it turned out that she and her husband, who had knowledge of the connection from the start, were engaged in systematically blackmailing Hamilton. Late in 1792, Reynolds and a man named Jacob Clingman, both then in jail, told Republican leaders they had proof that Hamilton had engaged in buying up old claims against the government—using Reynolds as his agent—and had amassed a large sum from these illegal transactions. Armed with letters and documents obtained from Reynolds and his wife, Hamilton was visited by three Republican Congressmen, James Monroe among them.

Hamilton recited his unhappy story of the low affair with Mrs. Reynolds, told of how he had been gulled, and then proved—from letters he had from the pair—that the sums Reynolds had received had been for the purchase of his silence and not to finance the alleged speculations. Hamilton's questioners were satisfied and left, promising not to return to Clingman or Reynolds the papers that sought to implicate Hamilton in frauds on the government. But the papers appeared publicly in 1797 when a Republican hack, in a work published in installments, called a *History of the United States for the Year 1796*, printed them along with other information that could have been obtained only from Monroe. Hamilton hoped that the three whom he had

seen in 1792 would come to his defense. From two he received as-
surances that satisfied him: they had nothing to do with the
disclosures. Monroe, on the other hand, was evasive; and it became increasingly clear that in one way or another he was involved.

Hamilton, to defend his public honor, exposed his private
shame, in a pamphlet he published in 1797, in which he retailed
all the incidents of the sordid business.[9] He printed the Reynolds'
blackmailing letters, the receipts for the moneys extorted from
him, his exchanges with the Congressmen, and an account of
Monroe's slippery part in the exposure. Hamilton cleared his
name, as a result, but the price to the peace and happiness of
himself and his family was a heavy one.

In 1799, Hamilton was ready to acquire a country estate. When
he returned to New York, the family took a house at 56 Pine
Street, then moved to 58 Partition Street (now Fulton Street),
and moved again to 26 Broadway, where they remained until
1802, "The Grange" then being ready. "The Grange" was deep
in the country—it was nine miles from Bowling Green—and
something of its inaccessibility may be gathered from the fact
that stagecoaches ran only three times a week from the tip of
the island to what is now Broadway and 42nd Street. The property was extensive—it stretched from the Hudson River to
present-day St. Nicholas Avenue and from 141st to 145th Streets
—and the house erected on it was a large structure of wood over
brick, embellished with the porches and columns that were the
fashion of the day. The building cost £1,550; this was a goodly
sum, as can be gathered from the fact that a workman engaged
on the house received, for three and one-half years, a total of
$424.50. The estate had a farm and an extensive garden with
glasshouses, where Hamilton raised tropical and subtropical
plants.

The house was filled with fine prints and books. Hamilton
owned a Dürer and a copy of Mantegna's "Triumph of Caesar";

his library included a collection of French books, Plutarch, Gibbon, Sterne, Bacon, Hobbes, Sir Thomas Browne, and Montaigne. He liked music and drove down to hear the Philharmonic Society when it gave performances at Snow's Hotel. Up to 1799, Hamilton kept careful household accounts, and from them we get some notion of his interests and activities. In 1795, he paid out £18.6.5 for French tuition for his children; in 1796, $60 for duties on a pipe of wine; the same year, $50 for books and $20 for a subscription to the Dancing Assembly. He was generous to the needy and gave sizable sums to individuals and the almshouse. On May 12, 1802, appears the sad little item: "Expenses Philip's funeral, $266.11."

Hamilton's return to the private practice of law was greeted by a series of testimonial dinners. At that held by the Chamber of Commerce of New York, where two hundred guests sat down, fourteen regular toasts and five voluntary ones were drunk. The company, among others, gave "Liberty and Law," "Social Order and Social Happiness," and "Integrity and Knowledge"; while Hamilton proposed "The Merchants of New York." Before long, Hamilton took his place at the head of the New York bar and by 1800 he was reporting an annual income of $12,000 and a worth of £10,000. This came almost entirely from his law work; the estate that he left, aside from "The Grange," was largely in wild lands in western New York and on his death brought very little to discharge his sizable debts. Hamilton's clients included such important figures in the city's business life as the British house of Constable, the representative of Willink, the Amsterdam banking house, the Holland Land Company, and the Georgia Company. In addition, because of his close familiarity with admiralty law, he played an important part in the growing insurance business of New York, as counsel. He rode the circuit, made frequent trips to Albany, by sloop or mail stage, and appeared as counsel for the State of New York and the United States. His old friend Robert Troup, watching him at work at this time, declared that Hamilton was progressing to "greater maturity," and that "his powers are now enormous." [10]

HAMILTON'S HOPE THAT HE MIGHT BE ABLE TO QUIT PUBLIC LIFE was an idle one; as the leading Federalist, the confidant of Washington, and the close friend of Washington's Cabinet and of his successor's, John Adams, he understandably was heavily involved in the country's concerns. During 1796–1800, despite the settlement with Great Britain and Spain, the threat of war was ever present. The French Directory, the successor of the Jacobins, continued to trouble the waters of American affairs—through the friends it had among leading Republicans, the activities of the Democratic Societies, and by open intervention in American politics. On the eve of the Presidential elections of 1796, in an effort to discredit Washington—for the Directory assumed he was to run again—the French Minister of Foreign Affairs announced the suspension of diplomatic relations with the United States.

Americans were told, almost in so many words, that if Washington were defeated, Jefferson elected, and a new treaty written with France to undo the work of the Jay Treaty, America would once more be back in the French favor.

Hamilton, wholly committed to American neutrality, saw that foreign relations were all of a piece. The Jay Treaty was the capstone of the entire structure; but an important part of it was putting the country in a state of defense. In the debates and deliberations in Philadelphia he was consulted constantly; again and again, he entered the lists as an active participant.

The Republicans were bitterly opposed to the Jay Treaty. Jefferson, writing in November, 1795, called it an "execrable thing"; and he went on, "I trust the popular branch of the legislature will disapprove of it, and thus rid us of this infamous act, which is really nothing more than a treaty of alliance between England

and the Anglo-men of this country against the legislature and the people of the United States." [11] It was to counteract Jefferson's influence, that Hamilton appeared in defense of the Treaty.

Beginning in July, 1795, and continuing into 1796, Hamilton wrote for two New York newspapers a long series of essays over the signature of "Camillus." [12] (Jay and King also took part.) These were a careful exposition of the Treaty, article by article, and they showed Hamilton's great command of international law and the realities of international relations. The intention behind this effort—that Hamilton was striving desperately to keep the United States out of war—showed in the second essay. "Few nations," said Hamilton, "can have stronger inducements than the United States to cultivate peace. Their infant state in general, their want of a marine in particular, to protect their commerce, would render war, in an extreme degree, a calamity. It would not only arrest our present rapid progress to strength and prosperity, but would probably throw us back into a state of debility and impoverishment, from which it would require years to emerge." [13] This wise counsel finally carried the day; but it was not until April, 1796, that the House of Representatives—intruding itself into the treaty-making power on the ground that only its appropriations could implement the convention—voted 51 to 48 to accept it.

The Federalists had another opportunity to broadcast the same message; this was in Washington's Farewell Address (issued September 19, 1796), in which he besought his fellow Americans to support their national government. Washington was pleading not so much for isolation as for the integrity and independence of his country. (Hamilton had worked closely with Washington on the Address, and while the ideas in it were shared by both, the actual writing was Hamilton's.) The Address [14] said, in part:

Against the insidious wiles of foreign influence (I conjure you to believe me, fellow-citizens) the jealousy of a free people ought to be *constantly* awake; since history and experience prove that foreign influence is one of the most baneful foes of Republican government....

The great rule of conduct for us, in regard to foreign nations, is in extending our commercial relations, to have with them as little *political* connection as possible. So far as we have already formed engagements let them be fulfilled with perfect good faith.—Here let us stop.

Europe has a set of primary interests, which to us have none, or a very remote relation. Hence she must be engaged in frequent controversies, the causes of which are essentially foreign to our concerns. Hence, therefore, it must be unwise in us to implicate ourselves, by artificial ties, in the ordinary vicissitudes of her politics, or the ordinary combinations and collisions of her friendships, or enmities.

Our detached and distant situation invites and enables us to pursue a different course. If we remain one people, under an efficient government, the period is not far off, when we may defy material injury from external annoyance; when we may take such an attitude as will cause the neutrality, we may at any time resolve upon, to be scrupulously respected;... when we may choose peace or war, as our interest, guided by justice shall counsel.

France's reply was in effect an open declaration of war against American commerce. Ships were stopped; their cargoes were seized; and decrees were issued which ordered American ships forfeit if they tried to engage in any commercial intercourse with British ports or the British possessions overseas. From 1796 to 1800, when diplomatic relations were resumed, Americans reported 1,853 cases of spoliations by the French with a total damage in excess of $15 millions. The British offered to convoy American vessels; but this was rejected.

John Adams, now President, at this time saw eye to eye with Hamilton. An effort should be made to re-establish diplomatic relations with France; and the country should be put on guard. There was no war party in the United States. Hamilton, writing to McHenry, Adams's Secretary of War, early in 1798, declared, "There is a very general and strong aversion to war in the minds of the people of this country." At the same time he was opposed to an embargo and an alliance with Great Britain.[15] Defensive measures, however, required the arming of merchant ships, the building of the frigates authorized during the trouble with Algiers, the raising of a provisional army, the augmentation of revenues through new taxes, and the floating of a loan. The basis of foreign policy was realism. "Real *firmness* is good for every-thing. *Strut* is good for nothing," [16] Hamilton had written to Wolcott, the Secretary of the Treasury, in June, 1797.

Meanwhile Adams had sent, in the fall of 1797, a mission to France, made up of C. C. Pinckney and John Marshall, both of whom were Federalists, and Elbridge Gerry, who was a Re-publican. They were privately received by Talleyrand, who had become the French Minister of Foreign Affairs, but no official reception was accorded them. Long months of silence ensued, as French depredations continued and the Republicans at home charged the Administration with withholding vital information.

What was actually occurring was one of the most amazing intrigues in diplomatic annals. As the commissioners waited in France, they were visited by three agents of Talleyrand who, speaking for the Minister, demanded a bribe for Talleyrand and his associates and a "loan" to the French government; only then would a new treaty, respecting American commercial rights, be drawn up. Marshall and Pinckney received these overtures in-dignantly; Gerry temporized, succumbing to the French blandish-ments, which were particularly directed at him. In the spring of 1798, Marshall and Pinckney quit Paris but Gerry lingered on until July. In any case, the mission was over.

The dispatches of the commissioners, telling this outrageous story, did not arrive in Philadelphia until March, 1798; Adams, aware that their explosive contents might precipitate hostilities, sought to hold them back; but the goading of Republicans forced his hand. He sent them, entire, to Congress, at the demand of the House of Representatives, early in April, deleting only the names of Talleyrand's emissaries; these were designated as X, Y, and Z. In consequence, the incident has always been known as the "XYZ Affair."

The Republicans were dismayed at this evidence of cynicism

and contempt on the part of their cherished France; and the country, for the first time since 1792, closed ranks behind the Federalists. During 1798 and 1799, the United States was united, and the Federalists seemed secure; it was Adams's own desire to seek an accommodation with France that ended his party's short-lived triumph and inevitably led to the Republican victory of 1800.

Congress quickly followed Adams's lead and in the month of July, 1798, it put the country on a war footing. All treaties with France were abrogated; commercial relations with France and her possessions were suspended; the regular army was raised to 13,000 and a provisional army was set up; new taxation—this time on houses and land—was provided; the building of the frigates authorized in 1794, was ordered resumed. Fearful of internal dissention and even subversion, because of the large numbers of recently admitted immigrants in the United States, Congress also passed the four Alien and Sedition Acts. These stepped up the period for the completion of naturalization from five to fourteen years; allowed the President to deport undesirable aliens out of the country; imposed penalties for conspiracy against the government; and permitted the federal authorities to bring to trial persons writing against the government or its members, or even seeking to bring them into disrepute.

This is no place to discuss the Alien and Sedition Laws. The American government, again and again, when in the midst of war—and an undeclared war with France did last until 1800—has taken steps to protect itself against subversion. The Sedition Law of 1798 probably was too loosely drawn; remedies against personal slander and libel were always available under the state laws. Hamilton felt so, and, in a letter to Wolcott, he said of the Sedition Bill that there were parts of it "which, according to a cursory view, appear to me highly exceptionable, and such as, more than any thing else, may endanger civil war.... I hope sincerely the thing may not be hurried through. Let us not establish a tyranny. Energy is a very different thing from violence." [17]

The intemperate character of partisanship and class hostilities in the early days of the Republic has already been alluded to. There can be no doubt that this was one of the unhappy influences of the French Revolution on America; the general misunderstanding of Hamilton's intention and the unjustified assumption that his leading concern was the aggrandizement of men of wealth also played their parts. The attack on Hamilton's personal life, in connection with the Reynolds scandal, was only typical of the depths to which responsible men like James Monroe were willing to sink to destroy a political antagonist. Even Washington was not spared personal abuse and slander. Thus Benjamin Franklin Bache, a Republican editor, hailed Washington's departure from the Presidency in these words: "The name of Washington from this day ceases to give a currency to political iniquity." [18] And Thomas Paine paid his respects to Washington thus: "treacherous in private friendship, and a hypocrite in public life ... apostate ... imposter." [19] Washington was deeply hurt and he approved the writing and passing of the Sedition Act.

IT WAS TO THE NEW ARMY THAT HAMILTON'S CHIEF THOUGHTS WERE directed, however. It was obvious that George Washington must be its commander-in-chief; but who was to be second in command—in effect, in charge? For it was apparent that Washington would be only the titular head. Here that rift began to develop between Hamilton and Adams that was to contribute so much to the failure and collapse of the Federalists. Hamilton's friends reached the ear of Washington, Hamilton must be named his second; Hamilton's allies in Adams's Cabinet were equally insistent and began to intrigue behind Adams's back; but the President was obdurate. He was prepared to name Hamilton one of Washington's generals, but not the leading one. At this point Washington stepped in: Hamilton was to be his first major-general and at the head of the list; he let it be inferred that otherwise he would refuse to take the command. Adams yielded and never forgave Hamilton and his friends; Hamilton was named a major-general with the title of Inspector-General as well.

Hamilton was in his element. The expectation that Washington would not actually take charge of the army was justified, and it was Hamilton who set about the many tasks of recruitment, training, and supply with his customary vigor. If the French were to land on the American shore, if, perhaps, in combination with Great Britain, Spain was to be driven out of Florida and Louisiana, if internal disorders were to threaten, at least the government would have at its command a dependable armed force.

Is Hamilton to be condemned for this concern over his country's safety? Everywhere, France had become a threat to world peace; Napoleon's Italian triumphs inevitably presaged more glorious dreams of conquest; there was no assurance that the American continent would remain untouched. The United States already, to all intents and purposes, was at war, although its actions were confined to the sea exclusively. A large number, at least 45, warships were outfitted and sent out against French armed vessels; some 365 privately owned vessels were put in commission and authorized to capture French armed merchantmen; the new navy began to distinguish itself in combat. The sea lanes were kept open and America's commerce, upon which so much depended, continued to be carried on the high seas. Hamilton was no warmonger—he never advocated a war declaration—nor was he a Caesar; he was seeking to establish those reasonable precautions a patriot had to advocate.

Meanwhile Adams kept the door open for negotiation, and early in 1799 he was led to assume that Talleyrand this time would receive an American envoy. Taking no one into his confidence, Adams sent a nomination to the Senate; and suddenly the positions of the two parties were spectacularly reversed. The Republicans were gleeful, the Federalists—smarting as well from the censure heaped upon them because of the Alien and Sedition Laws—saw the end of their short period of power. In an effort to tie the President's hands—for he would not yield—the Senate insisted that a mission of three instead of a single plenipotentiary be named.

This was the origin of the second mission to France that set out in late 1799. It was formally received but negotiations lagged as France, with Napoleon now the chief of state as First Consul, laid its ambitious plans for European conquest. A peace between the United States and France was finally patched up in September, 1800; it was not more than a truce, for while it did suspend all the old treaties, it made no provision for the satisfaction of American claims. Hostilities, however, were terminated with the recognition of American commercial rights and a strict definition of contraband. Meanwhile, at the order of Congress the President had begun to dismantle the provisional army, and on June 1, 1800, Hamilton resigned his commission. He did not know it: but it was to be his last public office.

PERHAPS BECAUSE THEY SENSED THEY WERE FAILING AND THAT THE race was run, the Federalists turned savagely on each other. Adams, smarting from their indifference and contempt, finally got rid of Pickering, his Secretary of State, and McHenry, his Secretary of War, whom he regarded as "Hamilton's spies." Hamilton took up the cudgels in defense of his friends by writing a long, bad-tempered, personal attack on the President which he called *The Public Conduct and Character of John Adams, Esq., President of the United States.*[20] It was undoubtedly meant for private circulation among fellow Federalists; but when Aaron Burr, Hamilton's adversary in New York, obtained a copy and proceeded to distribute it among Republican editors, Hamilton was compelled to acknowledge his handiwork. The ill-advised document hurt Hamilton; it hurt Adams; and it seriously affected the chances the Federalists had in the election of 1800.

Badly disunited, the Federalists named John Adams and C. C. Pinckney as their candidates. The Republicans named Jefferson and Burr. There was some talk among Federalists of knifing Adams and advancing Pinckney's cause; all this was idle intrigue, for Pinckney himself would not be party to it. The contest was bitterly waged and for a time was close, but when Pinckney's own state of South Carolina voted for Jefferson and Burr, the Republicans were triumphant. Jefferson and Burr each received 73 electoral votes; Adams obtained 65 and Pinckney 64. Because of the tie—a contingency obviously not foreseen by the makers of the Constitution—the choice of President was thrown into the House of Representatives.

There were Federalists, in their profound dislike of Jefferson, who were ready to vote for Burr. Hamilton labored hard to dissuade them, but he was not too successful. To Gouverneur Morris, Hamilton wrote in December, 1800, "If there be a man in the world I ought to hate, it is Jefferson. With Burr I have always been personally well. But the public good must be paramount to every private consideration." [21] Too many Federalists were embittered over the equivocal role Hamilton had played in the preliminaries of the election; and not his advice but other considerations—possibly even a bargain with Federalists—won the day for Jefferson.

So ended Hamilton's public career. He may very well have been aware of it, although he was only forty-five years old. He read Jefferson's inaugural address with some satisfaction. Jefferson, he saw, was ready to assume the responsibilities of office, for he was pledging to devote himself to the "honest payment of our debts and the sacred preservation of the public faith; encouragement of agriculture, and of commerce as its handmaid." [22]

Hamilton had every reason to say that Jefferson's address was "virtually a candid retraction of past misapprehensions, and a pledge to the community that the new President will not lend himself to dangerous innovations, but in essential points tread in the steps of his predecessors." [23] The Federalist party was never to return to national office; but Hamilton's work was secure. Jefferson, too, now that he was President, understood that the "preservation of the public faith" was "the palladium of public safety."

Alexander Hamilton

& Aaron Burr

HAMILTON HAD RETIRED FROM ACTIVE AFFAIRS: HE WAS BUSY WITH his important and prosperous law practice, his family, and his beloved "Grange," where he spent long hours on the house and grounds. In late 1802 he wrote to his old friend C. C. Pinckney in South Carolina, half wistfully, half seriously, "A garden, you know, is a very useful refuge of a disappointed politician." [1] And in the same year, to Gouverneur Morris, he admitted he was out of the swim of things: "I often hear at the corner of the streets important Federal secrets, of which I am ignorant." [2]

He began to turn his thoughts more to religion. From the beginning, he had seen as one of the perils of the French Revolution its assaults on morality and churches. Hamilton had been a religious man in the eighteenth-century sense: he had believed in the doctrines of Christianity and yet had not formally bound himself to any creed. As a child, he had been brought up in the Anglican Church; and he now renewed his associations with that church. He believed that a sense of dedication had gone out of American life: its two great sustaining forces, God and country, seemed to be weakening.

In 1802, in a long letter he wrote to James A. Bayard of Delaware, he suggested that the Federalists try again, giving more attention to Christianity and the Constitution than they had heretofore. Human nature he continued to be distrustful of: "Men are rather reasoning than reasonable animals, for the most part governed by the impulse of passion." He and his friends had "erred in relying so much on the rectitude and utility of their measures as to have neglected the cultivation of popular favor, by fair and justifiable expedients."

Hamilton then proposed the creation of a "Christian Constitutional Society"—an organization of clubs throughout the country, devoted to Christianity and the Constitution, which, nevertheless would use "all lawful means in *concert* to promote the election of fit men." [3] It is easy to read a vicious intention into such a scheme; but that Hamilton did not mean it so we see from his further suggestions that "charitable" institutions be created as part of the general program. Among these were to be immigrant aid societies and free vocational academies. Bayard gave Hamilton no comfort, and we hear no more of the plan.

Hamilton was out of politics, and yet of it. In 1801, he helped found the New York *Evening Post* as a Federalist organ; he did not write for it under his own name, but much of its general position was inspired by him. He used the *Evening Post* to hail the acquisition of Louisiana in 1803, in the face of the opposition notably of New England Federalists who saw in the purchase a portent: the decline in influence of the old states as new ones, carved out of the territory, would be admitted to the union, was inevitable. There was a company of these New England Federalists who began to talk of secession: Hamilton sternly turned his face against them. They decided to negotiate with Aaron Burr in 1804, as some of them had in 1800. That Hamilton no longer was the dominant figure, even in his own New York City, may be noted from the fact that the *Evening Post* looked with favor on this alliance.

IN 1804, ONCE AGAIN AS THEY HAD IN 1791, HAMILTON AND BURR'S
paths were crossing politically. In certain ways, these two extraordinary men were alike; in others so different that antipathy was
bound to be their relationship. They were almost of the same
age—Burr was a year younger; they had matured early; they
were distinguished advocates and led the New York bar; they
were charming in manner, each having hosts of personal friends;
they were highly ambitious. But Burr had been wellborn and
carefully nurtured: he was the grandson of Jonathan Edwards
and the son of the second president of Princeton College. There
had been no obstacles in his way, when, after a distinguished
career in the Revolution, where he had risen to the rank of
colonel, he returned to New York to become an important and
dazzling figure in its social, political, and business life.

Yet Burr, despite his security, his aristocratic habits, his in-
quiring mind, was a man of no principles in the political sense.
He was one of Jeremy Bentham's early votaries in American and
to that curious man's elaborate programs for society's reforms
he gave lip service; but Burr was willing to tinker with change
only as it added to his own personal position. He was a Fran-
cophile when devotion to France was fashionable and popular;
he turned against France, and led his New York followers to
join the war party when the "XYZ Affair" shocked American
opinion into an awareness of its real danger. Burr could run
with the hares and hunt with the hounds: be an avowed Republican, and treat with the Federalists; support the Hamilton
program or not, as the exigencies of the moment and his own
advantage dictated.

With no convictions, Burr could become a successful politician;
in fact, he was a great power in New York City and New York
State for fifteen years. His strength was to be found in the Society of Tammany, which he did not help organize, whose titular
head he never became, but which he quickly came to dominate.
This club of the sans-culottes—the members were largely disfranchised because among them were to be found the humblest

laborers and artisans of New York who possessed no property—
Burr led. As the first "Boss" of Tammany, and by chicanery, he
helped his cohorts obtain the ballot; and Tammany proceeded,
increasingly, to dominate the affairs of the city. Burr was that
anomaly and threat to order one occasionally finds in politics:
the aristocratic leader of a popular party.

With such a devoted following, Burr could move in and out
of New York politics almost at will. In 1791, he challenged the
Federalist domination of New York when he suddenly appeared
as a candidate for the United States Senate against Philip Schuyler, Hamilton's father-in-law; he won, to go to the Senate at the
age of thirty-five. The next year, he struck another blow at
Federalist control, when he helped to defeat John Jay, running
for governor of the state. In the Senate, Burr opposed Hamilton's
financial program; soon he was close to the Virginia dynasty and
a member of that Virginia–New York coalition that was the
basis of the Republican party's strength. The Clintons, Livingstons, and Burr in New York, by joining hands with Jefferson
and Madison in Virginia, constituted a force to be reckoned with.

As early as 1792, Hamilton had formed his opinions about
Burr, and these he was to repeat countless times in letters and
private conversations. When he was asked about Burr and Clinton
as candidates for Vice-President, he minced no words. Clinton
he disapproved of; but he was solid and he possessed integrity.
Burr was something else again: "I fear the other gentleman is
unprincipled both as a public and a private man." [4] Burr was determined to be head of a popular party and climb to the highest
honors of state "and as much higher as circumstances may permit." Burr lived extravagantly, his private affairs were embar-
rassed, he was "bold, enterprising and intriguing." There was
nothing personal about these strictures: Hamilton's political principles, as their first requirement, demanded that only honorable
men be invested with public office.

Burr was not returned to the United States Senate; he was not
disconcerted, and stood for the New York Assembly, the legis-

lature's lower house, to which he was elected in 1797. In 1799, his friends in the legislature challenged Federalist leadership in still another sphere, that of banking. They chartered the Manhattan Company to provide New York City with a water supply —but also gave the company the right to use its surplus capital "in the purchase of public or other stock, or in any other monied transactions or operations not inconsistent with the constitution and laws of this State or of the United States, for the sole benefit of the said company." [5] To its promoters, this meant a bank; and, at once, the Manhattan Company did set itself up in the banking business as a rival to the Bank of New York and the New York branch of the United States Bank, both of which were being managed by Hamilton's friends.

The hue and cry raised against Burr and his friends, for their alleged duplicity, did not hurt them more than momentarily. In 1800, Burr was again roiling the waters, and so successfully that New York was snatched away from the Federalists and chose Republican electors for the Presidential election of that year. Not only that; Burr was also a real Presidential possibility. Hamilton tried to sound the alarm to his friends; Burr was the man to watch. Writing to James A. Bayard, in August, 1800, Hamilton said, "The latter [Burr] is intriguing with all his might in New Jersey, Rhode Island, and Vermont; and there is a possibility of some success in his intrigues . . . if it is so, Burr will certainly attempt to reform the government *à la Buonaparte.* He is as unprincipled and dangerous a man as any country can boast— as true a Cataline as ever met in midnight conclave." [6]

After 1801, when the Presidency almost seemed within his grasp, Burr's star began to fall, slowly at first and then precipitously. Jefferson turned against him, rendered suspicious by Federalist support of him in the balloting for the Presidency; none of Burr's friends could obtain federal office—the Vice-President was isolated. In New York, the Livingstons and the Clintons, with whom Burr was allied and with whom he controlled the Republican party, also broke with him. Thus things drifted until 1804, when Burr sought to rehabilitate his fortunes in New York: he would run for governor of his own state.

The Republicans would not nominate him. He could not openly run as a Federalist; but he encouraged Federalist support, and those desperate New Englanders, talking of secession, began to weave their web and spin their fancies, with Burr at the center. Burr would not openly commit himself; but the Federalist took up the canvass for him in New York, hoping thus to re-establish their power in the North. All but Hamilton, and it may be that his opposition was crucial. For Burr was defeated in a close election, and in June, 1804, he, too, like his great opponent Hamilton, stood at the end of a long road.

Although neither was yet fifty years old, could it be possible that Hamilton and Burr knew the race was run? Possibly Hamilton did, for he permitted himself to drift into a situation from which he could have extricated himself in the beginning; it is difficult to be certain about Burr. Hamilton was finding peace and consolation in religion, Burr's mind—as subsequent events were to reveal—continued to be filled with all sorts of extravagant plots and stratagems.

But Burr needed vindication. On June 18, 1804, after the election was over, he sent a letter to Hamilton by a friend. The letter, in effect, was a challenge to a duel. It ran: [7]

Sir,

I send for your perusal a letter signed Charles D. Cooper, which, though apparently published some time ago, has but very recently come to my knowledge. Mr. Van Ness, who does me the favour to deliver this, will point out to you that clause of the letter to which I particularly request your attention. You must perceive, sir, the necessity of a prompt and unqualified acknowledgment or denial of the use of any expressions which would warrant the assertions of Mr. Cooper.

Burr had waited almost two months before calling Hamilton out. The incident to which Burr alluded had occurred in April, at a dinner in Albany. Probably Hamilton had talked freely about Burr, as he had so many times in the past. Cooper had been present at the dinner; and he had written two letters afterward. In one, dated April 12, he said, "Gen. Hamilton ... has come out decidedly against Burr; indeed when he was here he spoke of him as a dangerous man and ought not to be trusted." In the other, dated, April 23, he repeated the same sentiments and added, "I could detail to you a still more despicable opinion which General Hamilton had expressed of Mr. Burr." [8] Both letters were printed in the Albany *Register*. It was clear, according to the code then commonly accepted by gentlemen, that Burr's honor had been impugned.

Hamilton took two days to reply; and then he entered upon a long and tortuous argument. He was convinced he could not "without manifest impropriety, make the avowal or disavowal" [9] which Burr asked. Burr did not inquire into the specific remarks he had made; they were then probably "within the limits to which the animadversions of political opponents upon each other may justifiably extend." He came back again to Cooper's report: what exactly had he said? "I stand ready to avow or disavow promptly and explicitly any precise or definite opinion which I may be charged with having declared of any gentleman ... I trust on more reflection you will see the matter in the same light with me. If not, I can only regret the circumstances and must abide the consequences."

Hamilton could have denied having said anything "despicable," and that would have ended the matter. He would not; instead, he asked for particulars, and Burr, of course, could not furnish them. Burr proceeded to broaden the terms of disagreement, and now Hamilton could not escape. Burr replied the next day: [10]

Political opposition can never absolve gentlemen from the necessity of a rigid adherence to the laws of honor, and the rules of decorum. I neither claim such privilege nor indulge it in others.

The common sense of mankind affixes to the epithet adopted by Doctor Cooper the idea of dishonor. It has been publicly applied to me under the sanction of your name. The question is ... whether you have authorized this application, either directly or by uttering expressions or opinions derogatory to my honor.

A further exchange ensued, part of it conducted between the seconds both men had chosen. The fact is, letters by the principals and their representatives were passed back and forth during the whole of the following week. In one of them, Hamilton's second made this statement, in effect, a disclaimer, as far as Cooper was concerned: [11]

... he would be able to answer consistently with his honor, and the truth, in substance, that the conversation to which Dr. Cooper alluded, turned wholly on political topics, and did not attribute to Colonel Burr any instance of dishonorable conduct, nor relate to his private character; and in relation to any other language or conversation of General Hamilton which Colonel Burr will specify, a prompt and frank avowal or denial will be given.

This no longer would do, as it might have earlier. Burr wanted to be told that Hamilton had never imputed dishonorable motives to him; while Hamilton, mindful of fifteen years of political controversy, wanted chapter and verse cited of specific instances so that intention might be examined. On June 27, Hamilton accepted Burr's challenge and the duel was arranged for July 11 at Weehawken, on the New Jersey shore across the Hudson River.

HAMILTON, ORDERLY TO THE END, PREPARED HIS WILL, WROTE TWO letters to his "dear Eliza," and drew up a statement of his motives for meeting Burr. His letters showed how fully religion was now his consolation: he was prepared for death. The first one ran: [12]

This letter, my dear Eliza, will not be delivered to you unless I shall first have terminated my earthly career, to begin, as I humbly hope, from redeeming grace and divine mercy, a happy immortality. If it had been possible for me to have avoided the interview, my love for you and my precious children would have been alone a decisive motive. But it was not possible.... The consolations of religion, my beloved, can alone support you; and these you have a right to enjoy. Fly to the bosom of your God, and be comforted. With my last idea I shall cherish the sweet hope of meeting you in a better world....

Later that day he wrote again. "My beloved Eliza," he began, and continued, "the scruples of a Christian have determined me to expose my own life to any extent, rather than subject myself to the guilt of taking the life of another." "But you had rather I should die innocent than live guilty." "God's will be done! The will of a merciful God must be good. Once more, adieu, my darling, darling wife." [13]

His final statement showed that he was perhaps trying to expiate the wrong he had done Burr. He started out by saying, "My religious and moral principles are strongly opposed to the practice of duelling, and it would ever give me pain to be obliged to shed the blood of a fellow-creature in a private combat, forbidden by the laws." [14] He had "no ill will to Colonel Burr, distinct from political opposition, which, as I trust, has proceeded from pure and upright motives." The meeting could not be avoided:

... because it is not to be denied, that my animadversions on the political principles, character, and views of Colonel Burr, have been extremely severe; and on different occasions I, in common with many others have made very unfavorable criticisms on particular instances of the private conduct of this gentleman. ...

As well because it is possible that I may have injured Colonel Burr, however convinced myself that my opinions and declarations have been well founded, as from my general principles and temper in relation to similar affairs, I have resolved, if our interview is conducted in the usual manner, and if it pleases God to give me the opportunity, to reserve and throw away my first fire, and I have thoughts even of reserving my second fire—and thus giving a double opportunity to Colonel Burr to pause and reflect.

One wonders why Hamilton fought: surely the good repute of his world was hardly necessary for a man who had proved his courage on the battlefield. Had Burr driven him into a corner and were old habit and belief in the code of honor too strong in a military man? Did Hamilton see a crisis in the offing? Was he afraid that Burr would succumb to the extremists among the Federalists and head a New England secession movement? There is no doubt the worry oppressed him, for the night before the duel he wrote to one of his friends, "I will here express but one sentiment, which is, that dismemberment of our empire will be a clear sacrifice of great positive advantages without any counter-balancing good, administering no relief to our real disease, which is *democracy*, the poison of which, by a subdivision, will only be the more concentrated in each part, and consequently the more virulent." [15]

Or was there a fatalistic sense of termination: his work was completed, for good or ill; he had left his mark on the Republic? At least one contemporary voiced the thought, some ten years later. In 1815, John Adams wrote, "He [Hamilton] thought he had answered the end of his creation, as far as he could see any use of his existence upon earth and was content it should come to an end, physically or politically, if it was the pleasure of the Supreme Being." [16]

AT SEVEN IN THE MORNING OF JULY 11, 1804, HAMILTON AND BURR and their seconds faced each other on the dueling ground at Wee-hawken. The ritual was punctiliously observed: pistols were in-spected and loaded, a coin was tossed for the choice of ground, the contestants were set at the appointed distance. At the com-mand agreed upon, two shots rang out; Burr's found its mark. Whether Hamilton's pistol went off inadvertently or was aimed, it is impossible to say; Hamilton believed that he had not fired, and so the surgeon who attended him reported him as declaring. In a statement by the surgeon a few months later, Hamilton is quoted as follows: "Take care of that pistol; it is undischarged and still cocked; it may go off and do harm. Pendleton [Hamil-ton's second] knows that I did not intend to fire at him." [17]

Hamilton was struck in the right side, rose convulsively on his toes, turned to the left, and fell on his face. "This is a mortal wound, Doctor," he said, and became unconscious. He was fer-ried back to New York and taken to the home of William Bayard, on Jane Street, where he lingered on for thirty-two hours in great agony. His Eliza joined him; so did his old friend Oliver Wolcott, who wrote to his wife as Hamilton continued to struggle for breath, "Genl. Hamilton has of late years expressed his conviction of the truths of the Christian Religion, and has desired to receive the Sacrament—but no one of the Clergy who have yet been consulted will administer it." [18] But Bishop Moore, the rector of Trinity Church and the Episcopal Bishop of New York, relented, and in the afternoon of July 11, he administered the Communion of the Sick. Hamilton died at two o'clock the next day, and on Saturday, July 14, he was buried in Trinity churchyard and a simple monument was erected with this inscription:

To the Memory of
ALEXANDER HAMILTON
The Corporation of Trinity Church has erected this
MONUMENT
In Testimony of their Respect
for
The Patriot of Incorruptible Integrity
The Soldier of Approved Valour
The Statesman of Consummate Wisdom
Whose Talents and Virtues will be admired
by
Grateful Posterity
Long after this Marble shall have mouldered into
Dust.

This epitaph might have been shorter. It might have said:

Here lies
ALEXANDER HAMILTON
The Builder of the American Nation.

Epilogue

WITHIN THE PRESENT DECADE THERE HAS APPEARED A SIZABLE literature seeking to define and describe the influence of the conservative and liberal attitudes in America. The conservative, presumably, accepts tradition and custom as the forces which bind a people together; he is aware of the weaknesses of men, and he seeks strength in the acceptance of other worldly values. Says Russell Kirk, a typical exponent, "Life is something more than the satisfaction of appetites. I think that variety and growth—not equality and uniformity—are characteristic of a high civilization." [1]

The liberal, on the other hand, concerned with social and economic inequalities among men and having confidence in their capacity to make choices, sees the need for change to achieve progress. Men must continue free, but they must ever drive on, not so much for personal as for social improvement, utilizing the full agencies of government toward such a realization. Says Arthur Schlesinger, Jr., also a typical spokesman, "The liberal believes that society can and should be improved and that the way to improve it is to apply the human intelligence to social and economic problems." [2]

It is interesting to note that modern-day liberals and conservatives regard Alexander Hamilton as alien to either tradition; because he had thought in European, and more particularly in seventeenth- and eighteenth-century British terms, to them, he really falls outside of the ken of American experiences and therefore significant influences.

Expressing the conservative position, Russell Kirk rejects Hamilton because he was "a mercantilist" and therefore looked to the past for inspiration; worse, his espousal of "centralizing and acquisitive principles" [3] introduced values that were bound to disorder a stable world of small property and local loyalties. Hamilton spoke for large capital and industrialization; he concocted a witch's brew responsible for all the world's present distempers—"captains of industry," "modern cities," "the power of industrial labor." [4]

Clinton Rossiter's charges are more explicit. Hamilton was a rightist but not a conservative: he was devoted to "monarchy and hereditary aristocracy, visionary in his schemes for an industrial America." "No man could be so indifferent to the established order, full of schemes for its alteration, dazzled by plutocracy, casual about centralized power, and biased toward economics, and still lay claim to the title of conservative." [5] And contrasting Hamilton with Adams, Rossiter says of the latter, "Here was no lover of government by plutocracy, here no rootless dreamer of an America filled with factories and hard-packed cities. Here was a man who loved America as it was and had been...." [6] Kirk sounds the same alarm in still another way: "The obsession with economics—a Benthamite and Marxist obsession—which has oppressed nearly all discussion of the wants of Americans for a good many years...." [7]

The liberals read Hamilton out of American life in much the same terms. According to Louis Hartz, Hamilton was an elitist, filled with "aristocratic frustrations," an exponent of "capitalist Whiggery"; and "the idea of a national capitalist partnership in democratic terms was outside the path of his vision." [8]

These are useful reflections about conservatism and liberalism and when they illuminate the nature of a moral life they are worth pondering today. What is significant, however, is that these representatives of conservatism and liberalism currently in America are joined in the doubts they raise of the economic processes of private accumulation and capital formation and through them

—indeed, only through them—the ability to attain economic progress. We are confronted by an extraordinary set of dichotomies: social welfare must be achieved, but "material aggrandizement" is reprehensible; private property is the basis of social order, but industrialization brings in its train so many evils—captains of industry, cities, organized labor—that it perverts our moral commitments. We must have social stability, but we refuse to admit that the maintenance of an orderly society is inevitably linked with the recognition of talents and therefore the creation of opportunity, frequently through change, so that men can rise—and fall.

These discussions of conservatism and Hamilton's place in the tradition, written by men informed in the political processes, strangely enough have lost sight of those problems of statecraft posed here. A man devoted to his country and desirous of seeing it endure; a man who, when in office, accepts the responsibilities of government and meets its problems by honorable means and not through short-lived accommodation; a man who realizes that the maintenance of stability is an important charge upon the statesman—and this is best assured through economic opportunity—such a person is a good citizen and, in its best sense of conserving traditional values, a real conservative. Such was Alexander Hamilton.

In his *First Report on the Public Credit*—his initial pronouncement as a public official invested with responsibility—Hamilton said: [9]

To justify and preserve their confidence [of the most enlightened friends of good government]; to promote the increasing respectability of the American name; to answer the calls of justice; to restore landed property to its due value; to furnish new resources both to agriculture and commerce; to cement more closely the union of the States; to add to their security against foreign attack; to establish public order on the basis of an upright and liberal policy—these are the great and invaluable ends to be secured by a proper and adequate provision, at the proper period, for the support of the public credit.

It was in this kind of perception—the encouragement of bold private initiative and the maintenance of sound fiscal policy—that the strength of America was to lie. When coupled with all those enduring influences of the past—love of country, devotion to religion, a common welfare, human dignity, the rule of law —here was a basis for continuing public conduct. The acceptance of change has been part of it; but change which is an orderly progress and ever linked with the demonstrated experience of the past.

That great British conservative statesman, Benjamin Disraeli, put this idea well: [10]

In a progressive country, change is constant; and the great question is, not whether you should resist change which is inevitable, but whether that change should be carried out in deference to the manners, the customs, the laws, the traditions of the people, or in deference to abstract principles and arbitrary and general doctrines.

We come back to the basic problems to which Hamilton, as a statesman, rose. The survival of his country was linked with the integrity of governmental fiscal action and that of the private accumulative processes: these were the two sides of the same coin. Progress—welfare, in economic terms—was realizable in the diversification of the economy; and as productivity improved standards of living would rise. Equality of opportunity (through free enterprise) and redistribution (through high real income and taxation) assured justice and therefore society's stability: so much was government's responsibility.

Hamilton, if he were alive today, would accuse us of muddying the waters—and therefore jeopardizing our own security—when we introduce the idea of equalitarianism of wealth and income; wealth itself has become suspect in many quarters. If we seek the benefits of industrialization—and it is idle to suppose that poverty and therefore injustice can ever be eliminated otherwise—then we must assume that accumulation will go on. The choice before us is not wealth or no-wealth, but whether capital

will be created by forced labor under tyranny or through unequal wealth and income (because the talents of men are unequal) under freedom. Because he knew these things and imple-
mented them through statecraft, Alexander Hamilton is alive
and meaningful for us today.

WE LIVE IN ANOTHER WORLD NOW FROM THE UNCERTAIN AND IN-
secure one of the 1790s: the struggling young Union, Hamilton
labored so hard to establish, is now a great and powerful nation.
It has imaginatively exploited its natural resources and skills to
push out constantly the frontiers of learning, welfare, and social
arrangements. Despite its bigness—in government, business and
labor—it has not lost sight of those essential qualities to which the
Founding Fathers dedicated themselves. The governmental processes have integrity; individual conscience is safeguarded; private
enterprise, the key to innovation, has produced both that wealth
and income so necessary to assure the well-being and maintain
the confidence of the growing American population. Americans
are united in their devotion to their country and their desire to
keep it secure.

Yet, curiously enough, uncertainty, if not insecurity, has become a characteristic of our times. We are involved in a great
debate that has two parts, one affecting domestic policy and the
other foreign. What shall be the agreements concerning our own
society, notably, what shall be the measure of responsibility assumed by government to defend our own institutions and way
of life? And in the foreign sphere, as we face the challenge of
international communism, what shall be our obligations to the
outside world of our allies and friends and what are the terms
we have the right to impose on them for our cooperation?

It is interesting to speculate where present-day Hamiltonians
and Jeffersonians stand as regards these perplexing problems. If
we start out with the concept of "equality," we shall be able, at

least as far as the domestic sphere is concerned, to point up the basic differences existing between the two viewpoints.

To the Hamiltonian, "equality" means only "equality of opportunity": given a free climate and the protection of law, then men of talents will rise to their proper stations and realize their capacities, whatever their chosen fields. Freedom, in this context, means a political society which protects the individual and his conscience against the oppression of the many or the few; it means an economic society in which private accumulation, as a result of unequal incomes, is encouraged, so that, because the fiscal processes are honorable, the investment function and therefore innovation can be defended; it means that the door of education will always be kept open.

There are limits, then, to government intervention. That "energy" in government that Hamilton sought in the 1790s has served its purpose magnificently: it had a political intention—the securing of the Union—and it has been fulfilled. To continue to employ government to assure the individual's protection against all the mischances and risks in our economic processes, and to see it grow to gargantuan proportions in consequence, is a perversion of the Hamiltonian intention.

Today, the Jeffersonian, because of his concern with social justice, has given another reading to the idea of "equality." Men are unequal in their capacities, it is true; but exactly because this is so and therefore some fall rather than rise, it is society's obligation to prevent their exploitation. All sorts of devices must be developed by government in this connection, starting as humbly as the guarantee of minimum wages and ending with the narrowing of differences in wealth and income. Equality sooner or later becomes synonymous with leveling; welfare is realizable only through the welfare state which pushes its concern into every aspect of our economic activities until—one cannot avoid the inexorable conclusion—the greater part of decision-making must become a public function.

This acceptance of the equalitarianism of leveling has great dangers: it may end in the weakening of the fiscal function as government leans more and more on the monetizing of debt to establish social benefits and maintain high levels of economic performance; it certainly will produce the monolithic state which, by reducing most differences, will at the same time destroy initiative and that innovation which has been the one sure guide to our progress.

It is ironic that the present-day Jeffersonian, with his profound commitment to the preservation of individual integrity and his original abhorrence of energetic government, in order to achieve his conception of "equality," is willing to run the risks of oppression. He falls back, of course, on his belief in the perfectibility of man; given the elimination of injustice from the world, man no longer will war on man. And yet, was not Hamilton closer to the truth with his acceptance of "the passions of avarice, ambition, interest, which govern most individuals" as the basis of human motivation? We are on surer ground if we place our reliance on all those forces for order we have developed—religion, love of country, tradition, the responsibility of leadership—than in accepting the assurance of the utopians that justice will prevail automatically once "equality" has been created.

In the area of foreign relations, the differences are equally significant. Hamilton's achievements were mighty: guided by its self-interest and the need for securing its place in a hostile and warring world, the United States had to make certain its territorial integrity was recognized, its frontiers guaranteed, and its trade maintained. This was accomplished without resort to alliances, although the good will of Great Britain was important to the success of the whole intention. At the same time, by refusing to give aid and comfort to France, as it sought to establish bases in America for the preying on British commerce, Hamilton and his friends kept the United States clear of the dangers of war.

Hamilton was pursuing no broad and universal scheme for the regeneration of mankind as he advocated these policies; he did not say—as Jefferson and his friends did—that American survival was linked with the triumph of the republican cause everywhere. He was solely devoted to his nation's interests and was prepared to bargain, to temporize, to concede, settling for half a loaf if he could not get the whole, as long as danger was kept away from the American shore.

No American, today, dare deny the fact that we live in a disordered world. Free nations have been destroyed and made satellites of the Communist power; by infiltration, propaganda, threats, and blandishments, Communist Russia and Communist China foment disorders and ceaselessly labor to weaken the loyalties to free institutions everywhere. New countries have arisen in Asia and Africa; many are both overpopulated and poor in natural resources. At the same time that they seek to protect their new-found nationality, they accept a mandate to engage in programs of glittering social reform despite that they have neither the wealth nor the skills to do so.

Where are our responsibilities? We must defend our own institutions of liberty and welfare; this is our first and always primary concern. At the same time we know there will be no peace and progress unless a voluntary international community is once more re-established where nations respect one another's sovereignty and in which labor, trade, and capital have great mobility. This does not mean that we do not participate in international organizations: they are necessary for defense against aggression. But do we follow the counsels of idealism, giving general commitments that we will move everywhere with men and funds to defend and advance free institutions? Or do we follow those of realism, where our own interests, broadly conceived, dictate whether we move or not?

A Hamiltonian would be a realist in foreign affairs today as Hamilton was in the 1790s; by the same token, a Jeffersonian would be an idealist, as Jefferson was then. Every question, to the realist, calling for a decision, would have to be examined in terms like the following: Does the new demand upon us fit into the broad and general scheme of our own safety? Are the risks we are called upon to take calculated ones, with the chances good that the commitment will be concluded successfully? Will we end up by having more friends rather than less, and thus strengthening our position in world affairs? Are we likely, by our actions, to widen the boundaries of the free world, and thus once more move toward that mobility of freer exchanges and the security of a world-recognized currency that existed prior to 1913?

Having power now, the Hamiltonian would maintain, we can make individual and regional bargains with mutually beneficial advantages. We can say, for example, to poorer and still under-developed countries that we will do everything we can to facilitate the movement of capital if they will not erect barriers to trade and prey on foreign capital and if they will do everything they can to maintain their fiscal integrity in a regime of law. Only so can they, in time, develop their own "peculiar advantages" of which Hamilton spoke and thus assure for themselves a fixed place in the intercourse among nations. We have much to offer in return: access to our own markets, our great technical skills, our protection.

Is this the counsel of political expediency that denies the claims of the rest of the world upon us? Not at all; we expand the frontiers of freedom by showing other peoples how they truly can secure their own. If they will safeguard their national honor, as we did ours in the 1790s; if they will recognize, too, that survival and growth are realizable in a "system of perfect liberty," internationally based; if they will enter into agreements they will respect, because such understandings accept their sovereignty, then the chances of the free world winning out in the long run are good.

These were some of the things Alexander Hamilton was saying to the young republic of the United States in the first decade
of its history. It is impressive to record how timely his advice
is today not only to a powerful America but to these new and
underdeveloped nations as well, whose decisions—whether they
try to establish societies founded securely on national faith or
plunge headlong into schemes of utopian renovation—will contribute much either toward re-creating a free world or forcing
us to sink into a wholly enslaved one.

Notes

PREFACE

1. Merrill Jensen, *The New Nation: A History of the United States During the Confederation, 1781-1789* (New York, 1950).
2. *William and Mary Quarterly*, 3d ser., vol. XII, no. 2 (1955), pp. 217-267; 245.
3. Russell Kirk, *The Conservative Mind* (Chicago, 1953), pp. 69-70.
4. Alexander Hamilton, *Works*, ed. H. C. Lodge (12 vols.; New York, 1904), X, 258.

INTRODUCTION

1. Arthur Young, *Eastern Tour* (London, 1771), IV, 361.
2. Hamilton, *Works, op. cit.*, III, 361.
3. Thomas Jefferson, *Writings*, ed. P. L. Ford (10 vols.; New York, 1892-1899), IV, 479.
4. Hamilton, *Works, op. cit.*, IX, 341-342.
5. *Ibid.*, III, 332; II, 232.   6. *Ibid.*, IV, 100.   7. *Ibid.*, I, 286.
8. *Ibid.*, X, 321.   9. *Ibid.*, IX, 341-342.
10. James Madison, *Writings*, ed. G. Hunt (9 vols.; New York, 1900-1910), V, 27-28.
11. Hamilton, *Works, op. cit.*, IX, 71-72.
12. *Ibid.*, IV, 230-290.   13. *Ibid.*, II, 27-28; 70.   14. *Ibid.*, I, 250.
15. *Ibid.*, I, 401.   16. *Ibid.*, I, 391.   17. *Ibid.*, XII, 206.
18. *Ibid.*, IX, 533.   19. *Ibid.*, X, 207.   20. *Ibid.*, X, 321.
21. *Ibid.*, II, 436.   22. *Ibid.*, IV, 100, 107.   23. *Ibid.*, IV, 149.

CHAPTER I

1. John Dickinson, *The Late Regulations Respecting the British Colonies ...* (Philadelphia, 1765), in *Writings*, ed. P. L. Ford (Philadelphia, 1895), pp. 227-230.

CHAPTER 2

1. Jared Sparks, *Life of Gouverneur Morris* (3 vols.; New York, 1832), I, 23-26. Quoted in A. M. Schlesinger, *Colonial Merchants and the American Revolution, 1763-1776* (New York, 1917), p. 331.

2. Schlesinger, *op. cit.*, p. 269.
3. Allan McLane Hamilton, *Intimate Life of Alexander Hamilton* (New York, 1910), pp. 24–27.
4. Hamilton, *Works, op. cit.*, I, 113.
5. *Ibid.*, p. 71.   6. *Ibid.*, pp. 18–19.
7. *Pennsylvania Magazine of History and Biography*, vol. XXVII (1903), pp. 138–139.
8. Hamilton, *Works, op. cit.*, IX, 71–72.

CHAPTER 3

1. Hamilton, *Works, op. cit.*, IX, 56–57.
2. George Washington, *Writings*, ed. W. C. Ford (14 vols.; New York, 1889–1893), VI, 238.
3. Hamilton, *Works, op. cit.*, IX, 129.   4. *Ibid.*, p. 115.
5. *Ibid.*, pp. 120–121.   6. *Ibid.*, p. 187.
7. *Memoirs of Lieut.-Col. Tench Tilghman* (Albany, 1876), pp. 89 ff. Quoted in Hamilton, *Intimate Life, op. cit.*, p. 95.
8. Hamilton, *Intimate Life, op. cit.*, p. 103.
9. Hamilton, *Works, op. cit.*, IX, 208.   10. *Ibid.*, X, 224.
11. *Memoirs, Correspondence and Manuscripts of General Lafayette* (3 vols.; New York, 1837), I, 366.
12. Hamilton, *Works, op. cit.*, IX, 232–233.

CHAPTER 4

1. Hamilton, *Works, op. cit.*, IX, 273.
2. *Journals of the Continental Congress*, 1774–1789 (34 vols.; Washington, 1904–1937), XV, 1060.
3. Hamilton, *Works, op. cit.*, III, 319–341; 320, 332.
4. *Ibid.*, pp. 342–387; 360, 362.   5. *Ibid.*, p. 362.   6. *Ibid.*, p. 387.
7. *Ibid.*   8. *Ibid.*, I, 282.   9. *Ibid.*   10. *Ibid.*, p. 244.
11. *Ibid.*, p. 246.   12. *Ibid.*, p. 249.   13. *Ibid.*, p. 250.
14. *Ibid.*, p. 255.   15. *Ibid.*, pp. 213–239; 218.   16. *Ibid.*, p. 224.
17. *Ibid.*, p. 224.   18. *Ibid.*, p. 268.   19. *Ibid.*, p. 272.
20. *Ibid.*, p. 281.   21. *Ibid.*, p. 286,

CHAPTER 5

1. Hamilton, *Works, op. cit.*, IX, 327.
2. Hamilton, *Intimate Life, op. cit.*, p. 199.
3. Hamilton, *Works, op. cit.*, IV, 283.   4. *Ibid.*, pp. 288–289.
5. *Ibid.*, I, 293.   6. *Ibid.*, p. 294.

7. Washington, *Writings, op. cit.*, IX, 103–104.

8. Hamilton, *Works, op. cit.*, IX, 333.   9. Hamilton, *Ibid.*, 341–342.

10. *Ibid.*, II, 188–189.   11. *Ibid.*, IX, 311.

12. Washington, *Writings, op. cit.*, X, 214–216.   13. *Ibid.*, IX, 326.

14. *Ibid.*, p. 331.   15. *Ibid.*, p. 337.   16. *Ibid.*, I, 305.

17. *Ibid.*, p. 307.   18. *Ibid.*, p. 311.   19. *Ibid.*, p. 312.

20. *Ibid.*, p. 313.

21. Davis R. Dewey, *Financial History of the United States* (New York, 1902), pp. 58–59.

22. *Documents Illustrative of the Formation of the Union of the American States*, 69th Cong., 1st Sess., House Doc. no. 398 (Washington, 1927), p. 925. (This work contains all the debates at the Constitutional Convention in a single volume.)

23. Madison, *Writings, op. cit.*, V, 27–28.

24. Noah Brooks, *Henry Knox, a Soldier of the Revolution* (New York, 1900), pp. 194–195.

25. R. L. Schuyler, "The Constitution or What Might Have Been," in *Hobart Review*, vol. V, no. 1 (May, 1954).

26. Washington, *Writings, op. cit.*, XI, 81.

27. Madison, *Writings, op. cit.*, II, 318.

CHAPTER 6

1. *Documents Illustrative ...*, *op. cit.*, p. 280.

2. Hamilton, *Works, op. cit.*, I, 336.

3. *Documents Illustrative ...*, *op. cit.*, p. 745.

4. *Ibid.*, p. 742.   5. *Ibid.*, p. 296.

6. *National Intelligencer*, Aug. 26, 1826. Quoted in N. Schachner, *Alexander Hamilton* (New York, 1946), p. 452.

7. *Documents Illustrative ...*, *op. cit.*, pp. 215–225; 776–783.

8. Hamilton, *Works, op. cit.*, X, 446.

9. *Documents Illustrative ...*, *op. cit.*, pp. 217, 221, 781, 783.

10. *Ibid.*, pp. 224–245; 979–988.

11. Hamilton, *Works, op. cit.*, I, 420.

12. V. L. Parrington, *Main Currents in American Thought* (3 vols.; New York, 1927), I, 285.

13. Hamilton, *Works, op. cit.*, XI, 38.   14. *Ibid.*, p. 59.

15. *Ibid.*, p. 116.   16. *Ibid.*, p. 75.   17. *Ibid.*, XII, 193, 206.

18. *Ibid.*, p. 261.

19. William Kent, *Memoirs and Letters of James Kent* (New York, 1898), p. 31.

20. J. Elliott, *Debates ... on the Adoption of the Federal Constitution* (5 vols.; Philadelphia, 1881), II, 257.

21. Hamilton, *Works, op. cit.*, II, 59–60; 67–70.

CHAPTER 7

1. Hamilton, *Works, op. cit.,* IX, 531.
2. *Ibid.,* II, 426–427.   3. *Ibid.,* p. 229.   4. *Ibid.,* p. 254.
5. *Ibid.,* p. 230.   6. *Ibid.,* pp. 228, 232.   7. *Ibid.,* p. 233.
8. *Ibid.,* p. 235.   9. *Ibid.,* p. 236.   10. *Ibid.,* p. 231.
11. *Ibid.,* p. 236.   12. *Ibid.,* p. 241.   13. *Ibid.,* p. 244.
14. *Ibid.,* p. 246.   15. *Ibid.,* p. 248.   16. *Ibid.,* p. 273.
17. *Ibid.,* p. 283.   18. *Ibid.,* III, 387.   19. *Ibid.,* II, 283.
20. *Ibid.,* IV, 126.   21. *Ibid.,* II, 229–230.   22. *Ibid.,* p. 288.
23. William Maclay, *Journal ... 1789–1791* (New York, 1890), p. 237.
24. *Statutes at Large ... 1789–1873* (17 vols.; Boston, 1850–1873), I, 65.
25. *Debates and Proceedings of the Congress of the United States,* 1789–
    1824 (42 vols.; Washington, 1834–1856), Jan. 28, 1790.
26. *Ibid.,* Feb. 9, 1790.   27. *Ibid.,* Feb. 18, 1790.
28. *Ibid.,* Apr. 22, 1790.   29. *Ibid.,* Feb. 9, 1790.
30. *Ibid.,* Feb. 15, 1790.   31. *Ibid.,* Feb. 19, 1790.
32. *Ibid.,* Apr. 22, 1790.   33. *Ibid.*   34. *Maclay, op. cit.,* p. 331.
35. Jefferson, *Writings, op. cit.,* I, 192.   36. *Ibid.,* p. 196.
37. *Ibid.,* VI, 102.   38. Hamilton, *Works, op. cit.,* X, 321.
39. *Historical Statistics of the United States, 1789–1945* (Washington, 1949),
    pp. 298, 306.

CHAPTER 8

1. Hamilton, *Works, op. cit.,* III, 361.
2. *Ibid.,* p. 419.   3. *Ibid.,* p. 410.
4. Adam Smith, *Wealth of Nations* (New York, Modern Library Edition,
    1937), pp. 304–305.
5. Hamilton, *Works, op. cit.,* III, 390.   6. *Ibid.,* IV, 124.
7. *Ibid.,* III, 391–395.   8. *Ibid.,* p. 394.   9. *Ibid.,* p. 402.
10. *Ibid.,* pp. 404, 405.   11. *Ibid.,* pp. 399, 401.   12. *Ibid.,* p. 423.
13. *Ibid.,* p. 434.   14. *Documents Illustrative ...,* op. cit., p. 563.
15. Hamilton, *Works, op. cit.,* III, 463.
16. Jefferson, *Writings, op. cit.,* V, 284–289.
17. Hamilton, *Works, op. cit.,* III, 455.
18. *Ibid.,* p. 447.   19. *Ibid.,* p. 446.   20. *Ibid.,* p. 448.
21. *Ibid.,* pp. 449, 450.   22. *Ibid.,* pp. 453, 454.   23. *Ibid.,* p. 454.
24. *American State Papers, Finance* (Washington, 1832–1836), II, 351.
25. Jefferson, *Writings, op. cit.,* V, 348.
26. *Ibid.,* VIII, 172.   27. *Ibid.,* VIII, 252.
28. John Adams, *Works,* ed. C. F. Adams (10 vols.; Boston, 1850–1856), X,
    375.

29. *Ibid.*, IX, 638–639.   30. Hamilton, *Works, op. cit.,* IX, 502.
31. *Ibid.*, IV, 5.

CHAPTER 9

1. Hamilton, *Works, op. cit.,* I, 268.   2. *Ibid.*, IV, 96.   3. *Ibid.*
4. *Ibid.*, p. 100.   5. *Ibid.*, p. 102.   6. *Ibid.*, p. 136.
7. Smith, *op. cit.,* p. 642.   8. *Ibid.*, p. 640.
9. Hamilton, *Works, op. cit.,* IV, 76–77.
10. *Ibid.*, p. 159.   11. *Ibid.*, p. 160.   12. *Ibid.*, p. 104
13. *Ibid.*, p. 105.   14. *Ibid.*, p. 71.   15. *Ibid.*, p. 73.
16. *Ibid.*, p. 74.   17. *Ibid.*, pp. 87–88.   18. *Ibid.*, p. 89.
19. *Ibid.*, p. 92.   20. *Ibid.*   21. *Ibid.*, p. 95.   22. *Ibid.*, p. 98.
23. *Ibid.*, p. 111.   24. *Ibid.*, VIII, 459.   25. *Ibid.*, IV, 115–116.
26. *Ibid.*, p. 116.   27. *Ibid.*, pp. 124–125.   28. *Ibid.*, p. 130.
29. *Ibid.*, p. 134.   30. *Ibid.*, p. 139.   31. *Ibid.*, p. 140.
32. *Ibid.*, p. 147.   33. *Ibid.*, p. 148.   34. *Ibid.*   35. *Ibid.*, p. 149.
36. *Ibid.*   37. *Ibid.*, p. 150.   38. *Ibid.*, pp. 101–102.
39. *Ibid.*, p. 97.   40. *Ibid.*, pp. 104–107.
41. *The Speech of the Right Hon. the Earl of Liverpool* ... (London, 1820), p. 16.
42. J. S. Davis, *Essays in the Earlier History of American Corporations* (2 vols.; Cambridge, 1917), I, 357–358.
43. *Newark Gazette,* June 1, 1796. Quoted in Davis, *op. cit.,* I, 498.
44. Thomas Jefferson, *Writings,* ed. H. A. Washington (9 vols.; New York, 1853–1854), III, 260.
45. Richard Hildreth, *History of the United States of America* (6 vols.; New York, 1849–1856), IV, 276.

CHAPTER 10

1. Hamilton, *Works, op. cit.,* VIII, 199–200; 201, 203.
2. *Ibid.*, X, 329.
3. *National Gazette,* June 18, 1792; Mar. 15, 1792. Quoted in Claude G. Bowers, *Jefferson and Hamilton* (Boston, 1926), pp. 161, 164.
4. Hamilton, *Works, op. cit.,* X, 217.   5. *Ibid.*, p. 321.
6. Washington, *Writings, op. cit.,* XIV, 101.
7. Hamilton, *Works, op. cit.,* IX, 459–460.
8. *Ibid.*, VIII, 426–427.   9. *Ibid.*, p. 428.   10. *Ibid.*, IV, 436.
11. *Ibid.*, pp. 457, 463, 464.   12. *Ibid.*, V, 49.
13. Jefferson, *Writings* (Ford, ed.), *op. cit.,* IV, 479.
14. *Ibid.*, III, 269.   15. *Ibid.*, VI, 3.
16. Hamilton, *Works, op. cit.,* IX, 518.   17. *Ibid.*, p. 527.
18. *Ibid.*, pp. 527–528.   19. *Ibid.*, p. 528.   20. *Ibid.*, pp. 531–532.

21. *Ibid.*, p. 533.   22. *Ibid.*, p. 535.   23. *Ibid.*, II, 460–461.
24. Bowers, *op. cit.*, pp. 166–174.
25. Jefferson, *Writings, op. cit.*, VIII, 394–408.
26. C. D. Hazen, *Contemporary American Opinion of the French Revolution* (Baltimore, 1897), p. 192.
27. *Works of Fisher Ames*, ed. Seth Ames (2 vols.; Boston, 1854), I, 136–137.
28. Jefferson, *Writings, op. cit.*, VI, 2.
29. Hamilton, *Works, op. cit.*, II, 435–436.
30. *Pittsburgh Gazette*, Apr. 26, 1794.
31. Hamilton, *Works, op. cit.*, VI, 353–358.   32. Hazen, *op. cit.*, p. 205.
33. *Abridgement of the Debates of Congress* (New York, 1917), I, 477.
34. A. T. Mahan, *Sea Power and Its Relations to the War of 1812* (2 vols.; Boston, 1895). Quoted in S. F. Bemis, *Jay's Treaty* (New York, 1923), p. 270.
35. Hamilton, *Works, op. cit.*, V, 109.
36. *Ibid.*, II, 436.   37. *Ibid.*, III, 201.   38. *Ibid.*, pp. 299–300.

CHAPTER 11

1. Hamilton, *Works, op. cit.*, X, 57–58.
2. *Ibid.*, IX, 500.   3. *Ibid.*, X, 457.
4. Hamilton, *Intimate Life, op. cit.*, p. 215.
5. *Ibid.*, p. 260.   6. *Ibid.*, pp. 232, 259.   7. *Ibid.*, p. 231.
8. N. Schachner, *Alexander Hamilton* (New York, 1946), pp. 391–392.
9. Hamilton, *Works, op. cit.*, VII, 369–479.
10. Schachner, *op. cit.*, p. 346.
11. Jefferson, *Writings, op. cit.*, VII, 40.
12. Hamilton, *Works, op. cit.*, V, 189 ff.   13. *Ibid.*, V, 201–202.
14. *Ibid.*, VIII, 209 ff.   15. *Ibid.*, X, 275–278; 280.   16. *Ibid.*, X, 268.
17. *Ibid.*, p. 295.   18. *Philadelphia Aurora*, Dec. 23, 1796.
19. Thomas Paine, *Writings*, ed. M. D. Conway (4 vols.; New York, 1894–1896), III, 213–252.
20. Hamilton, *Works, op. cit.*, VII, 309–364.   21. *Ibid.*, X, 401.
22. *Messages and Papers of the Presidents ...*, ed. J. D. Richardson (10 vols.; Washington, 1907), I, 322.
23. Hamilton, *Works, op. cit.*, VIII, 240.

CHAPTER 12

1. Hamilton, *Works, op. cit.*, X, 444.
2. *Ibid.*, p. 428.   3. *Ibid.*, p. 342–347.   4. *Ibid.*, p. 20.
5. Davis, *op. cit.*, II, 101.
6. Hamilton, *Works, op. cit.*, X, 387.

7. *Ibid.*, p. 460.   8. *Albany Register*, Apr. 24, 1804.

9. Hamilton, *Works, op. cit.*, X, 461–463.

10. *Ibid.*, p. 463.

11. J. E. Graybill, *Alexander Hamilton, Nevis-Weehawken* (New York, 1897), p. 47.

12. Hamilton, *Works, op. cit.*, X, 475.

13. *Ibid.*, p. 476.   14. *Ibid.*, pp. 471–474.   15. *Ibid.*, p. 458.

16. Adams, *Works, op. cit.*, X, 156.

17. Graybill, *op. cit.*, pp. 59–63.

18. Hamilton, *Intimate Life, op. cit.*, p. 406.

EPILOGUE

1. *The New York Times Magazine*, Mar. 4, 1956.

2. *Ibid.*   3. Kirk, *op. cit.*, p. 75.   4. *Ibid.*, p. 68.

5. Clinton Rossiter, *Conservatism in America* (New York, 1955), pp. 112, 113.

6. *Ibid.*, pp. 115–116.   7. *The New York Times Magazine*, Mar. 4, 1956.

8. Louis Hartz, *The Liberal Tradition in America* (New York, 1955), pp. 16, 89, 108, 205.

9. Hamilton, *Works, op. cit.*, II, 232.

10. Quoted in R. J. White, ed., *The Conservative Tradition* (London, 1950), p. 127.

Bibliography

GENERAL. Two collections of Alexander Hamilton's writings have appeared, both incomplete. They are John C. Hamilton (ed.), *The Works of Alexander Hamilton*, 7 vols., New York, 1851; and Henry Cabot Lodge (ed.), *The Works of Alexander Hamilton*, 12 vols., New York, 1904. A complete edition is now in preparation under the direction of Columbia University. There are many biographies of Hamilton, of which these are the most important: Nathan Schachner, *Alexander Hamilton*, New York, 1946; Henry Jones Ford, *Alexander Hamilton*, New York, 1929; F. S. Oliver, *Alexander Hamilton*, London and New York, 1906; William Graham Sumner, *Alexander Hamilton*, New York, 1890; Henry Cabot Lodge, *Alexander Hamilton*, Boston, 1882; John T. Morse, Jr., *The Life of Alexander Hamilton*, 2 vols., Boston, 1876. Also interesting are Gertrude Atherton's novel, *The Conqueror*, New York, 1902; and Allan McLane Hamilton, *The Intimate Life of Alexander Hamilton*, New York, 1910. The best background history of the period is Nathan Schachner, *The Founding Fathers*, New York, 1954. Earlier works are John C. Hamilton, *The Life of Alexander Hamilton*, 2 vols., New York, 1834; and his *History of the Republic of the United States, etc.*, 7 vols., New York, 1857–1864.

1. THE WEST INDIAN BACKGROUND. An excellent introduction is W. L. Burn, *The British West Indies*, London, 1951. See also Richard Pares, *A West India Fortune*, London, 1950, and his *War and Trade in the West Indies, 1739–1763*, Oxford, 1936; F. W. Pitman, *The Development of the British West Indies, 1700–1763*, New Haven, Conn., 1917; L. J. Ragatz, *The Fall of the Planter Class in the British Caribbean*, Washington, D.C., 1928. The older view of British imperial and mercantilist policy is in G. L. Beer, *The Old Colonial System, 1660–1754*, 2 vols., New York, 1912; and *British Colonial Policy, 1754–1765*, New York, 1907. For a newer view, see Louis M. Hacker, *The Triumph of American Capitalism*, New York, 1940. The real facts concerning Hamilton's birth are to be found in Harold Larson, "Alexander Hamilton: The Fact and Fiction of His Early Years," in *The William and Mary Quarterly*, 3d series, vol. IX, 1952.

2. NEW YORK IN THE REVOLUTION. These are important: Virginia D. Harrington, *The New York Merchant on the Eve of the Revolution*, New York, 1935; and Oscar Theodore Barck, Jr., *New York City dur-*

ing the War of Independence, New York, 1931. Very little of a systematic nature has been written on the role of the leftists in the preliminaries to and during the American Revolution. See Sydney George Fisher, *The True History of the American Revolution*, Philadelphia, 1902, for an earlier account. Clinton Rossiter, *Seedtime of the Republic: The Origin of the American Tradition of Political Liberty*, New York, 1953, is very good for the political thinking of the period. See also the following for background aspects of the conflict: A. M. Schlesinger, *Colonial Merchants and the American Revolution*, New York, 1918; O. M. Dickerson, *The Navigation Acts and the American Revolution*, Philadelphia, 1951; E. S. and H. M. Morgan, *The Stamp Act Crisis*, Chapel Hill, N.C., 1953; L. H. Gipson, *The Coming of the Revolution*, New York, 1954.

3. HAMILTON IN THE REVOLUTION. There is a vast literature on the military aspects of the Revolution. These are recent and good: Williard H. Wallace, *Appeal to Arms*, New York, 1950; Christopher Ward, *War of the Revolution*, 2 vols., New York, 1952; John Richard Alden, *The American Revolution, 1775–1783*, New York, 1954. See also D. S. Freeman, *George Washington*, 6 vols., New York, 1948–1954; S. F. Bemis, *Diplomacy of the American Revolution*, New York, 1935.

4. THE STATES IN THE REVOLUTION. See Allan Nevins, *American States during and after the Revolution*, New York, 1924; J. T. Adams, *New England in the Republic, 1776–1850*, Boston, 1926; T. C. Cochran, *New York in the Confederation*, New York, 1932; J. P. Selsam, *Pennsylvania Constitution of 1776*, New York, 1936.

5. THE CONFEDERATION. See Merrill Jensen, *Articles of Confederation*, Madison, Wis., 1940, and *The New Nation*, New York, 1950. Jensen takes issue with the older view of John Fiske, *The Critical Period of American History, 1783–1789*, Boston, 1888. See also E. B. Greene, *The Revolutionary Generation, 1763–1790*, New York, 1945; C. A. Beard, *An Economic Interpretation of the Constitution*, New York, 1913; D. R. Dewey, *Financial History of the United States*, New York, 1902.

6. THE CONSTITUTION. See the following: Charles Warren, *Making of the Constitution*, Boston, 1928; Carl Van Doren, *The Great Rehearsal*, New York, 1948; Max Farrand, *Framing of the Constitution*, New Haven, Conn., 1913; R. L. Schuyler, *Constitution of the United States*, New York, 1923; W. W. Crosskey, *Politics and the Constitution*, 2 vols., Chicago, 1953. For the Convention debates, see C. C. Tansill (ed.), *Documents Illustrative of the Formation of the Union of the American States*, Washington, D.C., 1927. For Hamilton in New York, see C. E. Miner, *The Ratification of the Federal Constitution by*

the State of New York, New York, 1921. There are many editions of *The Federalist*. A convenient one is E. M. Earle (ed.), *The Federalist*, Washington, D.C., 1937.

7. SECRETARY OF THE TREASURY. In addition to Nathan Schachner, *The Founding Fathers*, New York, 1954, see H. J. Ford, *Washington and His Colleagues*, New Haven, 1918; and L. D. White, *The Federalists*, New York, 1948. For the Whiskey Rebellion, see L. D. Baldwin, *Whiskey Rebels*, Pittsburgh, 1939. See also Frank Monaghan and Marvin Lowenthal, *This Was New York, The Nation's Capital in 1789*, Garden City, N.Y., 1943.

8. THE NATIONAL BANK. There is no systematic work on the First Bank. See J. T. Holdsworth, *The First Bank of the United States*, Philadelphia, 1911; A. S. Bolles, *The Financial History of the United States from 1789 to 1860*, New York, 1883; E. R. Taus, *Central Banking Function of the United States Treasury*, New York, 1943.

9. THE REPORT ON MANUFACTURES. See J. S. Davis, *Essays in the Earlier History of American Corporations*, 2 vols., Cambridge, Mass., 1917. An easily available edition is Adam Smith, *An Inquiry into the Nature and Causes of the Wealth of Nations*, New York, 1937.

10. DEFENSE OF POLICY AND DEFENSE OF COUNTRY. See C. G. Bowers, *Jefferson and Hamilton*, Boston, 1925; Irving Brant, *James Madison, Father of the Constitution*, New York, 1950; Nathan Schachner, *Thomas Jefferson*, 2 vols., New York, 1951; G. S. Graham, *Sea Power and British North America, 1783–1820*, Cambridge, Mass., 1941; S. F. Bemis, *Jay's Treaty*, New York, 1923; C. M. Thomas, *American Neutrality in 1793*, New York, 1931; C. A. Beard, *Economic Origins of Jeffersonian Democracy*, New York, 1915; Frank Monaghan, *John Jay*, New York, 1935.

11. THE CRITICAL YEARS 1795–1800. See V. H. Paltsits, *Washington's Farewell Address*, New York, 1935; Joseph Charles, "The Origins of the American Party System," in *William and Mary Quarterly*, 3d series, vol. XII, nos. 2, 3, 4 (1955); S. F. Bemis, *A Diplomatic History of the United States*, New York, 1936.

12. ALEXANDER HAMILTON AND AARON BURR. See Nathan Schachner, *Aaron Burr, A Biography*, New York, 1937; M. L. Davis, *Memoirs of Aaron Burr*, 2 vols., New York, 1852.

Index

About the Author

Louis M. Hacker has been since 1945 dean of the School of General Studies at Columbia University. Born in New York City of immigrant parents in 1899, he attended Brooklyn Boys' High School and in 1916 entered Columbia, where he received his bachelor's and master's degrees and where a meeting with Charles A. Beard and Benjamin B. Kendrick stimulated his interest in the writing of history. In 1935, after a period of free-lance writing, he returned to Columbia as a member of the department of economics, to become, fourteen years later, head of the university's largest division. He has lectured and taught at many American universities and at Oxford, Cambridge, and Hawaii University, the last of which awarded him the LL.D. degree in 1953. In addition, he has been on the editorial staffs of the *New International Encyclopedia*, the *Encyclopedia of Social Sciences*, and *Columbia Encyclopedia*.

A prolific writer, Dean Hacker is the author of more than a dozen books about American life, including *The United States since 1865*, *The Triumph of American Capitalism*, and the well-received *Shaping of the American Tradition*. The present work represents a lifelong inquiry into the sources of strength and integrity of the American nation.

Dean Hacker makes his home in New York City with his wife Mrs. Beatrice Larson Hacker. He has two grown children, a son and a daughter. In addition to his administrative duties—which include the supervision of some 7,000 students and 800 instructors—he is a board member of many civic organizations and is presently chairman of the Academic Freedom Committee of the American Civil Liberties Union.